Warfare

Warfare

Through the Storms

Gregory Love

iUniverse, Inc.
Bloomington

Warfare
Through the Storms

iUniverse books may be ordered through booksellers or by contacting:

iUniverse
1663 Liberty Drive
Bloomington, IN 47403
www.iuniverse.com
1-800-Authors (1-800-288-4677)

ISBN: 978-1-4759-4535-5 (sc)
ISBN: 978-1-4759-4536-2 (ebk)

Printed in the United States of America

iUniverse rev. date: 10/11/2012

Contents

Chapter 1. Going into the Storm 1

It's Storming..2

The Battle is Not Yours, It's the Lords...5

In Remembrance and Thanksgiving 21

From Cornerstone to Keystone 32

Kicked Dog Syndrome..38

Chapter 2. In the Midst of the Storm 48

God is not Bob Villa! 49

Spiritual Discernment 54

Self Control by Choice..57

Habit or Conscious Effort 71

God's Business or Your Will 80

Position or Power of God..85

Talking or Teaching...92

Congregation or Confusion..102

Chapter 3. Coming out of the Storm 108

Following the Blueprint 109

Trusting the Architect...120

Building God's Kingdom Brick by Brick 133

Torn Down to Build Up 144

From the Ground Up..154

When I Labor for God's Kingdom...164

I Set My Kingdom Upon This Rock 173
Jesus is My Laborer 188
Using the Right Tools 196
Pray In Faith 213

"If my people, who are called by my name, shall humble themselves, and seek my face, and turn from their wicked ways; then will I hear from heaven, and will forgive their sin, and will heal their land" 2 Chronicles 7:14

Acknowledgements

Much thanks to April, Denise and Connie
Special thanks to my best friend Noah

INTRODUCTION

By Presiding Elder, Rev. Willa Estell

Matthew 8:23-27 says, "Now when He got into the boat, His disciples followed Him. And suddenly a great tempest arose on the sea, so that the boat was covered with waves. But He was asleep. Then His disciples came to Him and awoke Him, saying, "Lord, save us! We are perishing!" But He said to them, "Why are you fearful, O you of little faith?" Then He arose and rebuked the winds and the sea, and there was a great calm. So the men marveled, saying, "Who can this be, that even the winds and the sea obey Him?"

The weather, as we know, can be truly unpredictable. We don't know from one day to the next what to expect. As a matter of fact in the same day, it can go from beautiful blue skies and sunshine to ominous gray clouds. However, this is true not only of the weather, but of life generally speaking. I am sure that many of us can attest to the fact that we have found ourselves in various storms.

The nation today is in an economic and political storm. Strong winds are blowing from the north, south, east, and the west and there is a sense of unrest and fear among us. Our children are experiencing emotional and psychological storms causing some to take their own lives at 12 and 13 years of age. Storms perpetuated by bullies who really don't possess a sense of their own self-worth and are trying to find it by belittling and causing harm to others. There are physical storms that come in the form of ill-health. Life is full of storms. Someone has said that we are all in a storm, coming out of a storm, or getting ready to go into a storm. Therefore, no matter what your position in life, you are not exempt from storms.

When I lived with my grandparents in Alabama, whenever the skies would begin to darken on the horizon, whenever the thunder would begin to roar, causing the rain to fall and lightning to flash, my grandmother would have everybody (and I mean everybody), sit down and be still for she said that "God was talking." Could it be that she, with very little education, was right? When the storms of life come upon us, could God be talking?

Could it be that God is speaking to us as God spoke to the disciples, “Why are you fearful, you of little faith?” Could it be that God is trying to tell us something? Could it be that we are putting our hope and trust in created things and people with limited power and resources, just like us, and not the Creator Himself? I believe that the God who spoke to elements, the wind and sea, and they obeyed is speaking to us today. “If My people who are called by My name would humble themselves and pray, seek My face and turn from their wicked ways, then I will hear from heaven, forgive their sin, and heal their land (2 Chronicles 7:14).” There is only one who can speak to the storms of life and the storms are stilled at the sound of His voice. It is God, self-revealed in Jesus Christ!

Rev. Willa Estell is the Pastor of St. Paul A. M. E. Zion Church in Maryville, Tennessee.

Going into the Storm

1. It doesn't matter who hit who first when you get caught hitting at all.

2. It isn't God who breaks up your family; it's when someone gives up.

3. When you find a new strength it allows God to do a new thing in your life

4. True diversity is accepting one another no matter what the ethnic, social, economic, or professional background.

5. Laughing at sin builds a tolerance for sin.

6. Do what is right and people will respect you even if they still don't like you.

7. We lose reverential fear through familiarity.

8. Pray you don't enter into temptation. Resist!

9. Your kids will serve with the same dedication and joy they see in you.

10. Don't confuse natural talents with spiritual gifts.

11. You must read God's promises to know God's promises.

12. Believing and following are two different things.

13. Believing, in and of itself doesn't involve action.

14. Following, in itself demands and is action.

15. A person's higher level of intelligence doesn't lessen their propensity or weakness to sin.

16. Don't use people to "practice" your sermons on.

17. Looking and seeing are two different things.

18. Fight back before disappointment turns into discouragement.

It's Storming

As I was heading out of the door one day my mother asked me, "Where are you going"?

"To work, I've got brick to get laid," I responded.

"There's a storm coming. You don't need to get caught out there in the storm!" she exclaimed.

How do we know when there is a storm nearby? Let's see . . . the wind begins to blow a little harder, the leaves on the trees turn upside down, and the clouds once as white and fluffy as cotton are now dark and ominous. In the distance we hear the faint roll of thunder. The sun, which earlier shone so brightly, can no longer be found. The trees, which earlier stretched toward heaven, are now bent like horseshoes. Even the birds, which rule the skies and the wind, have sought refuge.

There's a storm a comin'!

Nature gives us all of the signs well before the storm actually hits so we know what lies ahead. Wind, rain, hail sleet, or snow can usually be expected with any storm. In extreme conditions, nature will unleash it's fury in tornadoes, floods, hurricanes, and other calamities.

Experience, wisdom, fear, prudence, concern for our well being, and plain common sense dictates a possible danger to all of us.

If nature can warn us, and we can recognize, that there is a storm in our midst, then why would God not show us warning signs of a storm in our spiritual life as well? Could it be that God does show us the signs of a spiritual storm brewing in our lives? Can it be that we are too busy doing our own thing to recognize these spiritual warning signs? Are we so full of ourselves that we just don't care? Or can it be that we Christians are secure enough in our own knowledge, wisdom, and understanding that we don't realize that we are under attack?

God's Word teaches us to be ever vigilant, ever mindful, and ever prepared for these spiritual storms in our everyday lives. The Adversary travels the whole world over seeking out those to devour and destroy. The prince of darkness will use anything, anybody, or any means to separate us from the truth. You see, the truth is the way and the way leads to eternal life with our Lord and Savior. Only by living in spiritual light can we achieve our ultimate goal of spending eternity with our Creator. There is no other way except through the Son, who is the Way, the Truth, and the Life. Walking in spiritual light leads to life. Walking in spiritual blindness leads to death. Our eternal resting place can be determined by whether or not we know whether we are living in spiritual light or spiritual darkness. Can the answer to this question be put off, pushed aside, ignored, or avoided? Remember, there's a storm a comin'!

Now, here is the tricky part. Here's the place where we are sometimes confused or confounded. Here's where we sometimes stumble. Here's where we hesitate or even quit and go back to what we feel is a safe haven. You see, the thing is that we claim to know the difference between spiritual light and spiritual darkness in our lives. When we're in the spiritual light, surely we know it! By the same measure, when there is spiritual darkness, we assume that we can recognize that it is indeed darkness. But the thing is that though we are in spiritual light, safe and secure from all alarms, as we sing, do we realize the spiritual darkness creeping up on us, surrounding us, even invading our safe haven?

Now, here's what I'm led by the Holy Spirit to share with all of God's people. Those of us who not only want to walk in the light, but want to walk in the Spirit, need to recognize and be aware of that though we may be in the light, our own spiritual blindness may keep us from remaining there. You see, we can be in the light and not see the warning signs of this spiritual storm in our lives.

God, who has all dominion and power on earth and in heaven, empowers those who seek Him and who wish to enter the gates of heaven and dwell with Him. God will not let Satan or any other dark forces overtake you or me without giving us warning signs of the things or thoughts in our spiritual life that come from Satan, the ruler of spiritual darkness. There is a spiritual storm constantly in our midst. What are these warning signs?

Earlier I mentioned several warning signs of an approaching storm. Blowing wind, rustling leaves, dark clouds, and animals seeking refuge are a few of the signs. Now ask yourself just what is the most important warning sign of all? I'll give you a hint. I haven't mentioned it at all. You see, the most important warning sign of an approaching storm just may be, the calm before the storm. The calm before the storm usually involves a soft breeze. The calm before the storm has still and peaceful waters; the calm before the storm says all is well, all is good, and all is just as it should be.

During this time of seemingly peace and tranquility, everything is so lovely and so perfect that there is no visible turmoil lurking. This is the time where no one or nothing can disturb our little world or invade our personal space without being noticed. If I feel that all is well in my world then any problems must belong to others. If I can stay in my own little cocoon, not venture too far away from it, and keep a watchful eye out then I know that I will not be caught up in any kind of mess. In other words, the warning signs of any approaching storm lie within others and not within myself. Oh, but doesn't a prideful, self-centered nature go before a fall? Now the more I look at it the more I realize that I might need to look at my own self, at my own ways, at my own thoughts, at my own actions or lack thereof. My relationship with God is at stake. There's a storm a comin'.

The Battle is Not Yours, It's the Lords

The Lord said, "I knew you before you were born . . . in your mother's womb I knew you." How excellent is His Holy Name. How infinite is His wisdom. A child is His gift to parents, the most precious gift that we have been trusted with, to raise up, nurture, and teach the ways of the Lord. I repeat, to teach the ways of the Lord. Just as you as parents must trust in the Lord in order to grow in His ways, so too must your children trust and believe in you in order to grow. Are you there for them when they need you the most? Do you really listen to what they are trying to tell you, by word or actions or behavior?

The truth is that though we are there for them and we hear and may understand where they are coming from, we just don't have all the answers that they need for the pressures and complexities in their lives. They must deal with and overcome their flesh in order to grow into well-rounded adults. Try as we may, they at times just seem to get farther away from our teachings. It is in these times that we must ask the Creator for His guidance in order to guide our children. You see, you too were once a child brought up by parents who were brought up by parents, who were brought up by parents and so on. No matter who you are somebody at sometime had to ask the Lord, who knows all, for knowledge, wisdom and understanding in order to bring your bloodline up in the ways set forth by God. You must give this battle to the Lord for He alone knew all of us, even in the womb.

Again, the key words in raising children are trust and submit. As we trust in the Lord what we are saying is "Lord, I pray for your guidance alone." When we submit we are saying, "Lord, I totally accept and depend on Your Word and not my own." You see, by praying, trusting, and then submitting to His will what we have done is to step out of our own wisdom and ultimate mistakes and given the battle to the Lord who can do no wrong. Then when our children see who we turn to for strength and guidance then they in turn learn to trust us. Believe me, if your children cannot or do not trust you then they will surely not submit to your teachings. Now, you may punish them or spank them into submission, but all they will be responding to is the spanking or punishment. This will work for babies and toddlers, but as they grow older your words and your actions will be what they are watching and what they are learning. Are your words and actions of the ways of the world or are they the ways of the Lord? If your ways are the ways of the world then your own understanding is of the ways of the world. This will be all that you can possibly pass on to your kids. If all that you can pass on to your kids is worldly, then know that they will turn to worldly behavior. When they turn to, or conform to, the ways of the world then they are surely lost. When they are lost, just as you are lost, then who shall lead? Who can you trust to take the reins and steer your children in the way that they should go? His name is Jesus; for the battle is not yours, it's the Lord's. This I can testify to personally.

I was born in a small town in the south to loving parents. I was the second born of what would eventually be four children. I was taken to a small black church, taught in the ways of Jesus, and baptized in His Holy Name. Even as a child I had an immense understanding of what trusting was all about. Trusting to me meant knowing that though I was too small to look out for myself that someone older, wiser, and more experienced knew just what I needed and just what to do for my growing up in this exciting, but often times confusing world. How comforting this is for any child. There was Sunday school, vacation Bible school, the children's choir, and once I got to read the Bible Scripture during morning church service when I was no more than seven or eight. It seemed to me to be the most wonderful feeling that I'd ever known that morning standing on the sacred ground behind the pulpit reading God's Holy Word to this adult audience. Funny thing, I would recall years later, was there was no hesitation, no fear, only a feeling of power. Though I didn't understand it then, God had a purpose for my life. "Boy!" I thought, "My voice sure sounded crisp and so clear coming out from behind that pulpit, almost like God was speaking Himself. No wonder why mommy won't let me walk through there going to the choir box." Still yet, every now and then, when no one was watching, I would sneak into the sanctuary, stand with hands on the podium in that pulpit and daydream . . .

As I looked back at my life through the years it seemed as if I and that little boy were two different persons. There was just something so innocently magnificent about standing on that sacred ground of the pulpit that would often times draw this young child's memory back to that first wondrous moment. It was this memory of that first experience with God that would stay with him for all of his life. For he knew, though he didn't understand or wasn't old enough to comprehend as a child, that there was a strange power of blessed assurance in the reading and sharing of God's Word. It was this blessed assurance of the reading and trust in God's Holy Word that would be all that he had left to hold on to one day. It was that one moment as a child that would ultimately lead Him home. Folks have often said that home is where the heart is and though this child of God, given to earthly parents and earthly ways, would eventually stray his heart would always belong to and be bound to God.

An insightful and highly perceptive child, he would sit on the old wooden pews of the church and marvel at the behavior of those adults who at times would scream and shout for joy over these stories about a man who was named Jesus. Jesus, the Prince of Peace! Jesus, the Lily of the Valley! Jesus, the Lamb of God! Jesus, the Son of God! Savior! Jehovah! It often times really tickled him to see the church fans the friendly mortician gave out and little old women's wigs flying like geese while singing and shouting praises to their Lord. Though this child was too young to have a real personal relationship with God Almighty himself, he felt in his little heart and knew in his little mind that one day he wanted to feel what they felt. Sometimes they would even fall out in their pews, so powerful was His presence. And through it all, even before any of this would occur he always knew when the Spirit was there. He just knew.

The one thing this child noticed most was that some certain folks and some certain preachers that came to preach, at what were called Revivals, would seem to be larger than life. They seemed larger than even his own parents. These people seemed to bring a strange, wonderful, powerful presence with them. As a young child he didn't know exactly what it was, but there was always something about their eyes. Yeah, their eyes seemed to shine with an understanding of a certain peace, yet fire, of a power far past understanding. Whatever it was, it sure made them excited when they shared what they felt to others. This child would sit there on the edge of his seat, straining to see more, to hear more, and to know more about what arose so much passion deep down inside of his own little heart. He also noticed that at times while the preacher was up there preaching that he didn't get this same warm feeling inside and this often left him disappointed.

But boy, when he did get that feeling he wanted to feel like that forever. Higher and higher and higher, like a bird, his spirit soared as he daydreamed about that pulpit. "If mommy doesn't catch me I'm gonna sneak up there after the service," he would say to himself. No matter what, he realized years later, nothing else could satisfy him. Nothing could satisfy what was stirring inside of him. There was no place that he could go, no place he could hide, and nothing anyone here on this earth could do to comfort him, for on one of those nights long ago, he, as a child of about seven or eight, had met a Bishop at one of those Revivals. Looking down into this young boy's eyes that Bishop asked, "Would you like to preach someday son?" His answer was yes . . .

Looking up, as a young boy, into the kind and soulful eyes of this awesome man this child had said, "Yes." And looking back upon his life years later, after suffering through immeasurable pain, heartache, and sorrows he realized that when he said "yes" that he really meant it. For as a young boy he had noticed that something far more powerful than anything or anyone in this world was what was driving this frail yet strong, this worn down, yet powerful old kindly Bishop, who stood before him on one Revival night long, long ago. And for some reason he knew that he could completely trust this man of God when this Bishop had told him, "Just put your trust the Lord son and He will carry you." Little did this child know just how much these words would mean. Trust in the Lord would be all he had left. For little did he know, there was a storm a comin!

One day as I was outside playing in the woods behind an old rickety run-down apartment building, two houses from where we lived, I heard the loud and unmistakable bass voice of my daddy coming from the liquor and smoke filled "splo house" on the top floor. My father would often take me up there with him while he drank beer and rot-gut liquor. The urine smell of that place, mixed with the smell of smoke and perfume that those cheap drunken women wore would often times be unbearable.

Though this young boy loved his father he had a deep hatred for his ways, way down inside. It was a place where hatred had no right to dwell. That place being the heart of a child. All innocence was gone. All innocence eroded away from this child's world for he now understood the ways of the world, the awful, wicked, sinful truth of the ways of men. Even as a child I knew that the wonderful, peaceful feeling that I got while learning about the teachings of Jesus did not coincide with the hatred that I felt. And it was hatred for my father's hangouts that led me to tell my mother about over hearing my father brag about his "girlfriend" to all his ignorant drunken friends on that day as I played in the woods. All I wanted was to go to ma-maw's and live in peace. To this day though, over forty years later, I still can't understand why on one cold winter night my mother called me into their bedroom and with my father lying on their bed beside her said, "Now tell your father what you told me about his other woman." The fire in his eyes as he looked at me told me that my father would never forgive me and would resent me forever. And I wondered until his death almost forty years later.

This little child of God, feeling resented by his father would never trust anyone ever again. Not even his mother. Not even God, for where was He?

It was that cold and blistery winter night, while in the warmth of his home that this child of God went back to his once comforting bed, curled up under the covers, and cried himself to sleep. "Bet I don't cry no damn more," he said. Until now, you see, he had never known the feelings of betrayal or distrust, only and unconditional love born of the innocence of a child. He didn't know that once he told someone something they could tell it and his life would be at their control. From this night on this child of God would no longer be a child. He was of the world now, not knowing where he was going.

It seemed to him that his father would go out of his way to make him "be a man" for telling of his infidelity. Taking him to every "splo house", bar, and night club in east Tennessee he seemed to have a need to teach his son in the ways of the world, which corrupted all of the blessed virtues that his son was learning in Sunday school and church. He made sure that his son understood that, "All those folks that are running around up there at the church are just as sneaking, rotten, and dirty as they can be. They drink just as much liquor, gamble, and whore hop as much as anybody else then run up in the church falling on their knees, whooping and hollering like they're suppose to be so sanctified." And it was true. "You stick with me son and I'll make a man out of you."

It was right before my father died that he told me he loved me. It was also then, with tears in his eyes, he told me how a "Christian" teacher of his had wounded his spirit when even he was just a boy. That teacher had called him a little ragdoll at school in front of all the other children because his clothes were ragged, but they were all he had. And I mean he hated that man too! As I would look back as I had grown older I began to notice just how much my own once joyous spirit had grown cold.

On one Easter Sunday, 1969 this child of God sneaked off with an older friend, smoked a joint of pot, drank a bottle of wine, shared two six-packs of beer, then at his mother's instruction returned to evening church service. This lost soul was eight years old standing in the Lord's house . . . drunk! His momma cried like a baby. He didn't.

By the time I got to high school I had spent a whole bunch of nights up all night in yet another juke joint, "splo house," or pool hall watching, just watching. Satan knew this is how children develop an appetite for the world.

Now I sometimes don't know if it was a blessing or a curse being out, often left alone, on all of those nights long ago. One thing that I do know though is people. How to watch people; How to read people; How to see all the way through people; I could see into their hearts just by listening to them, looking into their eyes and watching their actions. As far as danger or safety goes, people never scare me and seldom fool me. Any person that has ever fooled me, or thought they did anyway, was only because it really bothers me to be able to see what's inside of a person and still not give them a chance to prove me wrong. This gift comes from God and how to use it is still a work in progress. One thing I do know is that God has a plan for my life and always has had a plan for my life. Not only that but in looking back I realized that I never really hated anyone, only their actions or the hatred in them.

"Why are people this way and why don't you do something to change it," I would often ask God. Little did I know that God was leaving me in the fire; a fire I willingly jumped into, in order to bring me closer to Him. God knew all along that one day this tragic story would be a story of triumph not only for His child in the womb, but ultimately for the very glory of God's power.

Now if anyone wonders why I'm leaving out a bunch of names and details from my life the answer is very simple. God doesn't want me to include names or personal details about people. God is a God of victory and triumph over this world. His Only Begotten Son secured the victory not only for me, but for all those who have also sinned against God. I will in no way be able to claim victory in my life except by giving glory to the One who ordained this victory.

How did this child of God come to claim victory over the world and his own sinful nature? Well first of all, since I am he, let me tell it just as the Lord, my Savior, would have me to tell it. I give praise to God. I thank God. I worship only Him. I love God for He first loved me. I now live to obey Him and to keep His commandments. Most of all I reverence my God. No, I don't fear men, I fear only God. Men may try to take my life, but I don't fear that because I know that men cannot touch my soul. Only God has the power to take my life and send my soul to eternal damnation. Only God has given me the power to take my life and turn it around to His glory. For that, I fear and reverence my God. For that, I made a commitment to follow Jesus and to obey His will. I had to learn that my will and His will were not the same. My will was of this world and in worldly behavior, which was totally opposite from what He has planned in His perfect will for me.

I've been in a lot of churches, listened to a lot of Pastors, and prayed with a lot of people, but was never satisfied for no one could reach me, much less teach me, until one Sunday morning a new little Pastor was appointed to the church which I had grown up in as a child.

Have you ever felt like no one could reach you? Have you ever felt like no one could reach that part of your being that keeps you in bondage? Have you ever felt that no one knew how to reach you? Have you ever prayed for that someone to come along, in the name of Jesus, and to teach you what you need in order to finally be free from whatever holds you in bondage? Well I have, and God heard my petition, saw through all of my faults, and provided me with a teacher, and a Pastor, who has brought me a mighty long way. But first and foremost I must give thanks to Jesus, my Savior, and to the Spirit that dwells within those who seek Him. Much thanks and love I give to Reverend Willa Estell.

It was one Sunday morning in the fall of 2001 that I decided to go to church at St. Paul A.M.E. Zion Church in Maryville, Tennessee when I first saw this anointed teacher of the Word of God. I never will forget seeing her standing in the pulpit before all of those strangers. Small, quiet, shy, bashful, and yet brave were my first thoughts. Now as I've said before I don't fully understand how this discernment comes, I just knew these thoughts were true. After introductions she began to speak about herself being sent here and finding an adequate home and when she would be back to fully resume her duties. "As cute as she was, she sure had certain boldness about her," I thought. I now know why.

I was sitting outside the church the next time when she pulled up with the valves just knocking in the engine. "Well she's either driven a long way and ran the engine hot or she needs oil in the engine," I thought. "Bless her heart she made it and thank You, God for guiding her," I said. There was just something so innocent about the scene that it always reinforces my belief that, "I can do all things in Christ who strengthens me." I knew right then that it was indeed the Spirit leading her. I just knew it! After her first sermon I thought, "Yes, she's my Pastor."

I had joined this church long ago but had strayed from the Lord. I had given my life to Christ when I was young. And knew what I was doing. For one reason or another or for one excuse or another I stayed out in the world for a long time. I'm not going to get into a lot of details about that here, but I will say that whatever I did was of my own free will. My will again was not God's will. My will consisted of drugs, drug dealing, drunkenness, fighting and self destruction. My will landed me in jail dozens of times, counseling several times, and even prison. Now that I look back, it seems so long ago.

New member's class was really an eye opener for me. For the first time someone had explained just what I was a part of in detail to me. I learned what it meant to be a member in this body of believers. I learned what was expected of me and how my personal behavior was important to the church. I'm not just talking about my behavior inside the church. I'm talking of my behavior outside of the church as well. Before long and way too soon I had to graduate and move on. But I sure had fun learning though! After being presented to the church we were later baptized in the name of Jesus.

This is where I learned a most valuable lesson about just how serious Satan is in separating us from the will of God. This is where I learned the same hard lesson as a child years ago. Going through the same lesson yet again, I still couldn't grasp what was going on in my life.

Now this is how God works. I stopped by the church one day to see how my Pastor was doing in this new environment, when she first asked me how I was doing. At the time I was going through some things, which I mentioned, when she said," You know, Gregory, Satan will use anything and anybody to separate us from God." And just like that I had it and understood it. It was over! I finally had the revelation I needed to not to resent or hate people for the things they do. When I asked, "How are you doing?" she simply smiled and said fine.

Faith in God's Word was all that she brought and faith in His Word was all that she gave me. I prayed to God constantly for her and I still do to this day. I knew that only the hand of God could carry her through this awesome vision He has given her. I learned there is power in publicly telling that which God has ordained. It takes obedience to lead God's children. This was how the Holy Spirit was able to use her to reach me. In the Spirit of God she was able to keep me from going back to what I knew as living without all the confusion of being close to people.

I had long ago given up on trusting people. Long ago I had given up on the hypocrisy of leaders and the hypocrisy of the school system. Long ago I had grown cold. The craziest thing was one second I might feel warmth for somebody and as soon as they crossed me it was gone! This confused me so much that I thought I had been just left for evil to do whatever it pleased to me if I didn't fight back the only way I knew how to fight. My way. I stayed in the principal's office at school for fighting. The year I started school was the first year of integration. I can remember in the third grade the principle telling me, "Boys like you end up in prison". But they never took up for me when kids were calling me everything but a child of God. It wasn't until I was grown that I realized that though we were from two different worlds, color wasn't the real issue. It was an issue of the heart. Until I learned God's Word these feelings would resurface time and time again in my life.

Where was the God I remembered? Where was my God!!

With mixed feelings, and under public examination and doubt, whispers and lies, I left the church and my teacher for almost a year. Never in my life have I been as miserable as in this time. Never feeling welcomed or a kinship with any particular group anyway, I was as alone as I had ever been. Don't get me wrong, there were people who would say something nice to me or to greet me with some kind of smile and leave me with a "God loves you," but you know what you are looking at.

For you see, their lips said one thing, but their eyes said another. I knew that they had given up on me. I knew that they were talking about me. I knew that they were saying, "I told you." I knew that I was weak. I knew that I was wrong. I knew where my strength was. I knew that surely Jesus loves me. I knew that my Pastor loved me. I knew that I had to go back to see her.

Sweet as ever she took me in. Gently as a dove she picked me up. Patiently she listened. Once I had poured out my heart she looked straight at me and said, "Gregory, God would not have brought you this far to leave you." And once again, God had welcomed me back into His house. I bless God and thank God for keeping my little Pastor safe and well while I was weak for I always thought about the gift of her everyday and how I had just left her. From now on I knew that I would never nor could I ever leave church again. From that day forward I vowed to study more, listen more, and to actually do what I needed to do in order to be free of whatever was holding me back. I decided right then and there that this was something personal. This was something between the Lord and me. Boy was I ever wrong. You see, what I didn't understand was this was a battle between the Lord and Satan over me. What I still had to learn was that it would be my will, or rather my willingness, to be obedient to God's Word that would allow God to free me from the chains which bound my soul from accepting His *perfect will for my life*.

I knew that Jesus loves me. I knew that I was saved. I knew a lot of scripture. I still read my Bible. I have always been friendly toward people. There's nothing I love more than children and elderly. I knew I could speak about the Lord without shame or hesitation, but

I always felt that something was missing. "Where was my joy? Yeah, that is it," I realized one day as I was reading one of the Psalms of David. "Where is my joy?"

"Lord," I prayed, "Please help me to find my joy. Please help me to find my peace. Please show me the way to peace and joy that only rests in You." Now this is where things really began to happen. Good things, bad things, good times, bad times were all mixed together so consistently that I couldn't get a hold on what was going on. Bible study and church service were taking me to levels of which I had never been before. I had what seemed like a thousand pieces to a puzzled in my mind, but couldn't see the whole picture, much less put them together. This was really the first time that I had ever really been confused on a spiritual level. At the same time I understood that I had never made it this far before. I needed help. My Pastor would always encourage me and even outright told me what I needed to do about settling an old court issue.

"Boy, now you know that you can make it to that class one day a week if they hold that class three times a week," is what she told me. I knew that she was right. I just did not like the person instructing the class, period. I had laid a hundred dollar bill on the table right in front of him and ten other people and picked up my change when he hollered at me, "Don't you ever touch the money!" And the hundred dollars was more than what was on the table! I told him that too. Being that I didn't like him, and if I don't like someone, I simply want away from them, I wouldn't go to class at all. I knew that when I went to court and couldn't show the judge my certificate for completion of the course that I would be found in contempt and spend a year in jail, but I didn't care. I didn't like that man and would rather be in jail for a year than to look at him once a week for two hours for twenty-four classes. That is how I saw it.

Knowing that I was going to jail anyway, come the court date, I began to prepare for it. I would save my money up, so that I would have commissary money and I would be fine. All I needed was soap, shampoo, toothpaste and hair grease in order to make it. The jail ministries gave out books, pens and paper, so I knew that

I would have all that I needed in order to survive. Besides, God is also in jails, I already knew, because I had been there enough times to know.

Jail is a strange place and a strange environment. It makes some people better. It makes some people worse. It breaks some people's spirit. It drives some people crazy. Some people are punished by jail. Some people learn from their mistakes and get out and live good lives. To some, like me, it doesn't matter one way or the other. Jail is no more than going to a different place; a new playground with new playmates. The thing is that I could always get along with them if I wanted to. The main problem I have in jail or the free world is boredom. I like to read, write, and draw. With work and the rat race of the free world I've always found jail or prison relaxing because I could do what I like to do while there. To sit and read, write, or draw in *one place* is just as good as *another* to me because when I am in my own little world nothing else matters. Well, where I choose to go and what I decide I'm going to do doesn't always fit into where God has chosen for me to go or what He would have me to do.

Now, I've got to take you back in time just a few months earlier. I was in jail, yet another time, with a cellmate whose life was basically over. He was around my age, but facing a life sentence for drug dealing. Life means at least thirty years before being eligible for parole. While talking one day he told me that he had been a heroin junkie for about twenty years, but had been clean for about ten years. All he did now was sell cocaine. I asked him how he managed to stay clean for so long and he replied, "I prayed and asked God to remove drug addiction from my life and the next day I woke up and never touched heroin again. I never even had withdrawals."

This was the first time, the first time in my life, that I had ever been jealous. Now I knew I had my answer! The problem was although I too had prayed this same prayer many times and many times I managed to stay clean or sober for a while I would always revert back to my old ways, just as a dog returns to his own vomit. This time I vowed I would make it through. This time I would overcome. This time I would show the world that I could prevail. I would show God how hard I would try. I would show God what I could do. I would show God just how much I was willing to sacrifice. Again I was wrong.

This time God would show me what *He* could do and what *He* would do for me. Bless His holy and righteous name. It was springtime and the Lord had already blessed me with enough money to pay off my court costs, fines, and fees for the anger management class, but I did neither because I wanted to go to jail. I was really tired of living with same old ups and downs. I was really tired of the same routine year after year. Spring, summer, and fall are the time of year when most bricklayers make their money. The trouble was what to do with the money and my time during winter and rainy days. Money equals freedom to do for myself whatever I wanted to eliminate the boredom. Money, boredom, drugs, alcohol, and a "who cares" attitude, do not mix.

My plan was to keep driving to DUI class and to see my probation officer until it finally dawned on them to ask, "Why is he driving to class when twenty other offenders are standing outside on their cell phones calling for a ride home?" The craziest thing is they never said a word! My plan was to get arrested, go to jail for a year maybe two and come out clean. I was dead serious. Now one thing I will tell you about me is that when I'm serious, I'm serious. I did not want to go through another summer and ultimately a year of alcohol and drug abuse. All I had to do was to drive to work and to drive back home and I would have been safe. This would not suffice. My plan was to get clean in jail, study the Word, come out and say, "Here I am Lord, do with me as you wish." The only problem was that God had another plan. The only problem was that God had a plan that included God's plan.

For you see, I kept pushing my will through until one night I finally saw the light. Blue lights! (Sorry I couldn't help that). But seriously, one night the police stopped me for my headlights not being on and discovered I had no driver's license and took me to jail. Now part of my plan all along was to get rid of my car because access to bad places or the convenience of getting there was too great a temptation for me. When the officer asked, "Would you like to call someone to get your car," I said, "No" Bless his heart, I bet we sat there an hour with him trying to get me to not lose my car, but I again said, "No." I knew that I would have too much time between getting out of jail and court and I wanted to begin to prepare for my new life right then. Have you noticed that I keep saying "I"? It wasn't but a matter of days before I finally received that "blessed assurance" that many sing about, but so few have experienced.

Although I was where I wanted to be and had the best bunk in the jail pod, being first in line for chow, I was miserably tormented. I mean my entire soul was tormented. I slept in fits. I would be talking one minute and then feel like something was laughing at me the next minute. Then I felt like something was driving me onward the next minute. Then I would feel like I was right one minute, then wrong the next minute. Then glad, then sad. Then with hope, then despair. I mean I would literally wake up in a cold sweat, kicking, and talking out loud. I had no idea what I was saying. What I do know is never in my life have I ever been as miserable; never. Then!

Then one night that I never will forget as long as my Lord gives me air to breathe, while I lay on my bunk in that jail cell asleep, an angel came to visit me. Right in the middle of another torturous night it put its arms around me without even touching me and simply said, "It's alright, Gregory." I was free from bondage at last after forty-five years. I was free! Thank you God for hearing my prayers. Thank you Pastor for interceding for me. I'm a new creature now, though I have much too pray about and much change to make in my life, but now I too know that, "I can do all things through Christ who strengthens me!" Never in life have I ever had a peace and a joy as I did at that moment and I still carry that peace and joy even today. I will never forget seeing my little Pastor's face that night, not ever. And I will never forget the night she baptized me again, but this time in the Holy Ghost and given a brand new prayer language.

Oh, I guess you're wondering about court. Well to make a long story short the judge on the driving without a license charge gave me an "own recognizance" bond and set me free with the stipulation of two additional months of probation plus court costs. My probation officer was in court, didn't object, and didn't even revoke my original probation for this violation! The second judge a month later said," I've given you over a year already to have completed this six month anger management class and you still haven't done it." This was in May. "How much more time do you need?" "Maybe a couple more months," I replied, expecting jail since that wasn't even enough time. "I'll give you until November," he said. Only God can do this.

You see, I didn't realize it at the time, but what I had done was to submit, fully submit, my life to God. This I had never fully done before, because I always had a fall back plan just in case I got tired of church people or someone judging me and letting me know "my place" in "their" church. See, I always knew that the church belonged to Jesus and that I belonged in church but I had never trusted God to make me fit in His plan. Trust me, I've had some folks to say the craziest things to me in church, thinking that they were paying me a complement! I won't get into that yet, for like I said, this is a story of victory. God claiming and Jesus bringing back one of His lost sheep.

"If you should have one hundred sheep and one should fall into a pit, then you leave the ninety-nine and go get the one." This is how precious I am to my God!!

Beaten down by sin and finally submitting my all, I was now ready for God to restore me to those days of my youth, worshiping with a heart of a child. No, I'm not the same now, as I had been for years. A lot of people thought that they knew me, but only Jesus did. Only God knows why He left me here, and in the fire for so long. All I have for Him is praise, for He knew me and loved me even in the womb. I will follow Him all the days of my life for now I have life.

The Spirit came to me and told me what I had finally done that opened up heaven's blessings for me and it is this. Genesis 22:10, "And Abraham stretched forth his hand, and took the knife to slay his son." Genesis 22:15-17, "And the Angel of the Lord called unto Abraham out of heaven the second time. And said, by myself have I sworn, saith the Lord, for because thou hast done this thing, and hast not withheld thy son, thy only son: That in blessing, I will bless thee, and in multiplying I will multiply thy seed as the stars of the heaven, and as the sand which is upon the sea shore; and thy seed shall possess the gate of his enemies . . ."

I was willing to give up all, willingly, in order to be obedient to my God. This was the key. This is why I can, "Enter into His gates with thanksgiving, and into His courts with praise," being thankful unto Him, and blessing His name. In all that God has brought me through, first and foremost I must give thanks to God and to His Only Begotten Son Jesus Christ, who died on Calvary's Cross for the remission of our sins and now sits in heaven at the right hand of God, and the Holy Spirit who has been my Comforter.

In Remembrance and Thanksgiving

In remembrance I can now even be thankful for the little things like the smells of starch, hair grease, and Kiwi shoe polish. Yes, you heard me right. Thanks to the smells of starch, hair grease and Kiwi shoe polish. You see sometimes in order to be thankful for what we are, where we are, who we are, and how we are today we must go back to the remembrance of what got us or what brought us safely thus far. We must remember that seed! We must remember what it took to motivate us. We must remember what it took to inspire us to look towards tomorrow with hope and expectation. We must remember what it took to prepare us for our Sunday morning worship services and Sunday school. In this case it simply boils down to starch, hair grease, and Kiwi shoe polish. I know that by now you must be thinking "that boy's weird or crazy." But here is what the Spirit of the Lord has shown this old boy and has led me to believe is true.

All worship must begin with prayer. All prayer should begin with praise to God our Creator and our reason for living. Any praise to God comes from our meditation for living. Any praise to God comes from our meditation of who He is and acceptance of His Holy Word. Now the question is where does this meditation come from? Where does our preparedness to praise God come from? And how can we prepare ourselves to become receptive to the reading, preaching, and study of His Holy Word. The answer is we must prepare to receive His Word by reading His Word, not at the invocation of the service, for this is an invitation for the Holy Spirit to enter the worship service and dwell in our very presence during that service, but before we even begin the invocation. Thus I have come to realize that this takes place even on the night before Sunday morning. This is a night of the smells of starch, hair grease, and Kiwi shoe polish. This should be our night of meditation and our night of getting prepared to be receptive to the invocation of the Living Spirit.

You see, I have witnessed and I myself have been guilty of not being prepared for worship on Sunday mornings. I myself have somehow just overslept. I myself have been just too "worn out" to make it to Sunday school even though I managed to make it to the 11:00 church service. I myself have squeezed in enough time to make it to the 11:00 church service, no matter that I may be ten or fifteen minutes late even for it every week. I myself have not been there to participate in the opening of the church service to the very One who gives me the breath of life.

Have you ever left church service and said to yourself, "I didn't get anything out of that." Or have you ever said, "The Spirit just wasn't here today." Or maybe even, "Oh well, sometimes He's here and sometimes He's not. Maybe He'll stop by next week". Which actually is an attitude that is saying, "Anyway when He does stop by it's always when I've got my collard greens simmering at home, with company coming over, and the Cowboys and Redskins are on at 12:00." Sometimes deep down inside we just don't want the Holy Spirit in our midst because, yeah I'll say it, we think that He drags out the worship service too long! You know, give Him some sort of superficial praise, song, and shout and expect our lives to be blessed and God to be satisfied with us. Do we really believe that the Spirit of God can indwell within us when we have not done the things to be receptive to His divinity in the first place?

Now, I'm getting mad at my own self. Running around blaming everything, everybody, and every failed venture on God not hearing my cry instead of looking at myself and asking myself, "Am I being receptive to hear His voice? He, Himself said, "I will never leave you nor forsake you," but am I not being abusive to my Creator by not being obedient through meditation, fasting, prayer, and preparedness. No, though it grieves Him, He cannot and will not be abused. The only one that I have been abusing is myself. It is my own spiritual growth that I have been stalling. It is you and I that end up going around and around in circles like a fly with one wing.

What God has shown me in looking back is that when I was a boy, Saturday nights were the nights that you took down the ironing board. Saturday night was the night that you got out the iron and the starch. Saturday night was the night that you pressed your clothes. Saturday night was the night that you got your nappy head combed. Saturday night was the night that you greased your hair and kneecaps. Saturday night was the night that you got your "real bath." Saturday night was the night that you got your razor line. Saturday night was the night that you got out the shoe kit. Saturday night was the night that you took out the rag and brush from the shoe kit. Saturday night was the night that you opened up that can of Kiwi shoe polish. Saturday night was the night that you polished and shined your shoes so that they would be ready for Sunday morning. Saturday night is when we would study our Bible verses. Saturday night was when we rehearsed in our choir. Saturday night was when we practiced reading our Sunday school verses out loud. Saturday night was our night to prepare for Sunday morning! Saturday night was the night that we set aside to render ourselves receptive to the Holy Spirit, submissive to His will, and filled with exceeding joy. Surely joy comes in the morning!

What I'm talking about here is attention to detail. That is why I spent the time to go into detail, step by step, telling you about those Saturday nights when I was a child. I remember not so much about a wanting to look good to people, but wanting to look my *best* for Jesus. Play clothes were for playing games outside in the mud. Church clothes were separate and set apart for God. It was a mind-set that we were expecting Sunday to be different and set aside as holy. What God deserves is far more than I should give to the world or even myself. God gave His best when He gave His only Son as the perfect sacrifice for me. I expect to give my best to God. I don't care if what I give or do is better than what someone else gives or does. Neither does God! What is important is whether or not I gave my best or did my best with a pure and thankful heart.

Detail is very important to your worship because the enemy, Satan himself, desires nothing more than for you to trample upon the Blood of Jesus as if it were a common thing. It is too easy to forget that it is Jesus who allows you to do anything. It is too easy to forget that it is Jesus who gives you mercy and grace when you forget to pay attention to detail and leave a window of opportunity open for the Devil to enter into your life. We like to think that we can just relax and enjoy living from our carnal thoughts and the Enemy isn't going to bother us.

We know we are God's children because we are saved. But the Bible repeatedly warns each of us to daily be on guard against Satan and his attacks. Satan will use anything and anybody to get you to take your focus off of God, and to focus on yourself, other people, or circumstances around you. He wants nothing more than for you to spend Saturday nights arguing with your spouse or kids or maybe even trying to drink and party the problems away and then come to church broken again. You see Saturday night was the night that our Lord's body lay crucified, dead, and buried in His tomb. Saturday night was the night that our Lord was no longer in this world or of this earth. Saturday night was the night that we were lost. Saturday night was the night that our Lord's body lay still in obedience to God's perfect will. Saturday night was the night heaven began rejoicing. Saturday night was the night sickness, disease, poverty, death and the curse were swallowed up in victory. Saturday night was the night that God prepared to raise His Son up in glory. Saturday night was the night of great expectation for the Light of the World to once again walk among men with the burden of all men's sin left on the cross!

Lord we bless your Holy Name. We glorify You. We magnify You. We honor You. We praise You. We lift You up, Father. We lift You up that we may remain in Your grace. We need Your guidance from day to day. Order our steps, Lord. Lead us in the path of righteousness for Your name's sake. Deliver us from evil and worldly thought. Keep us near O God to You. Forsake us not although we have from time to time forsaken You. Grant us new mercies Father, that we should not utterly be cast down. Just as Jesus has gone on to heaven to prepare a place for us, let us prepare our hearts to enter Your Kingdom through thankfulness and remembrance. Our hearts belongs to You and You alone. Father show us Your glory and teach us who You are. Amen

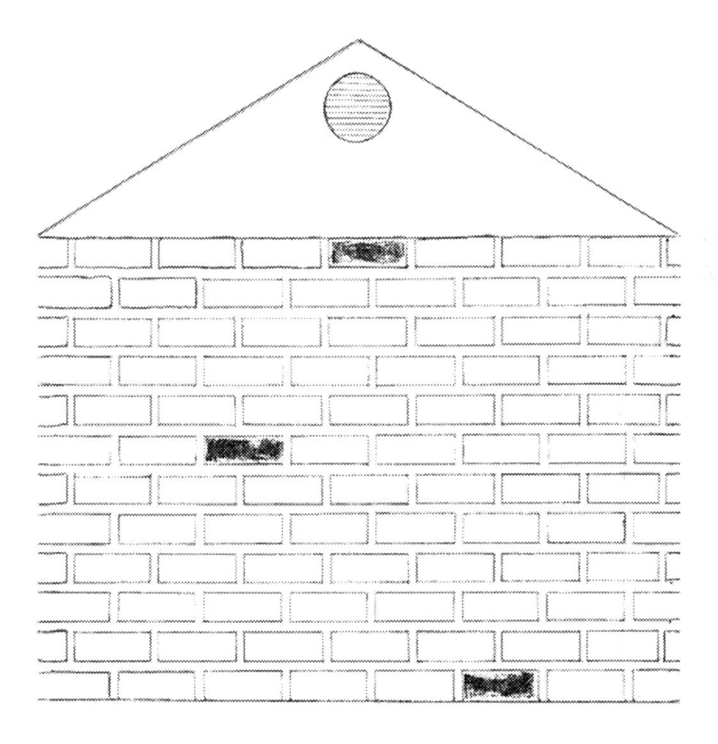

There are almost one hundred bricks in this wall from bottom to top. Which one of the shaded bricks has the most weight on it; the one on the very first course, the one in the middle, or the one on the very top?

I once had a masonry teacher to ask me this question when I was about sixteen; over thirty years ago. Since I'm a logical person and could easily spot the obvious I responded, "The brick on the bottom, because the rest of the bricks are laid on top of it."

"No son," he responded. "Actually there is no more weight on the very first brick you laid than there is on the last brick that you laid on the very top." He further explained to me that because of the mortar that binds all the brick together that they were no longer hundreds of bricks but one wall. "Now," he explained, "because of the mortar locking all the bricks together as one, all of the weight of this one wall rests on the foundation." Interesting I thought, and often times I would ponder this, as I grew older and wiser, always listening, and always learning.

One thing that's always bothered me is the divisive nature of certain Christians and churches. Jealousy, envy, selfishness, boasting, prideful, greedy, resentful, lack of compassion, no humility, and just plain unloving were a few of my insights. People, Christian folks at that, just couldn't seem to pull together as one. Everybody thinking that either they were doing all the work, carrying the whole church on their shoulders or that no one would let them participate, especially in the higher profile positions in the church. "He got his nose stuck in everything. She acts like can't nobody sing solo but her. I'm tired of cleaning up by myself." I've found out that attitudes like this are what stunts growth in the church, if really they don't destroy it altogether.

The more I pondered how we could fix these divisions in the people of God the more I thought about that lesson I'd learned long ago. Then the Lord revealed a very profound thing to me. What He revealed to me was that you, I, and the church family could be as one.

Just like that wall of bricks, if we Christians could understand and see ourselves, each one, as separate bricks bound together by the Holy Spirit acting as mortar, resting on the foundation of the Word of God then there would be no more burden on one of us than the other! It is clear to see, and we all know that we are to pray one for the other and petition our needs to God through Jesus in one accord. Your burdens become my burdens and my burdens become your burdens, which we can all lay at the feet of the Lamb. Notice I said to take our burdens, troubles, needs or our problems to Jesus, and *leave them there*. There's power in prayer and power in unity.

Now, some people may not like me saying this but I must say it anyway. Don't go running to your Pastor with a whole bunch of mess that you need to settle between yourselves. The Word says to go to your brother or your sister and personally work things out and forgive one another as God has forgiven you, before you even come to God with anything else. If you and I can't settle our differences and don't have enough maturity to leave it in God's hand, then what is the Pastor suppose to think about any of us!

Now I won't sit here and try to put words into any Pastor's mouth but I will tell you what happens. What happens is that instead of your Pastor being able to move forward relaying God's vision to you, he or she must now stop where they are in God's blueprint, a holy blueprint that calls for mature Christians. Coming together as one is essential, so vital, and so basic in God's instruction that it is imperative that we heed to the instruction. It's really a shame that our Pastors have keep going back over this basic point time and time again. It's written in the scriptures enough times and explained over and over enough that we all know what is required. We simply choose not to obey.

This squabbling will tear your church apart! It's not a matter of if this division will tear your church apart, but rather when this division will be complete. I am not talking about pad locking the doors and boarding up the windows here either. We just keep carrying on with the same mess year after year. But when you separate yourself from your brother, when you go and separate yourselves into your own little self-interest groups within the church, what you are actually doing is separating yourselves and the church itself from the Holy Spirit which should be binding us all together just like brick and mortar.

O Lord, let each of us examine our own heart. Let each of us study to show ourselves approved unto God. Let each of us have mercy, compassion, patience, and love for our neighbor. Let each of us show that same commitment, that same kindness and that same forgiveness to one another that You have shown to us. Let us move forward in Your grace, by Your Heavenly guidance, and in accordance to Your will for Your name's sake. O Lord, hear us when we pray and teach us to live our lives in one accord. Bind our hearts together with the Living Spirit so that we may rest on the foundation of your Holy Word. Amen.

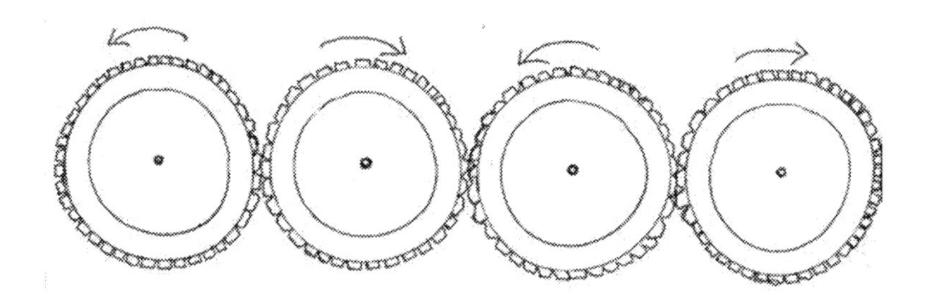

Thirty-four years of bricklaying has truly been a blessing to me. A blessing because of all the lessons I've learned about how to not only build, but also the lessons of building relationships. The many lessons I have learned have given me an insight into what it takes to build up God's Kingdom.

I studied the gears on my mortar mixer one day as I noticed the gears needed to be greased. The more that I looked at these gears the more my mind began to see a bigger picture. You see this was the mechanical world. A world where some things, once set in motion, although connected or intertwined, don't necessarily move in the same direction. Can they still attain a definite purpose or outcome that is beneficial? Is the fact that they are connected crucial to this?

One thing for sure is that it sure seems to be working with this mortar mixer.

If these gears were churches would this mechanical truth still be true? Can God's holy catholic church (universal church) be going in different directions and still be headed in the same direction all at the same time?

If different people of different Christian denominations are given spiritual gifts unique to them, can they all collectively come together? How can working together and seemingly going in opposite directions be one and the same? How can the holy catholic church (universal church) accomplish oneness with each denomination seemingly going its own direction? Is this truly a truth of God's will or merely no more than a riddle?

Well, God can not lie, so if these churches are seemingly going in opposite directions while still connected and still yet reach the promise of one universal church, then it's the connection itself that has to be the key to it all. Since God is a God of perfect order, Jesus is the Head of the church, and the Holy Spirit binds us all together, it then makes perfect sense that it is no less than God's perfect will, His perfect plan and vision that is this key.

Our thoughts are not always His thoughts and our ways are not always His ways. What people, even Christians, can do is of a finite realm when not done through the Spirit. What God can do and the manner in which He does it is of an infinite realm of being. Anything described to us or promised to us, although yet to pass has still yet been considered done to God who is perfect, who is the Great Architect, and who cannot lie or miscue. What the scriptures tell us is that we are to pray one for another, love one another as Christ loves us, keep His commandments, and obey His Word. If we ask the Lord to guide us then we all will indeed be heading not only in the same direction, but also in the right direction, which is toward an universal church; The holy catholic church of God's master plan.

Some things in life that seem contrary can often times surprise us in how well impossible situations, circumstances, or people, for that matter, become most possible after all. Could this come from whatever binds all of us together?

When I was in building trades school I had a masonry teacher that I really looked up to. A role model if you will. He seemed to always know what to do in order to finish any project no matter what obstacles were in our way. Most often these obstacles were weather, materials, correct measurements, or relaying the correct information along with making sure that everyone was using the correct and most effective tool for the task at hand. But what I most noticed was how he would handle discord, arguments, or students who couldn't seem to get along.

What he would do was to take a short piece of rope and tie both of the students together at the wrist! Then he would say, "You two don't seem to be trying to work together and get along with one another so now you don't have a choice. You'll either get along and do the job or you both are in trouble with me." The thing that I noticed about this situation was that while they were tied wrist to wrist they each had a free hand. One person's left hand was free while the other person's right hand was free. An impossible situation was now not so impossible after all. The only way to keep themselves out of trouble was not only to help the other person, but to get along as well.

In church or any other Christian relationship that we may have, that rope symbolizes the Spirit that binds us all. You see it's during these trying times, these times of trials, uncertainty, doubt, and pains of growth, that Christian folk need each other the most. You cannot, I cannot, and we cannot make it alone. "Do not forsake the assembly of my people!" When two righteous people are in agreement, praying in one accord for the Lord to assist or grant them that which in the abundance of His promises, it shall be given. He shall also be in their midst for His name's sake.

I've found out that there is power, power from on high, bestowed upon those whose purpose is based on unity, love and peace. I'm talking about the kind of unity that can only be brought together by truly fervent prayer and held together by the Holy Spirit Himself.

The thing is though, that unlike my teacher tying students together with ropes, the Lord leaves that choice up to us to whether or not we seek His guidance and togetherness. God expects us to expect to love our neighbor as ourselves. If we want to expect only the best for ourselves then we must also expect and hope for the best for our church family no matter who they may be.

So when we find ourselves bickering, gossiping, and unable or unwilling to get along all we need to remember is that the only time that we as Christians will be able to work together for the edification of God's Kingdom is when we are bound willingly by the Spirit.

The choice that we have to make is between accord and discord. Accord has to do with oneness or togetherness, or complete harmony with other persons or groups within the church. Discord is a divisiveness rooted in non-spirituality. I say this is because the two cannot both inhabit the same space at the same time and one or the other constantly dwells in man's heart. The heart of man is made by God to be a spiritual place set aside for Him. Only a non-spiritual existence is left as an option when man chooses to not allow the Holy Spirit to have His way. We cannot straddle the fence on this issue. We are either for the Lord or we are enemies of the Lord. The choice is ours to make. There will be no excuses that we can offer to the Lord on this issue. The thing is that when we are living in one accord then and only then do the fruit of the Spirit manifest in us into a mirror image of Christ. Discord on the other hand has absolutely nothing to do with Christ or any of His teachings. I've often wondered do jealousy, envy, strife, and hatred bring discord or does discord bring jealousy, envy, strife, and hatred. Or is it that discord and all worldly feelings are one and the same? One thing that I've learned is that in order for me to sustain any peace, love, and joy in my heart I must first make a conscious decision to let God work on my heart in the first place by remembering my strength comes from Him.

From Cornerstone to Keystone

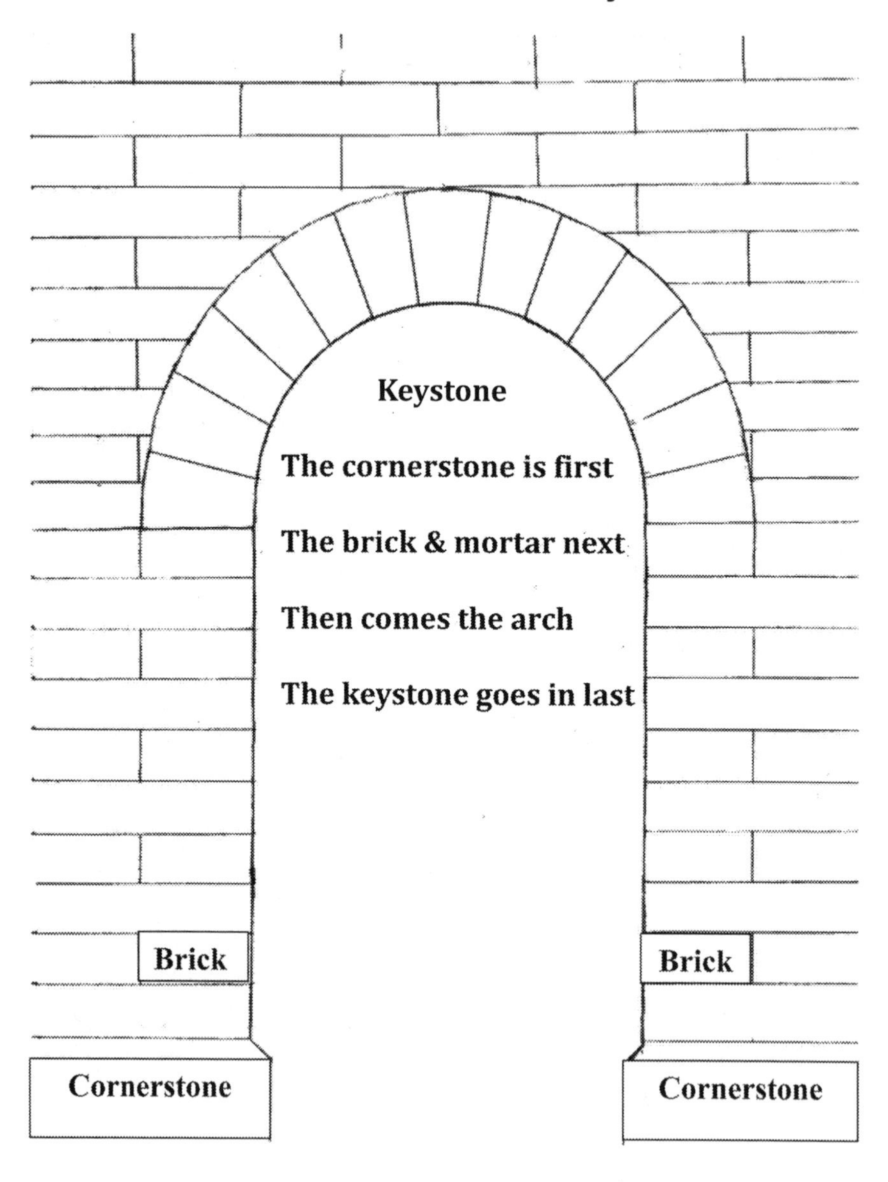

Cornerstone

N. 1. A stone uniting two masonry walls at an intersection.

2. A stone representing the starting place in the construction of building, usually carved with the date.

1. Something that is essential, indispensable, or basic.

Keystone

N. 1. A voussoir (piece of wedge shaped stone) at the summit of an arch.

1. Something on which associated things depend.

Template

N. 1. A pattern, mold, or the like, usually consisting of a thin plate of wood or metal serving as a gauge or guide in mechanical work.

1. Building a horizontal piece of timber or stone, set into a wall to distribute the pressure of a girder, beam or the like.

These are three words in masonry work that I've heard every since I began to learn this building trade over thirty years ago. Always having only to associate these terms to building structures out of brick, block or stone it took me until recently to realize and understand just how important these terms and my knowledge and application of these terms are to us in a spiritual sense as well as in an architectural sense. It is truly amazing just how many spiritual lessons one can learn just from his daily tasks or work. One thing that I have learned about this masonry business is that there is a general rule of thumb that any master mason will tell you, that is, "Never lay the first brick unless you know where the last brick is going." But is this true spiritually?

Now I will start you out with some basic tips on building an arch using cornerstone, brick, template, and keystone. First of all the strength of any masonry work is the corners. That strength comes from the fact that in a ninety-degree angle each wall supports other wall in that angle. In other words, the corner supports the corner. The cornerstone on a solid foundation needs no other support for it in itself is the main support for the entire structure. Once the cornerstone is set then the mason will begin to lay the brick on either side of the door or opening one brick at a time, course by course until he has reached the desired height at which the arch begins. This leaves two separate piers or columns, which will support the arch. In order to span this distance between these two columns, which will support the arch, the mason must use a template to temporarily hold the brick up as he lays them across the arch shaped template. In laying the brick across the arch template the mason must come from both sides equally and at the same time in order to keep the arch balanced and centered the same. Once the brick is laid from each column towards the center, using mortar to bind them together, the mason then sets the keystone or last masonry unit to lock this entire structure in place and together as one. Once the keystone is in place then he can continue to lay brick over and across the arch because now the arch itself is self-supporting. Once the mortar has solidified, or hardened, he can remove the template and the arch will not fall. So you see that it takes all of these things combined together to span any opening or obstacle in order to bring strength to the other. The cornerstone alone has nothing to hold up or to support. The brick alone produce nothing beneficial. The mortar alone has nothing to bind together. The template alone is useless and the keystone has nothing to strengthen.

Isaiah 40:12-14 puts it all in perspective for us this way; "Who has measured the waters in the hollow of his hand, and meted out heaven with the span, and comprehended the dust of the earth in a measure, and weighed the mountains in scales, and the hills in a balance? Who has directed the Spirit of the Lord, or being His counselor has taught Him? With whom took He counsel, and who instructed Him, and taught Him in the path of judgment, and taught Him knowledge, and showed to Him the way to understanding?"

Here is how God showed me this while I was working with an older mason, when I was about twenty or so, who was an excellent teacher. I remember that it wasn't that he taught me *what* to think or to do, but rather *how* to think any job *through* which was what contributed most to my growth and understanding. In teaching me *how* to think I was not only able to work *without* him standing over me, but I was able to overcome my fear of messing up. By learning *how* to think, I now had confidence in what I could do even if I couldn't see the *entire* picture in my head. What I learned to do was to think like he thinks. What I learned was at times there was *more than one* option in getting prepared for the last brick in a wall. If something that the carpenters had built was out of level or out of square before I started laying the brick then I learned to plan up front to make adjustments along the way by using thicker or tighter mortar joints, rowlocks, soldier courses, or even adding an unscripted design to the wall. Now, when I did this I knew that I *had* to make it pretty! Now instead of the homeowner questioning me about some flaws in their house, whether or *not* I was the person who caused it in the first place, I had now made a mistake in the building acceptable to them.

One of the funniest things about this was one day, when it was my own fault in the layout of the brick, the best builder I'd ever known came by one evening while I was still laying brick on one of the homes that he was building. Now, Jim really likes my work and me. He gave me my start, in owning my own business. He even bought me all of the equipment I needed and let me repay him as I could afford it. He is a good man and a smart one too. When He saw this fancy design in the middle of this straight wall, the first thing he said was, "What went wrong?" We both cracked up! Then he said, "Try not to do that no more, cause if somebody else sees that design they'll want it on their house too and then you'll be charging me for it." So what I learned most of all was not so much that when I wanted to change something I had to make it pretty but I had to have permission to change it at all!

So the truth is yes we need the same strength to finish our journey, as we needed in order to begin. And we need the same plan to finish that we use to start. God is the beginning and God is the end. It was He who chose to set Jesus as our Head of the church body. This is truly a blessed act of God for we alone could never hold the church together. All that we are vessels for Jesus to use. In order for Him to truly use us, we must obey Him and His teachings, but we don't always do this. Somewhere along the way we seem to revert back to our own worldly ways of bickering, arguing, and divisiveness. See, *along the way*, and I'm going to take this for granted, means that we have *started out* in the Word of God, with Jesus as our cornerstone, but are now standing as *many* separate columns of brick. When we separate then we leave a void or open space between God's other children and ourselves. Though we may continue to grow in certain areas *upwardly,* we are nonetheless *still* divided as a church reaching outwardly.

What template can God use to bridge this gap? Remember, a template is only temporary. Well I'm going to tell you that you can be God's template. Yes you! Whenever you bring two opposing sides together in peace and love, for the building up of God's Kingdom then you are acting as a template that crosses whatever brought this conflict or division about in the first place. God can use us to bring people together as long as Jesus and the Holy Spirit binds us together just like brick and mortar. Once, bonded together like brick with Christ acting as our Cornerstone then and only then will we have unity and strength as a people. Even when we, as God's template, are not present the church should *still* be able to function because Christ is not only our Cornerstone but our Keystone as well.

So we don't need to worry about what we think other folks need to be doing or where they should be in God's plan, for only He knows what He has in store for each one of us. *Trusting* in the Lord is all that we need to know. Having *faith* in the Lord to guide the church is what opens many doors where there once were obstacles. Having *love* for one another surely opens windows of opportunity to spread and to teach others what you have been taught. No crisis in the church is too great for Christ to overcome if the church is set on a solid foundation with Jesus as its cornerstone. In fact, what He will do is to turn this crisis or division *around* so that the church knows that it was Him that did it for His glory. Nobody but the Lord can bring people of all walks of life together under one roof and on one accord. Jesus mixes different people, weak and the strong together so that we can *support each other*.

Maybe you've been through some things that I am now going through. Maybe I've been through some things that you are faced with. Maybe there is a reformed alcoholic or addict in the church who can give you an insight into how to deal with your teenagers. Maybe someone in the church can teach you a different language while you teach him or her yours. There is a spiritual growth in sharing our lives and what God has done for us with *others*.

If your Pastor is anointed by God to lead you and your church then they are also a *template* that God has anointed, and Jesus has appointed to serve this church for the season set forth by the Lord. Here today, maybe gone tomorrow, your Pastor, with God's guidance and wisdom will be able to go about God's business without the church falling apart. What we need to do is to get started at the right place and with the Word of the Lord and the blood of Jesus as our foundation. By confessing our sins and repenting, asking for forgiveness, and accepting Jesus as Lord of our lives we set out on faith and faith *alone*. All that we can do is to follow one step at a time. Often times God will put something on our hearts to get done but we lack the vision to see the end, much less *His* purpose for what He has told us to do. Now if I, as only one brick in the wall, can't fully comprehend God's plan for my life then I know that I can't understand all that God has for you to do. What I have learned through the years is that God blesses those who bless others with a spirit of love.

Love conquers all. Love conquers hate. Love conquers jealousy. Love conquers fear. Love conquers the world's teaching. Love conquers loneliness. Love conquers depression. Love conquers anything that Satan uses against you. When you love as Jesus loves then there is nothing between you and Jesus. Isn't this what we want? If this is what we say that we want, then why is it so hard for us to love? Well, I'll start with me. You see, there are times when I simply choose *not* to love, truly love, everyone regardless of who they are. But in reflection it is during these instances that I have *come* to realize that I am of no use, and *can't* serve or be used by God for His divine purpose. So, we must make up our mind to let God mold us as He sees fit. If I do wrong I *expect* to be chastised or led in a different direction. Will this be good for me and for His vision of one love? Yes it will. You see, anywhere that you go, once you give in to let God do the work then not only will you find peace but you can also be a template for His church.

If you make the choice not to give up your will for God's will then you will always lack the power to lead others. The very control you want over others will always escape you. You will have given back to Satan the very authority which you have over him through the blood of Jesus. Only your salvation gave you power over Satan in the first place. You are now to do the works of Christ. If you don't use your authority over Satan then Satan is still in the driver's seat through your flesh. There must be a change in your thinking in order to change your actions or behavior.

What I have learned is that problems are created once, and then bred over and over. But they all come from the same source or seed. What I call one main type of this behavior is the "kicked dog syndrome." See, we all have an opinion but our opinion really only shows what or who our faith is in. Either we are made whole or we have a problem in our Christian lives. We are only made whole by establishing our faith in God and the Word by acknowledging the power of His might in our lives.

Kicked Dog Syndrome

Syndrome: n.1 a group of symptoms that together is characteristic of a specific condition, disease, or the like. 2. The pattern of symptoms that characterize or indicate a particular social condition.

When I was a young boy growing up during the sixties and seventies I had a paper route. My paper route covered my entire neighborhood, downtown, and parts of other neighborhoods outside of where I grew up. I had a lot of people on my paper route that I knew personally or at least knew who they were. Another thing that I knew was their dogs or where their dogs were most of the time. You see, during this time there were no leash laws or laws to keep your dog locked behind a fence, so as a paperboy you had better know where the dogs were! Now dogs have teeth and dogs will bite. Everyone always told me, "Don't worry he won't bite" even as the darn thing had me by the pants leg. Then they even had the nerve to get mad if I tried to kick the dog off of me. "He doesn't bite. Just stand still and don't run. Quit kicking my dog!" People are crazy and so are their dogs are what I decided before long. "Never again," I vowed. The trust was gone. "I'll look out for me," I thought.

Before long when I encountered a dog that wasn't already proven friendly to me I would just kick the mess out of it. I was taking no chances with any one of them or even going to give them the benefit of the doubt. Some were lying down. Some were standing up. Some were big. Some were little. Some growled, and some didn't. Some of them looked rather peaceful enough without their hair standing up on their necks or not even paying me much attention, but if I wanted to make sure that I was safe in my own mind, the poor creature was kicked. Many a day did I kick a dog but the strangest thing is that I never felt any safer or like I had any power or control the situation. The truth is that what I had was the "kicked dog syndrome." I now realize that what I did was to often times kick an innocent dog. In kicking the dog first I had put myself into a vicious cycle, for now I always had to wonder, "Did I kick him hard enough to be afraid of me, respect me, and not bother me, or did I kick him just hard enough to make him mad?" Needless to say now I felt I had no choice but to kick the dog every time that I saw it, out of fear.

Now what was the poor dog thinking about me? What was he suppose to think? What did I think he would think or feel about me? Should I really expect the dog to forgive me and to love me? What did God think about my actions?

These are some of the questions that we need to be asking ourselves as we go out into this world as disciples for Christ. For the truth is that I could have avoided certain houses or situations along my paper route or even quit but when we, as disciples for Christ, go out into the world we are committed to preach the Word unto all of God's children no matter where they are. Now there is certain spiritual discernment involved, which I won't get into here, but the bottom line is that we must have the heart, strength, compassion, boldness, and steadfastness to continue on in spite of our fears or how often *we* are attacked for Jesus' name. To put someone down, ignore someone, or to intentionally hurt someone in order to remove him or her from our path so that we are more comfortable is wrong because though we may be afraid of them or situations, these may be the very lost souls that God would have us to speak His Word to. I myself have made a vow to consciously look at the person and not the circumstances from now on. I pray that any person that I have "kicked" forgive me for my sins against them in order for me to move forward in Christ.

Now, if I have the dreaded kicked dog "sin drome" and admit that I do indeed have its symptoms then I must now examine the social condition that it creates. The truth is that every action has a reaction whether it is good or bad. Since God is good and doing wrong to others is bad then how can I expect any person that I "kick" to see God's Spirit in me? How can I speak in His name for His name's sake?

When we "kick" someone we are separating him or her from us. We are saying, "you are not like us" and "you are not acceptable to us" and ultimately that, "God favors only us and has left it up to us to determine who else is worthy or acceptable to Him." Whether or not they believe that we are God's disciples is now unimportant because the disease of the kicked dog "sin drome" has now taken root. Once taken root this syndrome itself has now been given the power by us to undo or hinder anything that we try to accomplish. Everybody has a constant battle of good versus evil going on inside of them. Everybody! So now that we have "kicked" someone for no reason, what happens next? One thing for sure is that they don't believe that God's Spirit is leading us. They also learn to stay away from us, or to seek others like themselves or withdraw from any person who comes to them in the Name of the Lord. So if we can't see the love of Christ in people and they don't see the love of Christ in us then where is Christ in the midst of any of this? We need to know because there is a storm a comin.'

I often wonder what would have happened if only I would have given those dogs a chance. I wonder if we could have gotten along. I wonder if the poor creature approached me out of hunger. I wonder if they approached me out of loneliness. I wonder if they were afraid of me first. I wonder what would have happened if I could have given them a chance to make first contact. I wonder what they thought about me in their turf or their yard and then treating them like they were the enemy. I wonder if all I had to do was to throw them a snack and to pet them, maybe stroke their ears or rub their belly. One thing that I know for sure is that I'll never know what type of relationship we could have had because I never gave them a chance to show me their heart.

I for sure showed them mine and in looking forward to my journey with Christ, I now know and understand that I must first and foremost become more Christ-like before I speak or go out into the world in His name. So do all of His disciples, so that He may draw all men unto Him, who is the only One worthy to pass judgment.

Matt. 7:18, "A good tree cannot bring forth evil fruit; neither can a corrupt tree bring forth good fruit."

Matt. 10:16, "Behold, I send you forth as sheep in the midst of wolves; be ye therefore wise as serpents, and harmless as doves."

Matt. 13:29-30, "But He said, nay; lest while ye gather up the tares, ye root also the wheat with them. Let both grow together until the harvest: and in the time of harvest I will say to the reaper, Gather ye together first the tares, and bind them in bundles to burn them; but gather the wheat into the barn."

Now, know that there are many different ways that we can "kick" a person who also is made in the very image and likeness of God. This doesn't have to be a physical "kick." Damaging another person's will to seek a personal relationship with Jesus is far worse. Attacking their essence or assassinating the Spirit, which dwells within them is of the worst transgression. Now I ask you, who is innocent?

To put a person down to destroy their character is to destroy the spirit in a person. Telling lies on a person, one of Christ's own, is to tell a lie on Christ. To twist a truth that you know about a person so that it tears them down instead of building them up is to tear down what Christ is building up. To publicly mock someone is to mock the Spirit in them. Even to mock their sin is sin itself. To belittle an unbeliever shows that you too are an unbeliever. Christ does the calling and choosing in His time not ours. To intentionally hinder someone or to put a stumbling block in their path, when the Lord is working on them or through them will not be without consequences. Gossiping about folks or their business only tears churches apart. Telling a person, especially a child that they are worthless tells them that they aren't precious to Jesus. Telling someone that you hate him or her is worse than any curse word. Waving your arms in church one minute then getting off in a circle with your buddies talking about, "white folks are the devil" only shows your ignorance.[Ephesians 6:12] Destroying someone's character only destroys your character along with his or hers. The point is once we "kick" someone or kick back, instead of continuing to "kick" them out of fear or ignorance, what we need to do is to look at our own selves and ask, "Am I my brother's keeper?" Then repent. Only the Devil is the devil and people are people! Your works show who *you* belong to though. [St. John13:34-35, 8:44, 47]

Lawyers or attorneys are a fine example (some anyhow) of people with this "kicked dog syndrome." Either hired by the defense or prosecuting for the plaintiff or the state, their main goal is to win their case. I said "win" and not prove because to "win" is to get their client off of the charges or lawsuit against them for the defense, or either to convict them for the prosecution. The prosecutor's job is to prove the defendant guilty, period. A lot of the time these judges or spectators don't know any more actual facts at the end of the trial than they did at the start of the trial.

In both lawyers trying to win their case they must convince the jury of the merits of their case. Not actually knowing either plaintiff or defendant these sworn public servants will still yet set out to destroy one or the others character. Additionally if there are any other witnesses, their character is also up for public assassination. It's all part of the game. They will dig up and use any dirt that they can against a person no matter how irrelevant it is to the case being tried. They will embarrass, ridicule, belittle, insinuate, and even enter an outright lie against someone in order to tear their character apart. By tearing this person's character apart they are feeling that this person is no longer a threat to their case, livelihood, or most of all, their ego. They don't want to give up their "stature."

It is all truly one big faithless act. Tell part of the story and leave part of it out. Call certain witnesses to testify but leave others out. Claim to be sane one minute but insane the next. Claim to be insane one minute then sane the next. If faith were involved we would just tell the truth and say, "Let God's will be done."

Here's faith. "Now faith is the substance of things hoped for, the evidence of things not seen." [Heb.11:1] See, since faith has substance means that it has weight with God. It is actually tangible to Him like holding something in our hand is tangible to us. Since God says faith is evidence in and of itself lets us know that it is our faith which we present through the blood of Jesus before the Judge, who is God, who then renders the verdict which always lines up with His promises for your life! So Jesus is actually your lawyer, or Advocate, or Mediator who presents the real evidence (faith) before the judge in court. Your faith in God is what determines what is truly admissible or thrown out of judgment! Not manipulation. It is the manipulation which God hates. Faith is the only exhibit admissible! There is no exhibit "A" and exhibit "B" or exhibit "C". Faith is its own proof. Now if I say I have faith and God looks in His hand

and it's empty, then all I have is hope, assumption, or a sense of entitlement.

The same thing is true for us in the church when we need to help nurture, train, or teach someone else what we have been taught so that they too can go out and teach someone else. Only by repeatedly lifting up our baby Christians in *faith* they will grow up to be disciples. They don't need pity! So yes, I am my brother's keeper just as Jesus keeps me.

And then there's the old faithful "I knew them when" syndrome of the kicked dog "sin drome." This one is guaranteed to bring these new converts, struggling, and up and coming baby Christians down to their "place." Funny how their place is always beneath us; their place is always decided by us; Us, the Father, the Son, and the Holy Ghost.

Time and time and time again we remind them of what they were. Again and again and again we let them know that we only see them as they were. Over and over and over we kick their legs out from under them for no reason. This is a sickness and this is also sickening to those that are hindered from moving closer to God. We can spread our sickness around so often and in such a hurtful way that these babes just lose hope and die inside. The sad part is that you too are dead inside spiritually if this is you. It takes a spiritually dead person to even think that they can judge others and that they themselves, will not be judged by the same measure by God. We are not above God!! Help these lost, new, struggling or baby Christians or shut up! You hurt them when you say, "I've got your 'number'." You hurt them when you accuse them of things that they haven't done just because it "fits" what you know about their past. It hurts them when you whisper around the church "I know how they are." It hurts them when you let them know, "I remember you and your whole family way before you were born and they weren't any good then and you ain't no good now and never will be any good." Over and over and over we "kick."

Now, let's get down to the other manifestation of this all destructive "kicked dog syndrome." We've looked at the physical and spoken parts of this disease so now let's look at the unspoken parts and psychological aspect of this disease and see how it directly affects the church and the churches growth. You see this is probably the most damaging manifestation of this "sin drome." This is where we are able to say, "Oh well, it ain't my fault. I didn't do anything." Well you got that right. You didn't do anything. You didn't do anything at all! You didn't even pay them any attention. You didn't even greet them. You didn't even introduce yourself. You didn't even introduce them to your friends. You never fellowship with anyone other than your own family. You never even personally invite them back. If they happen to come back on their own, then all you did was treat them the same way as before. You never even ask them anything about themselves, but sure burn up the telephone lines asking all of your gossip buddies what they had heard about them through your gossip grapevine. All you did was to ignore them time after time. All you did was to roll your eyes when they looked your way. All you did was not to give any acknowledgment to their questions or suggestions again and again. All you did was to grin in their face and then talk about them like a dog on the phone with others as if the person that you've been "kicking" in church is in your house in your way.

Well, let me tell you something "on the heart" brothers and sisters. You can cry "I didn't do nothing" all you want to but the truth is, and God knows it, that you played a psychological game of the kicked dog "sin drome" until you ran them out of the church and you don't care. You don't care if they tell others and you don't care if anybody else joins the church because you think that the church is all about you! Why invite someone into the church and be mean to them? I hope that you're not thinking, "I ain't invited them!!"

Life is not all about us. Love is not all about us. Fellowship is not all about us. Church is not all about us. And Jesus is not all about us. As a matter of fact the only truth in any of this is that God wants us, but He doesn't need us. If we don't praise Him the rocks will cry out praise for Him. And He can raise up an Abraham generation from these rocks to do His will. With that being understood only then can we begin to find a cure for this "kicked dog syndrome." It really doesn't take much. Confess, repent, and ask for forgiveness from Christ and then turn from sin. That's it.

Stop "kicking" people. If you are afraid of them then get to know them first. If you are afraid of not having control then give it to Christ. If you don't like the way someone looks then quit staring. If you don't like the way someone acts, guide him or her. If you want all the responsibility just pray for your calling. If you don't like the way the pianist plays, then play what you want to hear at home yourself. If you don't like the way the choir sings then sing to yourself. If you don't like the way the church looks then offer to help decorate it. If you don't like being around new people then pray for joy. If you don't like change then pray for a renewed spirit. If you have a problem with the Pastor then pray for them. If you have a problem with me then come to me before going to everyone else. If you have jealousy in your heart then pray for your purpose. If you are a stumbling block then turn to follow the Word. If you have a snide comment to make then pray for a transformed mind. If you are afraid of progress then pray for God's vision. If you have nothing good to say then say nothing at all. If you want to pass judgment on others, then first look in the mirror. If you don't love your neighbor then pray for a clean heart. If you don't know Jesus then seek Him. If you still can't help but to run someone off then simply submit to God because if you don't this syndrome will be stopped by God Himself.

If you know someone's sordid past don't continue to insult him or her or to hold him or her back by approaching him or her or talking to him or her in a non spiritual manner. Comments like, "Man look at the body on that woman" or "Honey, I bet that it wouldn't take much to have him," only serve to let the new Christian know you feel that their heart hasn't really changed. What you are actually saying is, "Aw, I know you may be trying but you are what you are and we will just keep it our little secret. You can confide in me." Then run and tell everything they may be struggling with.

They know that they have a new heart and that Jesus brought about this change but being "new" they also need your support, encouragement, and confirmation of their change. They need someone to tell them to "Come on." They need someone to tell them, "You can do it! Yes, you can conquer all of your iniquities through Christ which strengthens you." They need someone to tell them, "Greater is He that is in you than he that is in the world." They need someone to tell them, "Don't look back for now your sins have been removed from you as far as the east is from the west." They need someone to tell them, "Jesus loves you, this I know, for the Bible tells you so."

Just because one man sows and another man waters doesn't mean there has to be a long gestation period before we see the new creature in folks! So pick our new Christians up and let's stop tearing each other down. I need you and you need me. We all need the blood of the Lamb. Lord, pick me up, and help me stand by faith on God's own tableland. No higher plain than I have found. Lord, plant my feet on Higher Ground. Amen.

In the Midst of the Storm

1. Spiritually we learn to stand from our knees.

2. The purpose of God's Word is to bring clarity.

3. Hope turns to faith when you trust good to come no matter how dark it seems right now.

4. Give God your will.

5. Overcome evil with good.

6. We learn to trust God when He doesn't answer right away.

7. Privilege must give way to God's authority.

8. Constructive criticism doesn't involve assassinating someone's character.

9. You don't "do what you gotta do." You wait on the Lord.

10. Our actions add to or take away the blessings.

11. The seed of un-forgiveness becomes the root of bitterness.

12. Don't allow the exercising of your liberty to become a stumbling block to others.

13. Love isn't so much an emotion as it is a God-like quality or virtue.

14. Your faith acts as your witness and evidence before God.

15. Realize the value of your blessing.

16. Move on from good habits to the full character of Christ.

17. Don't live by what "they" say.

18. Don't let your plan's turn into schemes.

19. Learn who can decree a thing and it come to pass.

20. Don't confuse authority with total autonomy.

God is not Bob Villa!

We learn in the book of Exodus 20:23-25 that "Ye shall not make with Me gods of silver, neither shall you make unto you gods of gold. An altar of earth thou shalt make unto Me, and shalt sacrifice thereon thy burnt offerings, and thy peace offerings, thy sheep and thine oxen; in all places where I record My name I will bless thee. And if thou wilt make Me an alter of stone, thou shalt not build it of hewn stone; for if thou lift up thy tool upon it thou hast *polluted it."*

"And He gave unto Moses, when He had made an end of communing with him upon Mount Sinai two tables of testimony, tables of stone, written with the finger of God." (Exodus 31:18)

"And the Lord said unto Moses, Write thou these words: for after the tenor of these words have I made a covenant with thee and with Israel. And he was there with the Lord forty days and forty nights; he did neither eat bread nor drink water. And he wrote upon the tables the words of the covenant, the ten commandments." (Exodus 34:27-28)

These few verses from Exodus sure tell us what not to do. But when we look at these verses through spiritual eyes we can see also what God would have us to *do* also. You see with spiritual eyes we should see that it is not only that God tells the people and Moses what not to do but also that which he doesn't need them to do in order to serve him. Now I'll get to the point of what the Spirit has shown me: In the midst of the storm you had better know who God is and what He expects of you for yourself!

There is nothing that I can make that will please God. By the same measure no monument, writing on the wall, or public display should comfort us or be considered by us to be our only way of spreading the Gospel. Now if God Himself wrote the Ten Commandments on stone and then gave them to Moses that should be a clue. If God says *not* to take your tool upon the altar made of stone then what we should understand is that everything we want to offer up to God isn't consumed by Him. We must be sure our sacrifice is acceptable to Him! This is how Jesus stayed in God's plan. Jesus lived sinless and He spoke the Word.

If God would have *wanted* Moses to go around with tools in order to spread the Word then He would have given Moses a hammer and chisel, but He didn't. He said go and *tell* the people. Jesus says for us to go and tell the people of the Lord. He never said to anyone, to go by the Home Depot, buy hammer and chisel, and go around chiseling up stuff with His commandments on them.

I've watched Bob Villa and his home improvement show plenty of times and I've listened to him tell us what tools that we need in order to do a job in home building. But I must tell you that God ain't Bob Villa! The tools that we need don't come from any store. If they did God would have set church up in Lowe's, Ace Hardware, or Home Depot. Then we could go there and chisel and mark on the walls until our hearts were content. But God is not *content* with that, so get prepared to study, learn, pray, fast, worship, fellowship, comfort, witness to, intercede for, and disciple others just as Jesus did. Or could it be that we're just too lazy to be obedient?

Jesus did exactly what the Father would have Him to do. Jesus never built, nor worshiped, nor accepted any graven images, for this is sin. Set your sights on Jesus and turn neither to the left nor to the right. Wide is the road of disobedience and spiritually blind are those who walk this road. Straight and narrow is the path of the Kingdom of God. Keep on going. Stay on your way. Stay on this path even when it gets dark from time to time. Stay on the path even when your friends desert you. Stay on the path even if your family turns their back on you. Stay on this path even when you're lonely.

Stay on the path even if you are poor. Stay on this path if God's enemies abuse you. Stay on the path if only a *few* understand what God has chosen you to do.

This is obedience. Deuteronomy 6:9 says, "And thou shalt write them upon the posts of thy house and on *thy* gates." This is a reminder to the children of Israel to do as the Lord God commands as they come and go from *home*. He tells them they are to *teach* His commandments diligently to their children and to *talk* of them in their homes and remember to do the same when they leave home to go about their daily lives.

Moses never went around passing out hammers and chisels to the children of Israel in order for them to spread God's Word. So why is it that we hit the panic button when our own government disallows public display of the Ten Commandments? Don't you know them in your in your own heart by now? Do you have trouble remembering them? Or is it that by seeing them or merely knowing that they are on display is our comfort? Is God not still on His throne? Is Jesus not still sitting at the right hand of God? Didn't Jesus send you a Comforter? How easily we give in and give up what we have been taught.

Do you really think by our chiseling into some stone or writing on some wall will change people? What if they can't read? Seriously though, if Moses had these laws in his hands, written by God Himself, and the children of Israel would not receive them into their hearts after knowing that God gave them to Moses, then what makes us think that any person will follow His teachings by merely looking at something that we've made with our hands? God even wrote them down a second time and the children of Israel still wouldn't obey.

Believe me brothers and sisters when I tell you to watch who you follow. Many false prophets, teachers, and doctrines are in the world. Be careful of what they teach. Read and study for yourselves. Don't just go blindly after them like a sheep to slaughter. A lot of these so-called leaders will end up like the uninvited guest at the king's wedding party. You see, many are called but few are chosen. As you grow you will, or should if you are indeed growing, be able to discern whether or not your chosen spiritual leader has been called, chosen, or anointed by the Lord to preach or teach in His name.

We cannot play act our way into heaven. There is no big show to perform. There may not be any applause for our "performance", but know that God sees and knows each of our hearts. We will be judged by how we've kept the faith, persevered, and taught others about the ways of our Lord. This is what matters most: Have you accepted Christ as your personal Savior? Have you loved, truly loved your neighbor as yourself? Have you taught others and fully trained them to spread the Word?

Disobedience leads to the destruction of lives, whether intentional or not. Aaron let the people talk him into building a golden calf with his own hands. See, what you consider to be a little out of order, is completely out of order to God. Disobedience, whether turning to the left or to the right has consequences!

"Let me alone, that I may destroy them, and blot out their name from under Heaven, and I will make of thee a nation mightier and greater than they. So I turned and came down from the mount, and the mount burned with fire: and the two tablets of the covenant were in my hands. And I looked, and behold. Ye had sinned against the Lord your God, and had made you a molten calf: ye had turned aside quickly out of the way, which the Lord had commanded you. And I took the two tablets and cast them out of my two hands, and broke them before your eyes. And I fell down before the Lord, as at the first, forty nights: I did neither eat bread, nor drink water, because of all the sins which ye sinned, in doing wickedly in the sight of the Lord, to provoke Him to anger. For I was afraid of the anger and hot displeasure, wherewith the Lord was wroth against you to destroy you. But the Lord harkened unto me at that time also. [Deut. 9:14-19]

Don't let pride lead you into worshiping the works of your own hands! Make sure you memorialize Jesus by telling the Good

News wherever God leads you and pray for the gift of spiritual discernment in order to recognize the truth. The truth is our memorials are designed to honor our heroes, our loved ones, our leaders, our ancestry, events or wars, etc. It is our human way to share our love and memories of those things or persons who have left some sort of an impression upon our lives. It is our way to keep this person or history of our particular background or interest alive for all posterity to see, and study and learn from. Whoever or whatever has touched our hearts, we want to remember. There can be much healing of the spirit through our reflections of the past and those souls who have gone on before us. If we have learned to model our own lives after someone gone on before us then we should reflect on how they treated others. If they are worthy enough to be honored then surely they lived an honorable life or performed many noble deeds for others in need. We should remember not so much who they were, but what they were, by whose they were. Who they were encompasses what our kinship, or affiliation was with them. Who they were in Christ is what matters though. What they were encompasses how well they treated those they met along the way in their lives. What they were encompasses whether or not they loved their neighbor as themselves. What they were ultimately begs the question of did they have an intimate relationship with God and Jesus and did they share His Holy Word with others.

This is not meant to sound cynical or mean spirited for God knows that in our humanity and in our carnal thinking that we as humans and of the flesh tend to cherish those that we feel were either close to us, thought like us, or whom we aspire to imitate in our own lives. The difference is that Jesus still lives and gave them life! So the truth of the matter is that God meant exactly what he said through various scriptures, that being, "I will not share my glory with anyone." and "Be you holy for I am holy."

So what this tells us is that we are forbidden from glorifying anything or any person that are not a reflection of God's own very image and His likeness. You notice that I said, "of His *image and His likeness*." No one on this earth or who has ever walked on this earth are worthy to be memorialized if we have not completed our only purpose for being created in the first place. If we are created to love one another, do good works, spread the Word, and worship the One God who created us, accepting His Son as our Savior with baptism and communion and don't do what God expects of us then we have ultimately done nothing! Only those faithful in His Word are worthy of any kind of memorial at all. But even then if we covet man's praise more than we seek God's rewards we have surely missed the mark!

So brothers and sisters, let your actions reflect those of the Most High God. Let your words be tempered, your tongues be bridled when you are tempted to say unkind, degrading, humiliating, or hurtful things to another person, who also was created in the very image of God. I've seen for myself the truth in Scripture that only a life devoted to loving others can possibly bring peace to this troubled world. It takes spiritual discernment to recognize the difference between the peace of God and the false peace which the world gives.

Spiritual Discernment

Spiritual discernment is a very powerful and special gift from God and can be a very powerful gift in your life. A gift that you will find is more profound with your season of maturity. Just as a flower blooms so does this gift appear. This is indeed a gift and not some *milestone* that you have achieved. Rather this gift is a *stepping stone* to help carry you through turbulent waters and troubling times or situations. Know that you did nothing to earn this gift nor have anything to brag about, but that the Living Spirit has bestowed this discernment, spiritual discernment, upon you for God's purpose only. If granted one time and on a permanent basis we would think that we have "arrived" and that we no longer need God's help. Know that just like a flower needs the sun that you need the Son. Know that just as a flower needs the rain that you too need to continually go back to the flow of the anointing. The power is in the Son and in His fountain. There is growth when a flower has sun and rain. But at the same time know that sun and rain are not enough and can in fact be too much. Know that darkness is also important in a flower's *growth*. Know that too much sun will wither a flower. Know that too much rain will drown out its roots, so don't be discouraged when God leaves you in darkness.

God will not lead you into darkness but may leave you in the darkness you feel for a while in order to give you an insight into the fact that you aren't in total control of your life or the lives of others. God and God alone is in control. You are no more than a vessel for Him to use when you speak His Word. Know that God's covenant is with us and we don't initiate our own covenant with God, for we all have already been found out to be no more than sinners saved by the blood of Jesus. Can an Almighty God trust repented sinners with total autonomy in spiritual matters? Can we say we will sin no more? Will we be found to be more than the redeemed because He chooses to bestow spiritual gifts upon us?

We are only more than over-comers because we are saved. We are now the over-comers He says we are through Him and need to listen to Him. We should appreciate the gifts that He provides to protect and guide us, and use these gifts in order to build up His kingdom. Know that the blessing or gift of spiritual discernment does not give us the right or the power to claim to have God all figured out and are now mistake proof. Only God knows what God will do next or when He will do it, or how He will do it. Never, ever, count yourself equal to God because of any gift that you have been blessed with. The thing is that God is never in any darkness but we are always in darkness unless He reveals the light to us. Know that your flower although from time to time is in the darkness and maybe you feel alone and insecure, that God and the Holy Spirit will bring about its comforting grace when you need it most.

He tells us plainly in Isaiah 50:10, "Who is among you that fears the Lord, that obeys the voice of His servant, that walks in darkness, and hath no light? Let Him trust in the name of the Lord, and stay upon his God"

The Word also tells us in Hosea 12:5-6, "Even the Lord God of hosts, the Lord is his memorial. Therefore turn thou to thy God; keep mercy and judgment, and wait on thy God continually."

Acts 10:4 says, And when he looked on him, he was afraid, and said "What is it, Lord?" And he said unto him, "thy prayers and thine alms have come up for a memorial before God."

So just because God doesn't tell you everything doesn't mean He doesn't see everything! And it sure doesn't mean that He isn't already acting on your or your loved ones behalf! It is God's love towards you which brings you the blessings.

Matthew 26: 12-13 says, For in that she hath poured this ointment on my body, she did it for my burial. [13] Verily I say unto you, Wheresoever this gospel shall be preached in the whole world, there shall also this, that this woman hath done, be told for a memorial of her.

We can learn from these scriptures the Biblical definitions of memorials. These also represent the Biblical reasons for memorials. These are not contradictory to the "two greatest commandments." To love the Lord thy God with all thy heart, mind, soul, and strength. And to love thy neighbor as thyself. Remember that each of us have the same Father who is in Heaven. God chose to create you as you look and everybody else as they look. You have a purpose in your life and everyone else has a purpose in their life which comes from God. God hasn't asked anyone to bring division among His people, no matter what your ancestors taught you. There will be no excuses anyone can offer to God for a lifetime of pretending to love all of His children if in *fact* all they have done is lift up color, race, gender, or class and not lift up God. Remember, the very ones you secretly hate in church may just look like the ones you spend eternity with in hell! You choose to love or hate. You don't have to know why God created each race of people. You don't have to know why God created man before woman. You don't have to know why the wicked seem to prosper. You don't have to know all of what God is doing.

See, Isaiah 50:10 says it all. You can fear the Lord. You can obey the voice of His servant. And even then walk in darkness and have no light. So when you have done all you have been asked by God to do and still don't know everything just stand still! Just trust in the Lord! Just keep your eyes on God! The truth is that God doesn't tell us everything at once. The truth is that God doesn't *have* to tell us everything in order for us to trust Him. If He did tell us everything at once then we would forget all about talking to and listening to Him *daily*. The Lord wants you to seek His counsel and to acknowledge Him as your *constant* source of growing spiritually mature. God ultimately wants you to look to Him for everything. Everything! He leads us in ways which teach us to trust Him.

Far too many people in the church today believe they have spiritual discernment from God when all they have is their *own* judgment of right and wrong. It has become too easy for people to draw their own conclusions about others when they don't even know all the facts. Too many folks listen to a bunch of gossip, add their *personal feelings* to the gossip, and call this "*behavior*" discernment. Never forget that the one you ignore or pass judgment against as unworthy may be the very one God sent to teach you about some bad habits of your own. The very choices you make are seen by others just as their choices are seen by you. So either way those choices either line up with the Word of God or they don't!

Self Control by Choice

[2 Peter 2:15-16] Which have forsaken the right way and are gone astray following the way of Balaam the son of Bosor. Who loved the ways of unrighteousness; [16]: But was rebuked for his iniquity: the dumb ass speaking with a man's voice forbad the madness of the prophet. Amen. We should bless God and His righteous judgments with all that is within us.

"Which have forsaken the right way" lets us know that Balaam had to have, in fact, *known* the right way. Not only did he *know* the right way but the very word "*forsaken*" lets us know that he *was* walking in the right way beforehand. Now when you forsake the right way, you have gone astray from God's teachings and His commandments. When you go astray from his teachings and commandments then you are separated from God. You are going backwards. That's where we get the term "backslider" which is going back towards what you were before you were saved. Know that only the saved can be a backslider. The unsaved can't be a backslider because they haven't chosen to "slide forward" into salvation yet. Backsliding is so subtle you don't even notice it at first. That's why it's not back jumping, back hopping, or back skipping, but "backsliding." We determine our destiny by our choices.

"Who loved the *wages* of unrighteousness" lets us know that not only was Balaam separated from God's will, but that he loved what he was doing in sin and that he loved being in an *intimate relationship* with Satan. See, you can't have it both ways. When you live the way God wants you to live, in prayer, studying your Bible, attending Sunday school and church, loving your neighbor, walking in faith shunning all evil, then you are in an *intimate relationship* with the Lord. When you walk in sin you are in an *intimate relationship* with the Enemy. "*Wages*" are something received for work or services. Wages are pay. When you receive wages for what you do that is not of God then you are reaping the rewards of iniquity, sin, or wickedness. It pays you. You pay for it! It works both ways. It is a trap! Ultimately the wages of sin is death.

God loved Balaam enough to open the mouth of a dumb ass to teach him about his choices. [Numbers 22:28-30] And the Lord opened the mouth of the ass, and she said unto Balaam, "What have I done unto thee that thou hast smitten me these three times?" 29 And Balaam said unto the ass, "Because thou hast mocked me; I would there a sword in my hand, for now I would kill thee."[30]: And the ass said unto Balaam, "Am I not thine ass, upon which thou hast ridden ever since I was thine unto this day? Was I ever wont to do so unto thee?" And he said, nay.

This odd conversation between Balaam and his own jackass is the same mindset that we have today when things don't go our way. Not only do we want to have things to go our way, but we want to have everybody else to just go along with us. In other words what we want is control. You can put a halter, bridle, bit, and lead rope or reins on an ass to control her, but with people, you can't control them that way. And you sure can't control God. You can put a leash or a chain on your dog to control it, but you can't control God. You can use the string on your yo-yo to control it, but you can't control God! Sometimes we want to do what we want to do and to go where we want to go and to associate with whomever we please. We want control even when God says, "No."

When our friends, parents, teachers or boss won't let us have our own way we become angry with them for standing up and saying "No, this isn't the right way to go about what you are trying to do." What they are telling you is that you are on the wrong path. When you are on the wrong path the first thing you have to do is stop. Don't kick the jackass! The jackass knows better. The jackass may be smarter than you think he is. The jackass may sense something or see something you don't. He stopped! Balaam was on the wrong path, going to do the wrong thing with the wrong *associates*. God had *already* told him in verse 22:12 Thou shalt *not* go with them; thou shalt not curse the people; for they are blessed. Balaam even went and delivered God's message to the princes of Balak and refused to go with them. What went wrong?

Even most teenagers are able to "just say no" the first time that someone comes up to them with an offer or proposition that goes against what their parents have told them to do. You say "no" because you know that what is offered is contrary to the teachings of Jesus. You say "no" because since you were a child you have learned that there are consequences for your bad behavior and even for a bad attitude. The problem comes when your friends or the world offers up something that sounds good, looks good, or feels good *right now* and say, "God will understand." This is temptation. What seems okay at first usually turns into a snare on down the road. This is why you must be obedient to the teachings of Jesus. He will never lead you astray. He will never leave you or forsake you when you are not so sure what to do because of peer pressure, the desire to make a good impression, or the lure of easy money.

See, after Balaam had refused to curse the people from out of Egypt and told the princes of Balak that the Lord refused him to leave with them, the princes told this to Balak who in turn sent more princes to talk to Balaam who were more honorable than the first. Again temptation. You can't get caught up in how honorable men say another man is. You can't get caught up in who men say are looking out for your best interests. You can't get caught up in *smiling* faces. You can't get caught up in folks bearing gifts. And you *sure* can't get caught up in anyone making you promises which are *less* than the promises that you have from God! Anything that the world has to offer will surely pass away but God's promises are eternally for us. "There's a storm a'comin."

Embarrass 1. To make uncomfortably self-conscious; cause confusion and shame; to disconcert; abash. 2. To make difficult or intricate, as a question or problem; complicate. 3. To put obstacles or difficulties in the way of; impede. 4. To beset with financial difficulties; burden with debt.

I know, there is *nothing* worse for us growing up as teenagers than to be embarrassed. The outfit has to be just right. The shoes have to be just right. Your friends have to be straight. "Cool" parents are a must. Ain't nothing worse than getting called out in front of your friends, especially when you have lied to them saying, "Mom said I can go." *Knowing* you're lying.

I don't know what Balaam's problem was. I don't know if it was the promises of honor, the lure of silver and gold, or just the thought of power at being offered whatever he asks for, but he sure "forgot" that God had already told him, "Thou shalt not go with these people; thou shalt not curse my people." He even told the *more honorable* princes, "I cannot go beyond the word of the Lord my God, to do less or more." [22:18] Then he turns right around and runs up in Gods' face with the same old mess! God does not change! He does not have to. He is God.

See, God is tired of Balaam now. God knows that Balaam is going to want to go against His will, so he tells Balaam, "Go with them, but yet the word that I shall say unto thee that *shalt* thou do." Not go and do what you *want* to do but what I *say* to do. Balaam was a lot like me when I was a teenager. If they told me "no" I figured that if I asked for the same thing or to do the same thing over and over and over again then Mom would get tired of hearing it and give in or either I could con her into believing that I knew what I was doing and everything was under my control. Balaam was right. God did get tired of hearing it. But He was in control.

How does this story relate to you? Blessings. [II Chron. 7:14] God's promises today are the same promises that He made to the children of Israel. "If my people, which are called by my name, shall humble themselves, and pray, and seek my face, and turn from their wicked ways; then I will hear from heaven, and will forgive their sin, and I will heal their land." God said, "Turn, O backsliding children, for I am married unto you."[Jer.3:14] God said, I will heal their backsliding, I will love them freely: for mine anger is turned away from him.". [Hos.14:4]

See, God has made a *promise* to the children of Israel. God made this *promise* before He brought them forth from captivity in the land of Egypt. God stays *true* to His promises. God is not a man that He should lie; neither the son of man that he should repent. What God has promised to each of you He will deliver. What stops the *flow* of God's *promises* in your life is your disobedience. You *must* be obedient to His Word. When God says to keep on walking *through* the wilderness, *through* the fiery serpents, *through* the scorpions, and *through* the drought, and *through* the hunger, know that He wants to *humble* his people, that he might prove thee; to do thee good at the latter end! [Deut8: 15-16] You then, have favor!

What Balak was trying to get Balaam to do was to use his gift or his blessings to curse the *very* people whom God had already blessed, called His own, and had shown *favor*. You see, once God has blessed you or has given you *spiritual* gifts then you had better be seeking *His* counsel concerning what *His* will is for that gift. Not what your will desires. Not what my will desires. Not what the world desires. Not what mama or daddy desires, but that which *God* desires!

I know that none of you that are driving have a car that can speak but boy, what if you did? You'd be leaned back pulling up in the parking lot in front of your friends trying to be cool, when the car just stops, runs in the ditch . . . three times. You're still, trying to be cool, cussing the car where nobody can hear. Then the car yells out, "Jesus said you *better get* home!"

What God did to Balaam embarrassed him. See, he had his two servants with him, whom he was surely thinking about them laughing at him when his jackass bowed up on him twice and then just fell down refusing to budge. Men are *proud* of their equestrian skills and here this jackass is acting up in front of folks. Then to chastise Balaam even more, the jackass asks him, "What I have done to thee, that thou hast smitten me these three times?" Dead wrong and blaming someone else. That's us. Not only are we embarrassed for sticking our foot in our mouth or doing something stupid we want to make everybody just leave it alone, now. He was so mad that he didn't even think anything about the jackass *talking* in the first place. See, God was showing Balaam even this dumb ass has more sense than you. "I *told* you, thou shalt not go, the *first* time. You should have stayed away from those princes." See, when God tells you something to do or not to do, you need to listen, be obedient, and stand on His Word and on His promises, even in the midst of pressure from your friends, boyfriend, girlfriend, teammates, or whomever. It is better to be chastised by the Lord than to be loved or accepted by the world. When you say no, *mean it!* Let your yes mean yes and your *no* mean *no*! You don't owe anybody any kind of explanation for your choice to be good. But now, hey, more glory to God when you are bold enough to stand up and tell anyone that "I am a child of God and I'm gonna walk like it, talk like it and act like it!" That is *self-control.*

Another point that I want to make here is the role of the servants. The servants were the property of, or given wages *from* the master whom they *served.* That is what a servant does . . . he serves.

He follows orders from his master. He is at his master's beck and call. When his master says, "go", he goes. When his master says, "come here", he comes. He is not the leader. What his life consists of is following. These servants want to please their master *whether* they agree or disagree with the master's command. In other words, they have no *choice*. Obedience from the servant is expected and also demanded by the master. Balaam's two servants may or may not have been willing accomplices but the Word says that, "they were with him".

You, young people, are going to always have to be mindful of *who* you *serve*. No man can serve two masters. You cannot serve God and the Devil. You cannot *walk* in righteousness by living in sin. Colossians 3:23-24 says, "And whatsoever you do, do it heartily as to the Lord and not unto men; Knowing that of the Lord ye shall receive the reward of the inheritance; for ye serve the Lord Christ."

Remember, when we started out, the *Word* said in 2 Peter that, "Balaam loved the wages of unrighteousness." The *Word* says also that the wages of sin is death. But this is not your reward! For yours is the reward of the *inheritance* because you serve the Lord Christ. You say "no" to drugs. You say "no" to alcohol. You say "no" to lying. You say "no" to gossiping. You say "no" to sex. You say "no" to jealousy. You say "no" to envy. You say "no" to pride. You say "no" to cheating. You say "no" to hatred. You listened to your parents and follow the teachings of Christ.

Whatever you do, do it for the glory of the Lord! Wherever you go, go for the glory of the Lord! Whatever you say, say it for the glory of the Lord! Whenever you sing, sing to the glory of the Lord! Whenever you dance, dance to the glory of the Lord! Whatever you teach, teach it to the Lord! Let your light shine to the glory of the Lord! *Lift up* your brothers and your sisters to the glory of the Lord! Honor your father and your mother to the glory of the Lord! And let all of your worship and all of your praise be done to the glory of the Lord!

You see, when you live your life to the glory of the Lord, you are walking *into* your inheritance. I'm not talking about some money, house, or land that your poor old grandma left you. That stuff may be nice while you are in this world. But what you have inherited is the Kingdom of God. You are heirs and joint heirs of God's Kingdom through the blood of the Lamb. You don't have to follow anybody on this earth except for Jesus. Cars are nice, but they rust. Clothes are nice, but moths will eat them. Riches are nice, but thieves are waiting to steal those. So store up your riches in Heaven and with Christ.

You are leaders and not followers. I'm not going to tell you that it is easy walking through the wilderness, but I will tell you that if you put your trust in the Lord, He will lead you through. That is His *promise* to you. Your inheritance is in Him and nobody can *take* this from you, no, not even Satan. Your inheritance is a gift from your Savior. All you have to do is *humble* yourselves and accept Him as your Savior and to walk in His righteousness.

Don't you give up your inheritance in Jesus Christ for anything or for *anybody* no matter *who* they are. See, this is a good lesson on embarrassment because when you look at this relationship and conversation between Balaam and his jackass it really says a lot and teaches us a lot about our relationship with each other. "Am I not thine ass upon which thou hast ridden ever since I was thine unto this day?" could be your friend saying, "Am I not your friend who has run around with you since we first met?" "Was I ever wont to do so unto thee?" could be your friend saying, "Have I ever done you wrong or brought you harm?" Well if we were in sin then, "Yeah, you did me wrong and brought me harm. And I did the same to you."

In the case of Balaam, the ass saw the angel of the Lord blocking the path and turned aside. The ass saw that the angel had his sword in his hand. The ass knew that there was danger on this road. So what did he do? He stopped. Balaam was blinded by his own will and his own desire to pervert the will of God. He *said,* "I cannot go beyond the will of the Lord my God to do less or more," while steadily *doing* exactly that!

In your case this same scenario, could go one of three ways. You could either be Balaam, the jackass, or the servant. If you have a true friend that friend should look out for your *well*-being and your Christian walk. When you get off-track a Christian friend will tell you "No, this is not the right path and it's not the thing to do." A true friend will be there for you and steer you in the *precepts* of the *Lord. Anybody* leading you, following you, or going right on along with you down the *wrong* path are giving up their own inheritance and playing a role in you giving up your *inheritance* for the wages of sin. If you are their friend and a friend of God, then you will not lead any of your friends astray from Christ's commands.

What you should do is to use all of your gifts of the Lord for the glory of God. These gifts from God are a *stepping-stone* for you to use to lift up *His* holy and righteous name! God doesn't give you gifts as a milestone of achievement or *self-righteousness*. You see, God is in *control.* What you have is the choice of whether or not to learn and to practice self-control. When you practice self-control then it will be God's will and not your will that takes precedence in your life.

A lot of people aren't *effective* Christians because they aren't practicing self-control. Self-control involves self-denial. You have to deny yourself those things of the flesh. You have to deny yourself that bitterness, that jealousy, that rebellion, and that unforgiveness that you keep holding on to. See, it's not about you; it's *all* about Jesus from whom our blessings flow. Only when you look to the Lord and keep your eyes on Him and ask for His direction and ask for His *purpose* for your life will you begin to see an *effective* outreach in your Christian life. In other words, a lot of people are *boasting* of gifts that they don't have or aren't using.

The Word says, "Whoso boasts himself of a false gift is like clouds and wind without rain." [Proverbs 25:14] This rain is your evidence of power from your gifts of God. See, when the clouds bump together you hear thunder, or *a lot of noise*. You may even see lightening and the wind may blow furiously. But still *nothing*! What the rain symbolizes in your *spiritual* gifts is exactly what the rain does. The rain makes things grow! The *rain* from your gifts brings *life*!! Christ wants a church that will bring *life* and *praise* before His throne and not a bunch of self-righteousness. There are a lot of folks who can learn a whole bunch from kids. Children may fuss and fight one day and then you'll see them playing together the next day or at least in a short period of time. Children are a lot quicker to forgive people and to move on than adults; especially once you have explained to them what Jesus says about forgiveness.

Adults want to hang on to old grudges and old hurt feelings, or embarrassment. We want to pick and choose whom we are going to forgive and even then we haven't really forgiven the person at all. We just *smile* in their *face* for economic, social, or selfish reasons. "I'll forgive you if something is in it for me." We want to put on our smiling faces so that the public *or* the church may hold us up to a high esteem. A child's love comes from innocence before all the bitterness and negativity of bad or hurtful relationships set in our hearts. Jesus said "Suffer little children to come unto me, and forbid them not*; for of such* is the Kingdom of God." Only Jesus can teach them without getting His own story twisted. Adults have subliminally twisted this for years until Satan won.

There's a lot of truth spoken even when the little children sing Mary *had* a little lamb; Whose fleece *is* white as snow; And everywhere that Mary went the lamb is sure to go! Then it gets twisted to where the lamb is following Mary, instead of the lamb leading Mary. Then we sang for years the lamb stirred up trouble at school. Now, just like then, the Lamb is not allowed at school. The Lamb *leads* you to school each day. The Lamb *leads* you to work each day. The Lamb *leads* you until you return home safely. The Lamb *leads* you to Sunday school and church. Mary's little Lamb is with each one of you, leading you, wherever you go. Mary's little Lamb is calling each and every one of you white as snow. Mary's little Lamb is your High Priest. Mary's little Lamb is your Advocate with the Father. Mary's little Lamb is your Savior. Mary's little

Lamb isn't who stirs up trouble at school. Your words have power! Mary's little Lamb will pick you up and turn you around! I know because he did it for me.

Teenagers are a special group because teens are directly in this transition period we are studying here. You are no longer little kids (you keep reminding us) who need someone constantly standing over you but you still aren't quite ready to fly on your own. It can be an exciting time in your life as you grow into your own person and your own identity. You have been brought up with teachings of honesty, truthfulness, patience, faith, and love. Your parents or guardians have devoted their lives to the day that they can see you mature into a loving, intelligent, independent, and prosperous young adult who can not only survive *in* this world, but to live *above* this world. This is the time in our lives when parents and our guardians must loosen the reins a little bit; and let each one of their most precious gifts *develop* his or her own personality and identity. You are now able to think for yourselves and to make choices for yourselves. It is yourselves that will have to live with your choices and your choices can affect others. And God sees your choices.

When you were younger, your parents or guardians brought you up in church. You have been *taught* right from wrong at an early age. You *know* what is right and what is wrong. What is right are those things which are acceptable and pleasing to God. What is wrong are those things that are unacceptable and displeasing to God. It is that simple. What isn't so simple sometimes is making the *right* choices when everybody else is *pulling* you this way or that way while telling you God won't mind your behavior. I've heard adults say that kids nowadays are lost and don't know where they are spiritually. I say that you do know where you are spiritually because you are seeking the Lord. It was Jesus himself who said "Of those You have given me, I have not lost one." He was talking about His own disciples, whom He also had to raise up spiritually. You will make it as long as you don't allow yourself to get influenced by ungodliness.

One day while working on an old block building, I witnessed a very profound act. This act was between a mother squirrel and her babies. This act was also brought about by myself. You see, it was as I sat resting one evening when I noticed this mother squirrel walking along the *side* of the block wall without falling off of the wall. Across the wall, along the top of these sixteen-foot long sliding doors, to a hole in the block on the other side of the wall she went ever so purposefully. Then she came back across the door and wall to the first hole where she began. Now this time when she came out of the hole, I noticed something in her mouth. It was a baby squirrel! Her baby. One of God's creations.

Back across the wall and door she went again, only this time more slowly. Not because of any fear of falling off of the wall, for she was equipped for journeys like these. The claws on her feet are sharp and curved to fit any *tiny* rough spot. She was lightweight. Her bushy tail is the main key to her survival in nature because a squirrel's tail is what they use for balance. By raising, lowering, or straightening out her tail, she could adapt to most any terrain. No, she was being cautious because she had noticed me watching her, and she didn't want me so see where she was taking her babies. Every few steps, she would stop and look at me before taking a few more steps. Not wanting to risk her babies' safety she went the long way to her new nest this time to try and fool me. So I moved to a different spot, where she could tend to her business. Now, she moved really fast into her nest and back out to her old nest again and again. Four little babies I counted in all. When she was finished moving them, I came and sat back down in my chair. Now, she was smart. She would look at me, go to her old nest, *bypassing* her new nest, and go into yet another hole in the block, all the while checking to make sure I was "buying" it. Yep, she would do whatever it took for the well being of her babies, for she knew that was her job. She knew that there was a storm a comin'.

Even in the midst of a storm she know by instinct, discernment, or experience that she should look out for, and put her babies welfare first and foremost. The world with all its dangers, toils, and snares is already in motion. The world even with all its dangers, toils, and snares is *ultimately* in motion for the *will* of God. God *is* in control. God *will* allow the sacrifice a few to save many. Read: [Numbers 16:31-35, Acts 1-11]. Have heart and *understand.*

In a *worldly* sense, the job *must* go on. The job *will* go on. The job is on a schedule. The job is on a schedule that we believe is determined by *us*. The job will not deviate from this schedule discerned by us to be *correct*. O, but doesn't our *worldly* "discernment" make such a mess of not only our own lives but those of others as well. Right, wrong, and sin are of utmost importance no matter how we want and try to blur the lines that separate these issues, which encompass the very core of our being, from that which is within the will of God for the edification of His kingdom.

In the midst of an attitude that "the job must go on," I, with an immense love for nature and especially babies, did not take the time out to *fully* understand or to fully comprehend the *ultimate* consequences of my actions. Am I accountable? Yes. Was I accountable? No. For you see what I did was to look down into the cell of the block of which I thought the mother squirrel had taken her babies and upon not seeing them, proceeded to "patch" the wall of its holes. I would not hurt those babies for anything.

The next morning when I came into work the shop owner said, "Gregory, look here and see where that mama squirrel has torn up what we "fixed" just yesterday." Upon looking, I discovered that she had torn out a big chunk of the wood lintel, which spanned across the two windows and door to his office. "Oh no!" I thought, not because of the damage to the wood, but because of the realization that I had maybe blocked her path and prevented her from reaching her babies. This is where I really learned what God would have for me to learn. What I learned about myself was that the "job" was more important to me than that mama squirrel's babies. For you see, *I* could have taken apart what I had built the day before in order for the mama squirrel to get to her babies. But I did not do that. No. What I did was to tell and to *convince* myself that *surely I* was not mistaken nor the blame for the welfare of *that mama's* babies. It would have taken me maybe an hour to take those boards out, plus the waiting time to give the mama time to move her babies, but *my schedule* was what dictated my actions or lack thereof. Guilt, shame, worry and dread were my companions for the next week. It only got worse when each morning I could see where the mama squirrel had, the night before, tried to scratch and chew her way to her babies. "Surely not," I pleaded.

"Of those you have given me, I have lost not one" stayed in my spirit. More than a week later, while I was up on the roof working, he hollered, "Gregory, there goes the mama with her babies in her mouth!" Oh happy days! They were alive. They had survived. She had not given up. God had not given up. God knew. God's will was done. What she did was to wait until the office door was open, go into the office, climb the *interior* wall, chew and claw and scratch and bite her way through to reclaim her babies.

Day after day we watched these squirrels, for now they were old enough to venture out of their nest on their own. Now, baby squirrels, or even babies for that matter, all look the same to me. So upon only seeing one or two heads at a time, peeking over the channel guide of the door I was still trying to distinguish one baby from the other while deep down inside trying to count how many there were. Never being able to fully count *exactly how* many babies there were I *resigned* myself to being thankful and to console *myself* in the knowledge that God had done all that He could to fix *my* blunder.

One of the babies came out of the nest, crawled down the wall about three feet and couldn't make it back up to its nest. The owner and I got a ladder, put on gloves, and picked up the baby squirrel in order to return it to its nest. He had the squirrel. I held the ladder. Well, the baby started squealing, mama came charging, we took off running with the baby ending up falling to the ground and then scurrying off! Funny as it was, the truth was that we had gotten ourselves in over our head. We were out of order. If that baby squirrel had remained right where it was on the side of the wall his mama would have rescued him for this was not only her responsibility, but her child. Sometimes we need to simply be still. What we deem as help or to be the right thing to do may be the wrong thing to do.

Two days later, while building a fence, I heard one of the dogs barking and looked to see what the commotion was all about when I noticed that the dog was barking at that same little baby which we had lost. After getting the dog away from the baby and rescuing him we found out he was wounded and paralyzed in his hips and couldn't use his hind legs. All he could do was drag them behind him as he struggled to crawl along. It was a pitiful sight. We put him in a box, then a cage and tried our best to comfort him. Even in his mother's sight, she wouldn't come to reclaim him this time. He died the next day. No more storms for him. Sometimes our habit of thinking we can just do what we want and then fix everything we mess up later, often hurts others and can't be fixed.

Habit or Conscious Effort

[Roman 3:10] As it is written, there is none righteous, no, not one: "There is none that understands, there is none that seeks after God. [12] They are all gone out of the way they are together become unprofitable; There is none that does good, no, not one."

[Psalm 14:2-3] The Lord looked down from heaven upon the children of men to see if there were any that did understand, and seek God. [3] They are all gone aside, they are all together become filthy: there is none that does good, no, not one. Amen

Now I realize that these scriptures may hurt your feelings and make you want to justify your behavior but God is God and He is God all by Himself, so get over it. We can't justify our behavior before God anymore than anyone else can justify their actions before a Holy God! What we call righteous is as filthy as rags before Him. What we call understanding is nothing but foolish pride before Him. What we call seeking God is seeking God after we chased after the world and our own personal agenda while *using* His name to achieve our own will. The scriptures tell us that after we have done all that

God has asked us to do, still all we can say is that we are nothing but unprofitable servants. "There is none that does good, no, not one."

Why would God say this about *everyone* when there is such a wide disparity between "believers" relationships with God? I believe it is because of the *manner* in which we *claim to seek God.* See, God searches the heart and tries the reigns of men. God is searching for a people who seek His face and seek his own heart. God knows all of the secret places in our hearts that we don't see or won't acknowledge. God says in Psalm 119:2, "Blessed are they that keep His testimonies, and that seek Him with the *whole* heart." The problems arise in your life, no matter your spiritual level, when you count and brag on your blessings as something you have earned by good habits that aren't necessarily from the heart!

Habit n. 1. Customary practice or use. 2. A particular practice, custom or usage. 3. Compulsive need, inclination; or use; addiction. 4. A dominant or regular disposition or tendency; prevailing character or quality. 5. An acquired behavior pattern regularly followed until it has become almost involuntary.

Conscious adj. 1. Aware of ones own existence, thoughts, surroundings, etc. 2. Fully aware of or sensitive to something (often followed by of): conscious of ones own faults. 3. Having the mental faculties fully active. 4. Known to oneself. 5. Aware of what one is doing. 6. Deliberate or intentional. 8. Inwardly sensible to wrongdoing. Conscious implies to be awake or awakened to an inner realization of a fact, a truth, a condition, etc. Conscious means that you are aware of your very own inadequacy.

From the very beginning God had a plan for mankind. God breathed His very Spirit into man and Adam became a living soul. Adam and Eve entered into sin, which separated man from God. There had to be a perfect sacrifice to God for man's sin and iniquities. Jesus, the Lamb of God, is that Perfect Sacrifice. Jesus has done what the law couldn't do for mankind. Jesus shed His precious Blood so that His one sacrifice would reconcile us back into a right relationship with our Father, who is our Creator. We did not create ourselves or predestine anything in the heavens or on earth. All things were created by God for God and without God we are nothing. We can never get to a point in life where what we did yesterday is sufficient for today or tomorrow. With each new day there comes new struggles. With each new day comes new trials, temptations and tests. God's Word tells us that only by faith in Him do we have hope. Only in recognizing our own inadequacy can we have renewing of our thoughts and mind to fully humble ourselves before God and seek His face with our whole heart. No matter what your service, or even prayer life is, if you don't have love you have done nothing!

God has laid a burden on my heart for His church. The Holy Spirit has given me revelation into why we are not reproducing more disciples of the cross today as the church should be producing. The Holy Spirit has shown me that we are doing a lot of stuff to look busy but when it gets down to it all that we do is not out of love towards Him. By not doing all that we do and by not speaking all that we speak out of love, we are saying no more no less, "I will be the judge of how to approach God and I will approach God without going through the Blood of Jesus." You see, you cannot go to God without going through Jesus. Jesus is love just as God is love. When you leave your love walk you lose your faith walk because "faith worketh by love." [Gal.5:6]

What I am led to show you is the difference between the habits you have been led to trust in and having the conscious effort required in your Christian walk with Jesus. What you should learn is the difference between fact and truth! It is a fact that good habits can be beneficial to you. That is fact. The truth is that good habits will not save you nor will good habits *please* God. The truth is your good habits are *pleasing to* God but only faith *pleases* God. It is fact that good habits can help you stay on the right path. The truth is that good habits can be controlled by circumstance, people, or environment. It is fact that good habits can be a good routine for your life. It is truth that says good habits can easily become ritualistic routine. It is fact that bad habits are hard to break. The truth is good habits are just as hard to break and are works and not faith. There's a storm a comin!

You see, birds, animals, and fish think and can feel as this is how they were created by God. They also praise God is what God's Word tells us. That is fact. The truth is they have no choice but to praise God because they were created to praise God. It is fact that birds, animals, and fish can live long, good lives by their habits and in their habitat. The truth is that other animals roam, seek, and destroy or kill that same creature in its habitat by knowing the habits of its prey. Know that the Devil roams the whole world over, as a lion, seeking those he may devour. Now do you put faith in your habits? It is fact that you need to read the Word of God every day. The truth is that only the *knowledge of the truth* will set you free. You must have God's Word rightly divided!

Jesus is your example of how to live and how to treat others. Jesus shared the greatest truth in John 19:11. [10] Then saith Pilate unto Him. "Speakest thou not unto me? Know Thou that I have the power to crucify Thee, and have the power to release Thee?" That was fact. Then Jesus spoke truth!! Jesus answered "Thou couldest have no power *at all* against me, except it were given thee from above: Therefore he that delivered Me unto thee hath the greater sin." Amen

The problem with "good habits" arise because habits can be subject to intent, motive, or agenda. These can easily produce an unwillingness to change or even recognize when change is absolutely necessary to get to the next level. My good habits benefit me but what does that do for others? If all I ever do is rely on and count my good habits as my walk of righteousness then I am using myself as the standard for what is right and wrong. The fact is I am to use my spirit to determine if what I keep doing is the right thing to do or say. The truth is that my thoughts are not necessarily His thoughts nor my ways necessarily His ways. The truth is I must make a conscious effort in my Christian walk to seek Jesus' voice and God's will every day. Jesus said, "You can do nothing without me!" This is the same Jesus who told Pilate, "You could have no power *at all* against Me unless it were given to you from above." [1]

Now, I can have good habits, which are certainly better than bad habits, but I am still without any life changing, Kingdom building power because works without faith in God is dead. See, good habits are good for *my* vertical relationship with God because God will not hear me with iniquity in my heart. But if I am to follow His command to *go* out *into* the harvest then I need a deeper relationship and knowledge of God which comes through my *conscious effort* to do more and more instead of the same old ritualistic routine. God's desire does not begin or end with me at all. Jesus said, "I came not into the world to destroy the world but that through the Son the *world* might be saved."

My salvation came through a people praying for me before I was even born. My salvation came through a people who spread the gospel to others who in turn spread the gospel to others. You see, the gospel was kept alive by a people who knew what discipleship was all about! That's what Kingdom building is all about! It's me taking my eyes off of myself, putting them on God, and, and teaching "baby" Christians to become mature Christians. In plain language my vertical "up reach" to Jesus *gives* me power and justifies my outreach but it is my *conscious* effort to *use* that power that changes any lives other than my own! "There's a storm a comin'.

I have a good habit of reading my Bible every day. I have a good habit of praying before bedtime. I have a good habit of going to church. I have a good habit of attending all Bible studies also. As a matter of fact these good habits are the integral part of any Christian life. Now here's the problem: I love reading my Bible. I love my prayer time. I love going to church and Bible studies, and being on *time* for these meetings, and "alone time" with God. How is that a problem you ask?

The problem is there are too many "I"s involved here. See, when it's *time* for me to read my Bible, I'm going to read my Bible. When it's *time* to pray, I'm going to pray. When it's *time* for church, I'm going to church. When it's time for Bible class, I'm going to class. Those are my good habits! But, you ought to know there's a "but," every now and then the phone rings. Every now and then there's a knock at the door. Every now and then someone wants my attention. Every now and then all of my "good habits" are put right before an Almighty God and put to the ultimate test! Every now and then I am faced with a decision. Every now and then I have a choice to make. Every now and then I am faced with what matters most! Every now and then there is a precious life hanging in the balance. Every now and then I have to call upon the mighty name of Jesus. Every now and then all I am faced with His Words from His Great Commission. "Go ye into all the world, and preach the Gospel to every creature!"

You see, every now and then there will be somebody in your life. Every now and then there will be somebody in your face. Every now and then your "good habits" need a *reality check*! Because the truth is just as God has said it, "There is none that does good, no not one". The thing about your "good habits" is they can never replace a conscious effort of what matters most, church. You see, that person that you put off right now because you *always* read your Bible at 12:00 may be on their way to commit suicide and you with the very Word you are reading, are their last hope! That person you avoid answering the phone for and talking to may be about to abuse their child. That person you don't pick up for church because you like to get there fifteen minutes early and now are five minutes late may have been right at their breakthrough and are now back out in the world. That person you don't take to Bible class because you *always* go straight home to avoid temptation may backslide into drugs and alcohol. That person you don't have time to pray *with* because you have a "good habit" of praying *for* everybody else may be the very one God wants you to *nurture* into being a mature Christian disciple for His Kingdom!

We have got to grow as disciples of Christ! The way to do this is to love your neighbor as yourself. Your "good habits" may keep you *at* the cross, but God desires you to go *through* the cross to the place of power to *change lives* through His church! We have got to get to that place of consciousness of God's will that we *feed* his sheep and not just *show off* our blessings! Ezekiel. 34:2 says, "Woe be to the shepherds of Israel that do feed themselves! Should not the shepherds feed the flocks? [3] Ye eat the fat, and ye cloth you with the wool, ye kill them that *are* fed: But ye feed not the flock."

What happens is there are too many churches getting fat on tithes, offerings, and seed money but not hearing the cries of the flock who have gone astray because too many leaders count their own "good habits" as pleasing God. Only *faith* pleases God! Faith with a conscious effort towards God says, "Now wait a minute! I know we had three hundred people saved last year and only fifty of them are still in church. I am personally contacting each one of them to see why they are no longer in church attendance."

Now, here's the tricky question: Who are the leaders in the church? You! Any member of the body of Christ who is saved by the blood of Jesus should be able to lead someone to Christ and teach them how to live a holy life. This comes not only through teaching them Biblical lifestyles, but by living a holy and righteous life in front of them. This requires the ultimate sacrifice. This discipleship requires that we love, truly love our neighbors as ourselves. This requires that we put aside our prevailing character of "me first" and put on the mind of Christ in order to become fully aware of and sensitive to the needs of others in the body of Christ or lost in the world. I speak from my very own shortcomings and many times failures in the Great Commission of Christ. My prayer is that you will draw closer to God through my personal tragedies, triumphs, and victory in Christ. I tell you now that the road is narrow and there be few that find true Biblical love. Even fewer practice the love of Christ-like *servitude*. There's a storm a comin'!

In order to have spiritual strength to see a change in the lives of the people who God has placed in your life you have to always remember that you cannot measure an intimate level of obedience and servitude by your own standards! 2 Corinthians, 10:12-13 says, "For we dare not make ourselves of the number, or compare ourselves with some that commend themselves: but they measuring themselves by themselves and comparing themselves among themselves are not wise. [13] But we will not boast of things without our measure, but according to the measure of the rule which God hath distributed to us, a measure to reach even unto you."

Through my very own failure and blindness, God began to teach me of my shortcomings and my sinful, self-centered heart. It was through His divine revelation this book was birthed inside of me. I praise God and lift up the name of Jesus for keeping me through the storm, which almost completely destroyed me. You see, I could never see people as God sees people until I was taught by the Holy Spirit. Through it all I have had to face the truth that I can do *nothing* without Jesus! In the chapters to follow we will have the opportunity to draw closer to Christ as we learn to build His kingdom His way and by His *power* through the Word of God. But first I want to share with you how this book was birthed.

I was talking to a cousin of mine one day who told me that he was writing a book. I thought, "That's cool." Then I felt my spirit move. A desire that I had buried deep inside of me began to stir. Then I knew that the Lord was giving me not only the heart to help His children, but also the revelation of why so many lives remain broken. This endeavor has taken me to a deeper understanding of how serious the Enemy is in separating each of us from God. I have learned that the Devil will use anything and anybody to hinder your spiritual growth. For me this spiritual storm began in earnest when I first picked up this pen and paper. Here is how I learned just how wrong I could be while thinking that I was right where God would have me to be. All that I was doing for God, as I thought, turned out to be nothing because I had forgotten love.

See, my mother had been diagnosed with Alzheimer's a couple years ago. Now this was not really a shock to me and I quickly came to grip with this new information I had been noticing her forgetfulness and other warning signs so basically, I thought, "This is my mother. She has put up with me for years in drunkenness and drug addiction so now I'm ready to take care of her and serve the Lord." That was until reality set in my little cocoon I had built. I thought as long as I made sure she took her medication, ate her meals, and didn't go out walking alone that all I had left to do was to pray for her. Boy, was I ever wrong! What I had was a habit of doing the right things without having the conscious effort of knowing what I was doing was totally inadequate! What do you mean, Gregory?

What I mean is that it is a *fact* that she needed all of the things done which I was doing. But the *truth* is there comes a time when you better be sensitive to someone else's needs before your own! There comes a time when you better be aware of the *truth* that you don't even belong to yourself, but exist for the purpose set forth and predestined by the Lord! There comes a time when you better come down off your high horse and recognize your own faults! There comes a time when you better keep your mind stayed on the *love* of Jesus instead of pacifying people as you see fit! There comes a time you had better be fully aware that what you are doing is coming to an *expected end*! There comes a time when you had better be deliberate in your prayer life and intentional in following in every step that the Lord has ordered! There comes a time when you had better be inwardly sensitive to your own wrongdoing and stop and repent from your arrogance! There comes a time when you had better stay down on your knees in prayer until you hear the voice and instructions from the Lord! And always is the time that you had better realize that you have to *get up* off your knees and "*Feed my Sheep*!!"

You see, every time that I went into prayer, when beginning this book, my Mama would find her way down the stairs. Every time I began to write my Mama would come into the room and start talking. It made no difference if I was writing or praying. She just seemed to always be in my way. In my twisted mind she was interfering in God's calling on my life. And I resented it. I had little time for her. I had little patience for her. Now, here's the part that hurts the most. I had a friend who saw all of this tell me, "Gregory, you are rather short with your mother and for a man to speak about God and to be teaching me the Word of God you had better change your own ways before you even open your mouth to me ever again!!" And then God spoke the exact same thing to me! I had let *myself* get so caught up in *myself* that I really had no *true love* for anyone except *myself* while trying to convince God that I love him. He said, "No, son, there's a storm a comin'.

Then I realized as I looked at her one day that I had never truly forgiven her for telling my daddy I told her about that other woman forty years ago. At that moment I let it all go and from that moment on I loved her with all my heart. I have never been so blessed in my life as I was when God allowed me to be alone with my mother while she died.

It is this same love for God first which frees Pastors from the pressure the Devil tries to put on them concerning finances needed to run the ministry. It is a fact that there is seed time and harvest set up as a spiritual law in the earth. It is a fact that God blesses those who are givers. But the truth is God blesses us because He loves us! God blesses the just and the unjust. The truth is God blesses us for His name's sake! God blesses us to His glory that all may come to see His goodness towards all of His creation. So the truth is if we would preach God's love more, then people would give more because they would love God more!

God's Business or Your Will

Blessed be the name of the Lord. Blessed be all those who diligently and prayerfully and faithfully carry on with the business of His church on a day-to-day, week-to-week, month-to-month, and yearly basis. I pray for the guidance and wisdom from on high to order your steps. In you, the cohesion and well-being of each individual church rests. What you set in motion is what the rest of the congregation follows. The decisions that you make determine the course in which your church goes. Growth or decay will often times lay in your decisions. I pray that your decisions or rules are in accordance with God's master blueprint for the church. I pray that you realize that you are not officers of the church to tell your Pastor what to do or set up rules and guidelines outside of the established church doctrine of God but to follow your Pastor with God's established guidelines in order to keep the order of the church. This begins, from God, through Jesus to your Bishops, Elders, and/or Pastors.

You are God's servants. You are sons who serve. As you serve your Pastor *then* you are serving God. As God is a God of order I pray that you know and fully understand that your role in His various churches is to support that said church and not to lead your Pastor. Keep order in the church by your anointing or simply decline the appointment. Whether the Preacher Steward to the Trustees, Steward Board, Usher Board, Missionaries, Deacons, Elders etc, you are all accountable and under authority of your Pastor. Maybe elevated to a status above the general congregation you are nonetheless servants to this church body. Serve with the heart of one who is pleased to please the God who is the Architect of your church.

Although, often times, your duties and obligations are of the financial nature of the churches business, you must remember that all church monies come from the Lord to whom all the riches of this earth belong in the first place. Your job then is to put these monies to use for the edification of His church. You see, it's all His money, for His church, so there is no need for your decisions to be based on worldly or your own understanding. The matters of His church are of a spiritual nature. Pray and ask for His guidance and blessings, moving forward in blind faith oftentimes. You see, when God knows that you trust only in Him and that you know from where your blessings flow, then He cannot go back on His Word to provide a way out of no way. He will not go back on his Word to open doors that you cannot see. He will not let His faithful follower's labor go unrewarded.

Take care of His church business, His church, His church grounds, His people, and blessed will be your church body. Lean not unto your understanding on issues of the church but simply ask God to guide you. When you have turned all of your hopes over to Him, He will in turn sort out that which is in His will, His perfect will, from that which is from man. Sometimes what we want or what direction that we would have the church to go is not what God would have done or what direction He would have the church go. Our obligation is to edify the church body and not only ourselves. Our obligation is to edify the church so that God Himself is lifted up and exalted above all the earth. As an officer of His church what you have is *position* for all of the *power* is His which He gives to you to overcome the works of Satan. His power works through you! You are not the source of the power. Remember this last truth in all that you do for there's a storm a comin'!

[I Cor. 4:1-3] Let a man so account of us as of the ministers of Christ, and the stewards of the mysteries of God.[2] Moreover, it is found in stewards that a man be found faithful.[3] But with me it is a very small thing that I should be judged of you, or of man's judgment; yea I judge not mine own self.[4] For I know nothing by myself; yet am I not hereby justified; but He that judges me is the Lord. [5] Therefore judge nothing before the time, until the Lord come, who both will bring to light the hidden things of darkness, and will make manifest the counsels of the hearts: and then shall every man have praise of God. Amen

Let all that you do bring glory to God's name. All that you do will be done in faith. How can it not be done in faith? You were born with nothing. All that you are in charge of you received from God. Since you received it from God, what do you have to glory in as if you didn't receive it from God? See, it is your heart that makes you able ministers of the church. It is your giving glory to God that shows men you are working for His kingdom. Only God can take nothing and create something for you to take care of in the first place. He took His redeemed children, set Jesus as Head over them, and called it His church! People often learn of God by seeing your obedience in serving the church as if serving Christ himself.

Faith in Christ to lead releases power in your life when you don't know what to do next. Your faith in Christ and your giving Christ the glory releases you from any penalty of public scorn and judgment. When you know that you are hearing Jesus' voice for yourself on how He says to do His will then you don't have to worry about complainers in the church. There will always be someone looking over your shoulder. There will always be someone waiting to tear you down. There will always be someone passing judgment on every move you make whether or not you know it.

Paul says that man's judgment of him doesn't matter to him. How can he say such a thing? Because he knows in his soul that he is a minister of Christ and he has not put his will before Christ's will! Moreover, Paul *knows* that he has been faithful. See, when you know that you have been faithful you don't worry about what men think or say about you. When you are faithful you have shown by your actions that you can do nothing by yourself. In acknowledging that God is the Righteous One who judges, Paul is saying that no man's condemnation of him is going stop him from doing God's will. He even goes on to say "Yea I judge not mine own self." See, this can be taken one of two ways, but I believe that Paul meant it both ways. "I judge not mine own self," means that he doesn't esteem himself to be more than what he is as a minister of Christ. When he says, "I judge not mine own self," he is also saying "I'm not going to put myself down. I'm not going to dwell on my faults. I'm not going to look back at missed opportunities. I'm not going to let Satan make me feel guilty. I'm not going to count myself as less than what God tells me that I am!" See, what Paul is saying is that what we see and what God *knows* He placed in us may not always be evident right now.

As church officers and stewards of the ministry all you can do to please God is have faith and to walk in His instruction with obedience to His *timing* for bringing things to pass. Keep God first. Keep love for others especially your family second. Then make sure that the things of your heart concerning the church are pleasing to God. God has a perfect will for your life and his church. Find it! Then all men may have praise for God. Never become prideful that you have been operating in his permissive will for this is actually not His will but your will. This is His mercy being extended to you until you grow up. God's perfect will is that all men be saved and none should perish. God's desire, perfect will, is to draw men closer to Himself in order to restore and cleanse them. You should have the same will as God as church officers and stewards of the ministry. Integrity is an important part of your job. What you say should build others up, not tear them down. There is nothing worse than church officers or ministers of the church gossiping about others. Don't you know that you are judged by the same measure? And I'll tell you something else too. Children also judge your behavior. Nobody likes to think they are being betrayed by the very ones who claim to have their best interests at heart! What do I mean? I'm talking about confidence. What someone tells you in private should remain private! What is discussed to the leadership should remain confidential! That is if the counsels of your heart are built around servitude. The church should be a place of love and forgiveness. But what happens? Some immature church member runs to some church officer with revenge or mischief in their heart. They come with "concern" for someone else in the church. This really isn't concern at all. This isn't a prayer request at all. What it is, is that spirit of Ham. See, Ham wasn't concerned about his father, Noah, being drunk and naked. No, he was mocking his father's one fall into weakness. He wasn't trying to help at all. Ham wanted his brothers to know that, "Daddy done messed up. So now daddy can't be telling anyone else about God anymore. Now daddy will not be able to speak of the Lord and correct us anymore. We don't have to mind him. Now we can just dismiss anything that comes out of his mouth as foolishness." After hundreds of years of righteousness, because of this one transgression in a moment of weakness, the attitude is, "Daddy finally fell weak just like I knew he would. Now let's go tell everything I saw."

Far too many church officers carry this same spirit of Ham. What they hear in counseling or a private meeting they run home and first of all tell their wife or husband who then get on the phone and gossips the "news" all over town. It goes like this. "Hey brother Bill. This is brother Joe. We need to get together with brother Don and brother Jim to pray for brother Sam. I'm worried about him. You may not know it but I heard his wife is cheating on him. I hated to hear that but you know they say he's been cheating on her for years too. But I'm worried about him, so we need to lift him up in prayer. They say he's been sick, but you know it ain't no wonder he's sick if he's laying up with that woman I heard he's been with and drinking again. You know they say she's got . . ." Then you wonder why there's a storm a comin'.

Position or Power of God

Pastors, I write this with joy and thanksgiving mixed with words of encouragement. The joy comes from knowing that someone with a higher calling than most is on this earth to lead God's people. The thanksgiving comes from the fact that you have heard God's calling and stepped into His ministry. This is a special calling, a calling to bring God's Word to God's people. In accepting this calling, and only those called should be a Pastor, you are not only required to spread the gospel of Jesus the Christ but also teach His people how to live and how to apply His Holy Word to their everyday lives. The words of encouragement come from the knowledge that just like everyone else there will be spiritual storms in your lives also.

The Spirit of the Lord will lead you. The Spirit of the Lord will guide your way. The Spirit of the Lord will tell you when to speak and when to listen. The Spirit of the Lord will give you the words to speak from your mouths so that none are offended, discouraged, or lead astray. (I know some are going to be offended no matter what). Your words will be tempered, tried, and true. The Holy Spirit will be your Comforter from day to day and from task to task. The Holy Spirit will keep you from harms way. The Spirit of God Himself will be your provider for His name's sake. Fear nothing or no one except He who has created you in His very image, but be very mindful that there's a storm a comin'.

Being Pastor of a church body is a lot more than most people understand. There is an undertaking of responsibility that leaves you accountable directly to God for your actions or lack thereof. There are a lot of preachers. The sad part is there are too many preachers showing up when Pastors are called for! Pastors are to preachers what masons are to bricklayers. Both perform basically the same work but one has more of an anointing for duty or obligation than the other. A bricklayer can show up for work, lay brick, and go home. A preacher can show up at a church, tent revival, or street corner and preach and go home. A mason has the added responsibilities of reading blueprints and the overall coordination of the bricklayers. The same holds true for Pastors. Pastors must coordinate all the other ministers in the church as well as teachers and officers and outreach ministries. This is along with keeping the church finances in order with God's will. Plus Pastors have the church property to look after. Church property is God's property! Then to top that off the Pastors calling is for church growth, both in members and spiritually maturing them.

Only in functioning by the unction of the Spirit of God can any Pastor keep his flock in one accord and in unity. We can have life and have life more abundantly here on earth but what we are doing on earth is preparation for entering Heaven. There will be no more fighting or arguing or gossiping in Heaven. God's Word tells us that we are "one in the Spirit and one in the Lord." Pastors have an awesome task from God to perform. This task is planned out and ordained by a God who has all majesty, all dominion, and all power. God who rules Heaven and earth. God who is Alpha and Omega. He is the pulse of life. He is the pulse even before there was a pulse and He will be the pulse even when there is a pulse no more. Since we measure our life by whether or not there is a pulse, then we know our God is truly Supreme. He is worthy to be called Master. God of Truth and Spirit. The King of kings! The Lord of lords! The Host of hosts!

What a mighty God you serve. He is worthy of all the praise we can offer Him. But praise is not enough. We must also do all that He says to do in order to serve Him. As Pastors, you are required to lift God up just as He lifts you up before men. This Good News is nothing less than Christ resurrected! This Good News is nothing less than faith in God's promises. This Good News is nothing less than love, holiness, and righteousness. You have been given a gospel of God's never ending love and desire and promise for each of His children. Being that this earth is a place of preparation on our journey home, know that you are anointed to keep order here.

Since Jesus is the cornerstone of the church then you are who He has chosen to carry the load of His ministry. You are chosen to be the pillars on which all other leaders depend. Dependence on you is based upon your willingness to hear, understand, and coordinate the will of God. The guidelines for the church are for the ultimate goal of the edification of God's Kingdom. Your goal should be discipleship! *Mature* Christians teaching infant Christians how to *mature as* Christians in order for them to go out and repeat the same process. This is what church is all about. Salvation is only the beginning. It is not God's ultimate goal. It is your duty to hold the church body together during hard times. It is your job to keep the church running smoothly during good times. It is your job to make sure the church body keeps a constant connection to the Holy Spirit and God's specific plan for your church body. Your mind, heart, soul, and spirit must yearn to see these heavenly and divine plans put in action, not according to your will but to God's will. You are God's vessel. God would not have chosen you if He didn't plan to use you as a vessel for His Kingdom. It will be your connection to God which will determine how far you are able to lead your flock. If you are not growing in the wisdom and guidance of the Lord, neither will your flock grow. If you are not walking in obedience to the Word of God then neither will your flock. If you are caught up in religion, then your flock will also be caught up in religion. If you are caught up in legalistic doctrine so will your flock. If you are caught up in tradition so your flock will be also "traditional."

Hosea 14:2 tells us to "Take with you words, and turn to the Lord: say unto Him, take away all iniquity and receive us graciously: so we will render the calves of our lips."

All of the limits are taken off when you submit to the Lord. Why do I say this? Because I know that my Word says "All men sin and fall short of the glory of God." The limits are taken off when you allow God to take away your iniquity through your submission to Him first. Then Jesus can clean you up, before you try to speak holiness to your flock. Most people, even Pastors, don't want to admit iniquity tries to rise up in their hearts. It will be your willingness to allow God to search you, instead of pride and selfish ambition deceiving you, that quiets the spiritual storms in your life.

You have to be graciously received by God *each day* until your calling is finished. Your praise should be from the truth that it will only be God's will that is done. The calves of your lips will then be unblemished and fit for offering to a Holy God. Psalm 66:18 says "But if I regard iniquity in my heart the Lord will not hear me." The Lord will not hear you when you are prideful and covet His glory! The Lord will not hear you when you seek recognition for *yourself* instead of Jesus being lifted up. The Lord will not hear you when you use *His holy Word* to justify your vain glory. Remember there's a storm a comin'.

Always remember that although you may gain the respect of men, Satan is unimpressed with you. The Enemy does not believe you are untouchable. So why give him the opportunity to mock God through your pride? What is my pride you ask? Your pride is in leaning on your own understanding and not acknowledging God as the source of wisdom and truth. The Lord says, "If *I* be lifted up from the earth *I* will draw all men unto me." "No man comes to the Father except through the *Son*." "And no man comes to the Son unless the Father draws him." Never forget that you don't save anybody. Jesus does! Not only can you not save anybody, but you can do *nothing* without Jesus. You don't have the words in and of yourself to make anyone get saved. Keep your faith in Jesus and don't get weary of doing what is right and pleasing before God. Then you won't get discouraged when no one comes up for alter call.

Don't forget your elders! Some were praying for *you* before you even heard God's Word. Many have witnessed the power of an Almighty God before *you* were even born. They have seen God's faithfulness for generations. They have never seen the righteous forsaken nor his seed begging for bread. They have persevered even before you were saved. They have endured until the end. They are a living testimony to the scripture, "The race is not won by the strongest or the swiftest, but to he who holds out to the end." They also have something that we also can have. And it is called long-suffering. The most important lessons I have learned in life have always come through these old soldiers patience with me. There is *nothing new* under the sun. It is all about the blood of the Lamb! It is all about our God who through love and *long-suffering* has not cast us away but draws us to Jesus. It is all about God reaching out to mankind as our

Father. You are His vessel and God has placed people in your life to help you do your duty.

You being a son who serves brings me to this second point, I am led to inform you about your elders. This is something you don't hear much about in the church today. This is something that has been overlooked or untaught for the purpose of not wanting to look "religious." This was the foundation of the building up of the church at Jerusalem. But now this is just not "cool." What I am talking about is what I remember growing up with. What I am talking about is something these old folks had. What I am talking about is what these young teenagers need to have today. What I am talking about is a thing called *reverential fear*. The church maturity level should be reflecting reverence toward God. The truth is God isn't our buddy! God isn't our good old pal! God isn't the old man upstairs! God ain't your "homeboy"!

Hebrews 12:28-29: "Wherefore we receiving a kingdom which cannot be moved, let us have grace whereby we may serve God acceptably with reverence and godly fear. For our God is a consuming fire."

Isaiah 66:13-16: "As one whom his mother comforts, so will I comfort you and ye shall be comforted in Jerusalem. [14] And when ye see this, your heart shall rejoice, and your bones shall flourish like an herb; and the hand of the Lord shall be known towards his servants, and His indignation toward His enemies. [15] For behold, the Lord will come with fire, and with His chariots like a whirlwind, to render His anger with fury and His rebuke with flames of fire. [16] For by fire and by His sword will the Lord plead with all flesh: and the slain of the Lord shall be many."

We should thank God that He always leaves a remnant of people to remind us that everything begins and ends with His Word. [Acts 18:24-26] "Apollos was an eloquent man, and mighty in the scriptures. He was instructed in the ways of the Lord, and was fervent in the spirit. He spoke and taught diligently the things of the Lord knowing only the baptism of John. Even as he spoke boldly in the synagogue, when Aquila and Priscilla heard him, they took him into their home and expounded into him the way of God *more perfectly.*" Allow God to use whoever He wishes to help *instruct you.* Stand with humility!

The Holy Spirit spoke this to me one night: Just as John the Baptist was the forerunner to the coming of Christ, so is this new false spirit of revelation the forerunner to the false prophet and the antichrist. There is a lie being preached that God is not in control. God is the Alpha and the Omega, the Beginning and the End! Not man. Man cannot extend mercy or grace unto himself when he does mess up. Men are all intertwined with one another in the earth and no man can be given total autonomy over another man's life. No man knows the future except for what God revels to him. Men receive the promises and provisions of God by their faith in God and God will not allow the destruction of one man's house, relationship, or marriage to bless even a man of faith when that man wants what doesn't belong to him and in fact belongs to another. Men of faith mess up too and need God's mercy and grace. The created will never be greater than the Creator.

Man being given dominion in the earth and control of his own destiny doesn't equate to him being given total autonomy in spiritual matters. And it sure doesn't mean because God has given us dominion and power in the earth and over Satan that God has given up any of *His* dominion!! God cannot be any more or any less God now that we have a little Word in us than He was before we knew anything! The Word says we are co-laborers with Christ! The one in control is the one who makes the law. The one not in control is the one who must obey the law set forth by the one who is superior. If you were in control with total autonomy, and God wasn't in control at all, then you could rewrite the law. You could cancel, amend, or even revoke the law or covenant, but you can't. If we were the one in control and God wasn't in control then we would be the ones who judge God instead of He, the Righteous Judge, judging us.

As you preach the Word you should always remember Psalm 18:22-24, "For all His judgments were before me, and I did not put

His statutes away from me. I was also upright before Him, and I kept myself from mine iniquity. Therefore has the Lord recompensed according to my righteousness, according to the cleanness of my hands in His eyesight."

We can know who God is by Psalm 22:28-29, "For the kingdom is the Lord's and He is the governor among the nations. All they that be fat upon earth shall eat and worship: all they that go down to the dust shall bow before Him: and none can keep alive his own soul."

The danger in making statements like "God is not in control" is that after far too many preachers say this, the ones hearing it are told that they are in control but "don't know how to be in control." Then the way they are told to learn to be in control is to "buy my books and tapes." Before long God is left out of the person's actual Bible study and prayer life as far as seeking God's face. Before long the person is following whichever speaker, preacher, or evangelist is telling them what they like to hear. Before long the average person isn't even reading the Bible for themselves anymore. Then the preacher or evangelist has become their god. Any person not reading along with whoever is preaching can be led to believe and follow anything. It's called deception. What they need to hear is God's way of doing things from God so they learn to hear His voice because there is a storm a comin'.

See, we can be in control of whether or not our names are written in the Lamb's Book of Life but it is God who writes them there, and it is only God who can bring any prophecy to pass. We cannot speed up the return of Jesus and we can't slow it down!

What we need to be preaching is the whole truth and not just enough of it to stir up the emotions of the flock to where they are whooping and hollering and don't even know what they are whooping and hollering about. See, God has given mankind power to rule in the earth but there are conditions attached to it which determine whether or not that power is available to *you*! It's all promise and principle. You live the principle, you get the promise. You don't live the principle, you don't get the promise.

Now, we teach "You shall also decree a thing, and it shall be established unto you." (Job 22:28) But we overlook the importance of the word "also". When you see the word "also" way down here in verse 28, that lets you know that verse 28 is in addition to something else in the preceding verses. So we must find out what these verses before verse 28 say in order to know what GOD'S Word really says! And that is found in verses 23-24 of the same chapter. Verse 23 starts it all, when it states, "*If you return* to the Almighty, you shall be built up, you shall put away iniquity far from your tabernacles."

"IF"!!! Verse 24 . . . "THEN!!! . . ."

So you can decree all you want to, but if you are not in fellowship with God and keeping His laws and commandments for living a holy and righteous life before Him, then the truth is your "decreeing" will turn to "*decrying*" and *defeat* and you ain't going to establish nothing except the fact that you have been walking in deception! I told you there's a storm a comin!!!

Talking or Teaching

Greetings in the name of Jesus to all of our teachers who are in charge of teaching Christians the way in which they should go. Blessed be those teachers who not only seek, understand, and learn themselves, but have been anointed to teach others in the ways of our God's instruction. This is not an easy task nor one to be taken lightly. What you teach is surely learned in one sense or the other. If what you teach is carnal, then what is learned is of this world. By the same measure if what you teach is spiritual then what is learned is of a spiritual nature. If you stay in the Word then you teach that which is already anointed, ordained, or established by God. His laws are perfect and just. His wisdom is holy. Man's knowledge is no more than folly.

Lift Him up at every opportunity. Lift Him up especially to the children for they belong to Him and not us. Show them the examples in scripture of His *eternal love* for them. Teach them to trust in His Word. Teach them to trust in His *promises* to them. Teach them faith. Teach them to be *still*. Teach them to *share*. Teach them *compassion*. Teach them *truth*. Teach them to *love*. Show them love. Love is the key. Love is what our children need most of all. Not only a love for themselves but also a love for God first and a love for others. It is too easy for a child to become selfish and self-centered and to think that life is about only themselves. Unless their parents or you teach them that their life revolves around God and not themselves then they will never make the connection of unity and loving their friends or playmates as themselves. Are you teaching God's Word? Be careful, there's a storm a comin'.

The same holds true for teachers of adults through Bible study, Sunday school, Discipleship class, marriage counseling, singles ministry, etc. Now, know that the ones that you are teaching are not children and should already have some semblance of self and who they are. Don't worry they will let you know! The trick is to teach them difference between *who* they are and *whose* they are in a manner which is *drawing* them closer to God as opposed to pushing them away or discouraging them. Surely an attitude of humility is required for this important task. You see, adults would not even be present if they weren't seeking a closer relationship with God or peace in their life. Although all biblical teachings are for all of us and for all of us to adhere to, the fact is that different people are, often times, at different levels of understanding in their own spiritual journey which should be going *forward*. How to reach everyone in one particular group takes time, patience, and participation from everyone in that group. Separating God's will from worldly thought or behavior, which comes natural to us, is of utmost importance. You have God to answer to when you begin to instruct in His name. Only God's instruction is perfect and to teach those instructions requires His constant guidance. You cannot teach God's divine blueprint without God *teaching you first*. What you know and understand will determine how for you can take your flock. Understand that you also must continue to study and learn all that you can about the

Lord in order to be prepared to convey His wisdom to others who seek Him. Do not be upset or surprised to find out that those you are teaching are often times teaching you. God *will* keep you humble if you teach in His name for long. You must study to show *yourselves* approved.

Young teachers must stay in the Word. Older and elderly teachers must stay in the Word. When you get outside of God's Word, then you open a window of opportunity for Satan to exploit and twist God's Word. God's Word, no more no less, must be the foundation and very essence of all that you teach or instruct. The rules of the church have got to be in line with God's rules for the church. Marriage counseling must be in line with God's purpose for husbands and wives first and foremost. If the talk show host's philosophy or world's philosophy aren't in alignment with God's divine purpose for family and the institution of marriage then you had better go with God and leave all other rationalization of worldly teachings to the deceived souls who are spreading these doctrines or opinions which come from themselves.

Bible study and Sunday school should also be an integral part of your own life. You cannot teach what you haven't been anointed to teach. In praying for wisdom and guidance and waiting for God to lead you, your teachings should be in one accord with those in your church connection. In other words we should be able to hold study sessions with other church members from different churches and still agree on viewpoints and goals through the Holy Spirit, which binds all of us together as one. Our vision should be God's vision and not our own. We are one in the Spirit and one in the Lord. Even as a teacher you cannot "go it alone." You too, are *part* of this assembly of people, not an island unto yourself. Are people drawn to your teaching *His* Word or your own? Sometimes it's not even what you say, but what you don't say which leaves the lasting impression. Sometimes it's not what you do, but what you don't do. You lead by example!

1 Peter 5:2-4 says to, "Feed the flock of God which is among you, taking the oversight thereof, not by constraint, but willingly;

not for filthy lucre, but of a ready mind. [3] Neither as being lords over God's heritage, but being examples to the flock. Or, overruling [4] And when the chief Shepherd shall appear, ye shall receive a crown of glory that fadeth not away." 2 Peter 1:20-21 says, "Knowing this first, that no prophecy of the scripture is of any private interpretation. [21] For the prophecy came not in old time by the will of man; but holy men of God spoke as they were moved by the Holy Ghost."

Get it? Let's read it one more time. "For the prophecy came not in old time by the will of man; but holy men of God spoke as they were moved by the *Holy Ghost.*" By the *Holy Ghost*! Not by pride, arrogance, or self-righteousness! Who gets the glory when you speak about God? Will God share His glory with anyone? The answer is no, God will not share His glory with anyone. Teachers, like everyone else are laborers. You serve the Lord by feeding His flock. Jesus stressed this point to Simon Peter by asking him, "Simon, do you love Me?" When Peter answered, "Yes" Jesus told him first, "Feed my lambs." Then He said, "Feed my sheep" after the second and third times He asked Peter the exact same question.

See, the point is you are also sheep fed by the Good Shepherd. But before you were sheep you were lambs, or babes, in Christ. You too had to be taught so don't try to take Christ's glory for yourselves by overruling His lambs. Don't lead Christ's lambs into bowing down to you or believing that you are somehow exempt from Matthew 23:9, in which Jesus states, "And call no man your father upon the earth, for One is your Father, which is in Heaven." Ain't nothing worse for myself than someone trying to tell me they are my "father" or "mother," spiritual or otherwise. I, like many others, have heard the Word before and have learned from many teachers or sources. Now I may feel someone is my mentor or spiritual "guide" but that is for me to say and not them to cram down my throat, as though I need them to hear from God for me, as far as my growth or trust of them is now concerned.

What I know to be true is that whoever is in my face right now doesn't know any more than the "men of old", who received the Word of God through the Holy Spirit, not by any private interpretation, and wrote that Word down for me to read for myself. This protects the teacher or Preacher from pride and myself from dependency on them. What I have found is there are far too many teachers teaching their viewpoint and not God's revelation. Then it becomes easier and easier for them to add their own personality or "cute delivery" of scripture to the point that it becomes no more than a *popularity contest or competition* among Bible teachers.

See, you have to be careful that you don't allow filthy lucre (money) to drive your ambition. Don't allow you being on the church payroll lead you into self pride. Jesus will raise you up in His time. There is no need for you to *pass up* the *very lambs* Jesus *wants you to feed* in order to keep certain others listening only to you, so you can be recognized by the "elite." You know. The ones who can brag on you to someone else with influence. The ones you feel can move you up in the hierarchy in your church. The ones you feel can get you that television show. The ones who may get you that radio spot. The ones you feel can get your books published. The ones who can get your child the microphone to "testify" when your boy comes back from the war. You have to be careful that you keep your *motives* for teaching in God's name pure! You have to keep your heart right with God. You have got to teach with the *intent* that souls are saved, the flock is fed and growing up, and God is getting the glory! I told you there's a storm a comin'!

Remember, there comes a time when your lambs become sheep and should be able to stand *on their own*. Are you preparing them for this or are you trying to keep them feeling dependent on you, for what they really are now able to do for themselves, so that you can appear more spiritually mature than anyone else? If a student asks for a meeting with you over a disagreement do you meet with them in a timely fashion or blow them off like they aren't worth your time? When you do meet with them do you listen to them or continue to ignore them just like before? See, I don't have to judge you or anyone else to know whether or not you are of God's business. No, I don't really have to pay you much attention at all as a person. That's not my place to judge you. All I have to do is look at the path you are on. All I have to do is look at your path, which you chose, to know whether or not you can lead me. If I judge that path to not be of my Father's business then you better know that I am not getting on it! I know that God leads me in the path of righteousness and that the Devil can't walk on this path because it is holy and there is no holiness in him. That's why he uses people to try to get you to step off of the path of righteousness into his territory. That was the only way he could get Adam to fall. You don't have to be the greatest teacher in the world. Just be what God wants you to be! The Word tells me, "For the time has come that judgment must begin at the house of God. And if it first begin at us, what shall the end be of them that obey not the gospel of God? And if the righteous scarcely be saved, where shall the ungodly and the sinner appear?" 1Pet.4:17-18.

One thing that I've learned, if I haven't learned anything else in life, is that there is a difference between being wise and having wisdom. Wise, no matter how you look at is shallow once the Holy Spirit shows you the deeper truths of God. Wise often comes from logic. Wise is limited to the certain areas of expertise of each person. Logic itself can be learned by studying a wise person's train of thought, doctrine, theory, reasoning, etc. who doesn't even know God. Wisdom comes from a higher more personal relationship with the only One who knows and understands all. You cannot separate God from wisdom or wisdom from God! You can *be* wise and not have true wisdom but wisdom in itself is what makes you wise because of the decision you made to seek, believe God, and walk in God's way of doing things. Proverbs 21:30 tells us, "There is no wisdom, nor understanding nor counsel against the Lord." The nature of wisdom is the very nature of God!

Proverbs 8:22-23 tells us, "The Lord possessed me in the beginning of His way, before His works of old. I was set up from everlasting, from the beginning, or ever the earth was."

I was at work one day laying brick when the discussion of homes came up. At the time I was around 40 years old. My boss, was no more than five years older than me. Now, the other two masons were 66 and 72 years old. CJ and Jack were some good old

God fearing men. They both really taught me a lot of lessons about life. I think CJ had six grown kids plus grand kids and great grand kids. My boss who has a few kids of his own said that since his youngest child was moving out on his own that he and his wife were contemplating selling their home and buying a smaller one since they would no longer need all that space. Almost simultaneously Jack and C.J. said, "Buy a smaller house! If you know what I know, you would be adding on! When they come back they'll be bringing wives, girlfriends, husbands, boyfriends, grand kids and all!" Everybody cracked up laughing. This type of wisdom only comes from experience. Just like you have to experience God. And know His Word!

One of the hardest lessons that I've watched up and coming brick masons learn is that to be at the top or the leader in one aspect of the building process doesn't necessarily make you qualified to teach someone else who is the lowest in another job position. Sound like trouble? It is. One great American statesman said, "You can't lead where you don't go, and you can't teach what you don't know. "The problem in building often times turns out to be a matter of order. Order, among other things, mainly consists of knowing your role and staying in it! When one worker or crew chief gets outside of his or her responsibility then they are also outside of what they are asked to manage. Often times, more than not, this leads to confusion, resentment, jealousy, and a whole lot of misinformation being passed around to the "laborers" in each crew.

I've watched many men hire on as labor or mason helpers. Their job, in starting out is simply to mix the mortar, carry brick to the masons, and make sure that the masons never run out of these materials while they are laying brick. Simple as it sounds this takes a great deal of planning, coordination, and alertness on the "helpers" part in order to keep the job running smoothly and without grinding to a standstill. Time is money. Since everyone's wages come from hourly rates and the bosses pay comes from the market price paid per thousand brick laid, then the masons must lay enough brick per hour to not only pay their wages but those of the laborers, as well as turn a profit for the boss, who must in turn pay out workman's compensation insurance and match social security withholding on each employee, plus pay state, local, and federal taxes and for the maintenance on his equipment while replacing old and worn out equipment. Amazing how the least of us is so important concerning the building process. I've watched many go from a general laborer to scaffolding leader in charge of setting up scaffolds. Some move up to be the forklift operators, saw man, labor foreman, or top out as a "laborer" as an apprentice.

You noticed I said, "top out" as a laborer. I didn't say that this was as far as they can go in the company, only that this is "topped out" in their area of expertise through study, training, and guidance from someone who knew more. The strangest thing is that for some reason we tend to think that because we have mastered our job then we surely know something (enough something) to begin telling the least or apprentice mason, who by the way is above us, what to do, what he needs to be doing, or how to do his job. If someone was my training supervisor when I began and I learned from them my job responsibilities and how to effectively perform them for the cohesion of the entire building process, then who do I think I am to try to take over the entire operation? Or who do I think I'm impressing or fooling by trying to teach that which I haven't been taught myself. You see, looking, seeing, and just watching things going on doesn't equate to being taught. Sometimes you can do more harm than good.

We were laying brick on an office building once that was located next to a Rescue Squad building, when the rescue units tore out of there with their lights and sirens blazing. When they returned a couple of hours later one EMT came over and said for us to be careful because they just had to rescue a bunch of masons who had fallen on another job. It was funny because one mason had noticed the scaffolding getting farther and farther away from the wall.

"Quick!! Everybody on top of the block, the scaffolding is falling!" he screamed. Then, crash!! They all hit the ground mangled among the block. When they looked up, there stood the scaffolds just as straight as ever. It was the wall falling the whole time and *not* the scaffolds!! So, you see, what we think we see and what we think we know has nothing to do with what's actually taking place in our lives sometimes, even though we may have warning signs of danger or storms in our midst. I didn't know any of those masons that fell that day but one thing I did learn was not to just follow anybody's instruction. I also learned that we need to be careful and pay attention to everything going on while building up God's Kingdom as well. Unlike the masons, who would recover from their fall and go on back to work, as Christians, we may not always be able to recover those whom we have led astray or caused to stumble. Again I say, "Study to show yourselves approved." A true disciple always puts Jesus first.

By study, fasting, and prayer you will know your job and your place in God's perfect order for the edification of His Kingdom. You will not or should not have to suffer the embarrassment of your Pastor having to tell you or remind you of your place in the church. Don't get tired of the Lord's chastisement for He chastises those that He loves. Remember that to stumble or to fall doesn't mean that you are utterly cast down for the Lord upholds you with His hand. Through you His Word shall be taught to those who seek a more personal relationship with Him. Teaching in one accord and learning in one accord leads to living in one accord, which leads to praying in one accord, which leads to God opening up doors that no power can close or even hinder us from walking through in faith. The Lord is with us in all that we do in His will for His Kingdom.

How many times have we been standing on God's Holy Word only to abandon His Word for our own understanding? For myself it's more times than I can count. If God's Word is solid and His knowledge given to us is sufficient then why do we forsake standing on His Word through the storms? Do we truly trust Him and the Holy Spirit to carry us or we merely "playing church?" If God says to go out and spread the gospel of Jesus Christ to the world then why is it that when we go out into the "world" that we only end up having a church service with each other and *not* the very ones we claim to be ministering to? We say that we're going to "take a park or city block or crack house back," but where are the lost souls who dwell in those places? More often than not they're sure not at this "church service". How can we even believe that we're ministering to anyone who is lost if we haven't even invited them to attend?

We cannot go on having these meetings or prayer vigils without *inviting* the very ones that we claim to go out in God's name to witness to in the first place! What God sees in all this is a bunch of folks "playing church." You know, "This is Rev. Running Late, my good friend and the Lord's servant, who I'm so glad could be here today. Rev. Running Late is an old soldier of the cross."

Then Rev. Running late says, "Well, thank you Rev. Good Grinning, you too are such a good Christian, just like me. You're a Christian, I'm a Christian, everybody is a Christian here today. That's why we're here today to pat each other on the back and eat some chicken."

You see, to God, we are not standing on His Word when we don't spread the love of Jesus to these drunks, drug addicts, whores, and other folk who may just not know who Jesus is or what He has done for us and will do for them. Just like those masons who jumped off of those scaffolds onto a wall that they themselves built so are we who leave out what God has ordained us to do in order to do what we think is the right thing to do. And just like those masons we will end up right back on the ground. Don't worry though, because God's Word will be preached and Jesus' name will be exalted above all the earth. It just may be without us. So don't think that we can stand on God's Word sometimes and on our own human understanding at other times, because we can't. The name of Jesus will be preached unto all the earth because He said it would be. Jesus is the same yesterday, today, and forever. God has already done His part. Jesus has already done His part. It is now time for mankind to do their part.

1 Cor.1:22-24 tells us we are set apart as His disciples.

[22]: For the Jews require a sign, and the Greeks seek after wisdom;[23]: But we preach Christ crucified, unto the Jews a

stumbling block, and unto the Greeks, foolishness;[24]: But unto them which are called, both Jews and Greeks, Christ the power of God, and the wisdom of God.

Dear Lord help me to die. Help me to bury my old self. Help me to let go of myself. Help me to give up my old nature to You. Grant me a newness of life for Your name's sake. I surrender my all to you and a newness of Spirit. I pray for the indwelling of the Holy Spirit so that I may grow in Your abundance. Amen.

Congregation or Confusion

In the mighty name of Jesus do I send greetings unto you my brothers and sisters of His church. Make no mistake about it, it is His church. I am His church. You are His church. Collectively we are His vision of *one* holy catholic church. The word catholic here means "universal" and is not to be confused with the Roman Catholic Church.

"Forsake ye not the assembly of My people," Thus saith the Lord. Why should we not forsake assembling together? Is it because of the word assembly itself? Is it because of the word My? Or is it because of *who* said both is speaking to a specific people? First of all let us examine what the word assembly insinuates or suggests in the first place; that word being congregation.

Congregation n.1. the act of congregating, 2. a congregated body; assemblage. 3. An assembly of persons brought together for common religious worship. 4. An organization formed for providing church activities; a local church society. 5. The people of Israel. Ex 12:3-6; Lev. 4:13 [a]6. New Testament. The Christian church in general.

I'll stop here to keep from getting off into specific denominational connotations.

Again I ask why is this "assembly of My people" so important that Jesus would command us to not to *forsake* it? Don't even think that I'm going to look up "forsake" for you! Well I have been led to believe that the words "assembly" and "my people" are all synonymous with Christ's will when He speaks. You see, Christ is about His church and saving the lost. For any other person, you or I, to speak of a congregation, we could mean anything from a little old ladies tea party to misled youth in a gang standing on street corners.

So, you see, that in Jesus' eyes, spiritual eyes, any and all assembly should include Him and His divine purpose for congregating in the *first* place. He will not play *second* fiddle to any of our whims or vices. He will not recognize us as His own if we don't recognize His voice as our Shepherd and follow Him. What we need to understand is that *any* and *all* that we do that is not with, of, about, or for Christ is worldly. Christ is not of this world. And although we were of this world we must strive to live *above* this world in order to truly be a *congregation* in Christ's eyes now that we are saved. Read 2 Peter 3:9-18.

Once we come together in His House of worship we should have one common goal; To praise God and to lift up Jesus. In lifting up our Savior, we are saying that He is greater than any of our problems. Whether our problems are personal or between each other, when we come together in one accord, in the name of Jesus, then and *only* then can we even be *considered* a congregation.

Now this may sting a little bit, but I know that it is true. Just because we have studied, showed up on time, and prayed together does not mean that we are on one accord in Christ's eyes. I told you that this may sting a little. For you see, Christ sees all of us right to the very center of our heart. We do not fool Him, nor can we offer any explanation to Him for any of our disagreements within His church, especially when *neither* side is even within His will.[1John 3:11-12] "For this is the message that you heard from the beginning, that we should love one another. Not as Cain, who was of that wicked one, and slew his own brother. And wherefore he slew him? Because his own works were evil, and his brother's righteous."

There is no power in smiling falsely in folks faces! There is no truth in backbiting. There are only the works of Satan in discord and hypocrisy. So roll up your sleeves and get to work. Get to work on yourselves. You see, in order to come to Christ we must all start within ourselves. No one can cross this bridge for you or me. The good thing about this journey is that the purpose for God's plan of a congregation is that you learn with me and that I learn with you in *one* love and *one* accord so that *His* name is *exalted* above all the earth. To gather and to whoop and holler does not impress our God one bit. *Be* where you *should be* spiritually, for there's a storm a comin'.

Where you should be is dwelling with the Lord. How do you dwell with the Lord? By keeping His commandments! What is His commandment? [1 John 3:23] "And this is His commandment, that we should believe on the name His Son Jesus Christ, and love one another, as He gave us commandment." What happens if I don't? [1 John 3:15] "Whosoever hates his brother is a murderer; and ye know that no murderer hath eternal life abiding in him." How is my hatred the same as murdering someone? Because your works destroy their spirit. Why are my works evil? Because Jesus laid down His life for your brethren also! Hatred brings spiritual death and abides in death. Lies, gossiping, slander, vengeance, and pride are evil because Jesus says they are evil!

One thing that we as a congregation must understand and acknowledge is that we are a congregation *under* authority. Under authority! Not the authority. Not the focus of authority. Not the ones to tell our Pastors what God has in His blueprint for them to build. God is the Architect. God is the engineer. God is the developer. God is the contractor. God is the banker, and God is the investor! How much more can you invest than the Blood of the Lamb? Be still and listen. Listen to our Lord. God does not holler nor does He force himself on anyone. In stillness and quietness does our Lord speak. In stillness, quietness, fasting and prayer, in sacrifice of themselves do your Pastors lead the church. The things your Pastors go through in order to lead their flock are immeasurable when done for the glory of the Lord. It takes the heart and spirit of a person who has not only received the anointing, but actively does God's will, to lead God's people. In their anointing your Pastors should already have God's blueprint within their hearts.

Do not try to lead your Pastor! Do not be mean to your Pastor. Do not try to rally congregational members together against your Pastor! Do not pry into your Pastors personal life history behind their backs. Don't give Satan a toehold in your church! Being anointed means they will tell you about themselves in God's timing. It is God's timing which will have no other purpose than the uplifting of God's Kingdom. Do not try to impress your Pastor with wild supernatural stories that you don't even understand which more often than not, are *not* even of God. Never forget that Satan is the great imitator and thrives in confusion. I will discuss this deeper, later on in the book.

If you feel that the Lord has put something on your heart to say or to do then don't be upset if what you believe is the direction in which the church should go does not correspond with what your Pastor tells you that God has told them to do within His church. We are the sheep. Our Pastors are the shepherds. Christ is the Good Shepherd.

You must understand that your Pastors spend many hours a week in prayer. Some Pastors spend hours each day in prayer because prayer is their constant connection to Jesus. What Jesus, as Head of the church body, would have your Pastor to do will come to your Pastor through Jesus. Where your Pastor should be, will come through Jesus. When to prepare for what God has in store for your congregation will come through Jesus. How to accomplish God's will and stay in God's will comes through Jesus. All of your Pastors *vision* will come through prayer, meditation and a commune with the Lord. Leading a congregation is easy if you listen to, and *follow* the very ones that you are supposed to be leading. There's an old saying, "When everyone is the leader, then no one is the leader." Everyone is under authority from the *top* on *down.*

Sometimes what is on your heart *may* confirm or be the same thing that is on your Pastor's heart but the timing of moving in that direction is up to the Pastor to decide, not us. If you tell your Pastor what you feel the Lord has in store for the church to do or what direction to go and your feelings don't match your Pastor's *vision*, then simply follow. Don't become angry or cynical towards your Pastor and start trying to pressure them into believing that they should follow you and your little group. If your Pastor tells you that the Lord hasn't revealed to them what you claim He as revealed to you to do then don't take the attitude that, "Who said that He has to tell you something. He might tell me first for me to tell you!"

Well, I'll tell you what a lot of Pastors are afraid to tell you. God ain't going to tell you nothing for your Pastor to do within the church your Pastor is leading before He tells your Pastor! Now, they may not have been listening to His voice, but He did tell them! In plain English, the anointing always flows from the top. So get over it! Your unwillingness to submit to your Pastor's authority is sin. It is called rebellion.

My Word tells me in: Cor.3:-3-8:, "For ye are yet carnal: for whereas there is among you envying and strife, and divisions, are ye not carnal, and walk as men?[4] For while one saith, I am of Paul; and another, I am of Apollos; are ye not carnal?[5] Who then is Paul, and who is Apollos, but ministers by whom ye believed, even as the Lord gave to every man?[6] I have planted, Apollos watered; but God gave the increase. [7]So then neither is he that plants anything, neither he that waters; but God that gives the increase. [8]Now he that plants and he that waters are one; and every man shall receive his own reward according to his own labor."

This is the Good News. Jesus has a plan and a purpose for your life. It is my sincere hope that you seek the Lord's plan for your life. I pray that you find your purpose for living. You are no accident. You are important to God. You are always on His mind. You, out of all His creation were chosen to worship and to serve Him. God has given you His Holy Word. He has given you the victory. I pray that you don't let the Enemy trick you into complacency. I pray that you don't just stand at the cross. My deepest desire is that you allow Jesus to come into your heart. My deepest desire is that your life is cleansed from corruption and carnal thinking. My deepest desire is that you go *through* the cross to have the Blood *applied* to your mind, body, and spirit. Without the Blood *applied*, you are just standing at the cross. We ain't a cult. But we're a bloody religion. I crack me up.

Coming out of the Storm

1. The difference between seasons is wisdom

2. We don't define reality; the truth does.

3. You must create the opportunity for the Holy Spirit to make you successful.

4. Make sure God consumes your sacrifice.

5. There is no need to search for signs. Your birth is the sign.

6. Believe God and others will be saved.

7. Ask God to increase your territory.

8. Forgive others while they live.

9. You must be in fellowship with God to decree anything with results in your favor.

10. Encouragement results in churches growth.

11. Get past amazed and into expectancy.

12. Tell the Good News and not the drama.

13. Don't waste time talking about the latest ideas.

14. You must defeat Satan in your mind.

15. Be as enthusiastic to teach before they fall, as you are to correct and gossip after they fall.

16. Do earthly good

17. God is wherever His thoughts are.

18. Trust God.

Following the Blueprint

And the earth was without form. And void and darkness was upon the face of the deep. And the *Spirit of God moved* upon the face of the waters. [Genesis1: 2]

[1:10] And God called the dry land Earth; and the gathering together of the waters called the Seas; and God saw that *it was good.*

[1:21] And *God created* great whales. And every living creature that moves, which the waters brought forth abundantly after their kind, and every winged fowl after his kind; and *God* saw that *it was good.*

Yes it *was* good! It *is* good! And it *shall be* good! God created it so how can it ***no*t** be good? Well I'm not even going to *waste our time* with some long drawn out explanation, making *excuses* for why men are so far away from God's blueprint. I'll just tell you straight up. People, even "church" people, have *given* God's goodness away to the Enemy. Just *gave* it away. What people have done is to *twist* what God *created* as good into something ugly or unholy. God brought the beasts of the field before Adam for Adam to name them and the *Word* says, Gen 2:18 ". . . *whatever* Adam called every living creature *that was the name* thereof. So if Adam said, "This is an ass," that's what it is. It's an ass throughout the Bible. So what is so bad about this creature of God being what Adam named it? There was nothing wrong with the Word, the animal, or *God* so that only leaves people. If men want to take what God *created* and *blessed* and twist it into some part of human anatomy, or whatever else they want to then that's their problem. Don't you ever give Satan or anybody else what God gave you! Now we don't expect to live our lives and never have to come in contact with the world. But we are not of the world. Our separation is a spiritual separation from darkness. Adam spoke through the Spirit of God to his surroundings! Adam named the animals *before* "the fall" so that tells you there was no sin in him at that point!

What's confusing is when religious folk will make a big deal out of the name of an animal in the Bible for the "children's sake." Then turn right around and load these same children on a bus and take them to the bowling alley or ballgame and watch people get drunk. I'm not saying that we can hide them from the world, but I'm sure they are not hearing the Word there. Do we even know what God's blueprint is what I'm left to wonder. Sometimes it seems that folks just do and go along with whoever fits in with their whims, notions, or philosophy. Right or wrong in God's eyes often has nothing to do with our decisions, behavior, or judgment. If we say it's wrong, it's wrong. If we say it's alright, it's alright. It's then the kids who are influenced. Influence is a funny thing in life. The issue with influence is that it never goes away. You always have influence whether you want it or not. You are always going to influence someone one way or another, for good or bad, whether you intend to or not!

When did God say to bring practicing sexually immoral Pastors, officers, or youth leaders into the church? He didn't! But still it goes on. These days, churches are even being sued over little boys being molested by priests and preachers. It took years and years for this abomination to be brought to light. Thank God it has been brought out in the open. But do I believe that no one knew it was going on all those years? No because I, even as a teen, witnessed perverted teachers actions being swept under the rug until someone's peace was disturbed enough to act against it.

Now after sin disturbs your peace and you turn to God then He replaces your peace with His peace. See, His peace flows from things righteous and holy. Your peace can more often than not come from whatever you agree on and allow. God should be the standard! If telling a teenager to shut up about some perverted youth leader is right, then who wants anything to do with "church people"? Even the unsaved know right from wrong!

The blueprint that God gave to us is His covenant towards us. His covenant is established in righteousness. His covenant, God's Holy Word, or blueprint is for living in peace, forgiveness, holiness, integrity, faith, trust, obedience, unity, and love. Without order all you have is a bunch of religious folks playing God with other people's lives. We must receive God's covenant, or blueprint into our hearts, souls, and minds and speak only on those things. When we allow the Holy Spirit to guide us we won't see self-exhortation, judgment, ignorance, and pride. Pride always comes before a fall. During these times of downfall it is too easy to get caught up in finger pointing. Too often many of us want to point fingers and say, "They are the ones who aren't like Christ." What we mean is "they are not like us and unacceptable to us and *we* need to change them." But *we* can't change anybody. We need to ask God to change us! I have been through that fire and have seen the power of God's transformation through *His* glory.

I pray you never change to follow anyone who you see doesn't even understand the very blueprint they profess to follow. Follow God who says in Isaiah 42:6-9, "I the Lord have called you *in righteousness*, and I will hold your hand, and I will keep you, and give you for a covenant of the people, for a light of the Gentiles; [7] To open the blind eyes, to bring out the prisoners from the prison, and them that sit in darkness out of the prison house. [8]I Am the Lord: that is my name; and my glory will I not give to another, neither my praise to graven images. [9]Behold, the former things are come to pass, and new things do I declare: before they spring forth I tell you of them."

You can read and study for yourself to find out God's will for your own life. You have right at your fingertips God's will for your own life. You have the Word of God at your own disposal to begin to build your own personal relationship with God. God wants you to know Him. He wants to talk to you. He wants to reveal his very nature to you.

When the book of Genesis opens and says in the second verse that, "the earth was without form, and void; and darkness was upon the face of the deep. And the Spirit of the Lord moved upon the face of the waters," it is saying that God is active even when He seems to be inactive. God is preparing a way for His holy blueprint to be brought into being or existence in a physical sense. Just the *thought* of bringing life brings life in God [Isa.14:24]. The Spirit of God is always moving. The Spirit of God is God and God is always moving. God is moving from eternity. What is nothing to us is everything to God. What is everything to us is nothing to God. Nothing just "pops in God's mind." God's Holy blueprint is sovereign. It stands alone. It stands alone because wisdom and truth are eternally with God. God cannot be separated from wisdom and truth! And there is no wisdom or truth outside of God.

God is so smart that He has faith in Himself! God is so wise that even if He told us everything, all the mysteries of God, we *would* be overwhelmed. How are we to comprehend how God can exist in nothingness? How can we comprehend how God can speak into nothingness and create what the human eye can see? How can we understand that when the Spirit of God moved upon the face of the waters that God was stepping out in His sovereignty with a desire to create someone to talk to and love and call His own tender possession? How can we comprehend the thought and planning that God had in creating mankind? How can we possibly understand that even when the earth was without form, and void, and darkness was upon the face of the deep that He already was preparing to send His only begotten Son into the world that the world through Him might be saved? The only answer is faith.

We *know* that from before the beginning that the Spirit of God was upon the earth without form, and void, and that the Spirit *moved*. The Spirit *moved* according to the will of God. The Spirit, God and the Son are One. And the Spirit, God and the Son shall always be One. We also can *know* that we will be in the presence of the Lord God Almighty in Heaven when this life is over. So we really can't wait, as Kingdom-minded people, to follow the *blueprint* from God.

According to Deut 4:16-20 God has shown me that I am not to make, draw, or worship or find *any* comfort in an idol made by man. God has shown me that these seemingly innocent, cute little figurines of angels or anything holy are no more than idols and graven images. You say they are not idols? Then throw them away. Why not? If you can't you may want to examine yourself. If man will worship the sun, the moon, and the stars, wind and sea, then he will surely worship these. What is the attachment that you can't let them go? What the Holy Spirit has shown me is that *even if* the *owner* of such figurines is *not* worshiping these cute little "angels" that someone else who doesn't know the precepts of God will end up putting more faith in and finding more comfort in these graven images than in Christ to the point that these objects *become* idols. The apostle Paul *repeatedly* warns to "*stay away* from idols!!" If *God* says to stay away from idols then why do people take what is *holy* and just *give* it to the Enemy? Because men are following man's blueprint for righteousness and not God's. I know that a lot of people will disagree with what I'm telling them but I can only serve the Lord in *His* truths and not ours. I've seen people smoke crack for days, doing all kinds of wickedness and sexual perversions and stick their Bible beneath their pillow to sleep on. Never *read* it! I even heard a preacher say one day, "That's a good thing." He won't be preaching to me.

You have to *know* the Word of God and that the Bible, as *intended* by God, ain't no *good luck charm* no matter what anybody tries to tell you! We should *know* that according to God's blueprint that we don't need any *accessories*, for *His* grace and *His* mercies are sufficient. If men want to hang stuff around their neck, call themselves religious, and do their own thing then that is between them and who they say that they serve. If men want to fill their shelves with graven images of the angels or hosts of Heaven then that is between them and whoever they claim to serve. If men want to paint or hang pictures of man's idea of Christ on their walls then this too will be between that man and God.

It is easy to take what is Holy before God and to turn it into something unholy or something that only serves to cause confusion, debate or lies. Jesus started out as the Messiah, King of the Jews, the Lion of Judah, the Prince of Peace but now is a caricature hanging on a wall. Some people have to *see* a white Jesus. Some have to *see* a black Jesus, while others want to *see* a more feminine Jesus or just *any* Jesus that resembles them. What has happened is that these *carnal* Christians have *forgotten* that God's blueprint calls for us to become *like* Christ in our words, deeds, faith, obedience and *love* for one another and have now tried to make Christ like us, or what we think He should be and then try to pass this off as Christianity.

"I got my picture of Jesus and my angels hanging on the wall. I got my cross tattooed on my shoulder. I got my little angels (they even come in black or white) on my desk and coffee table so, yes, I am a Christian!!" Don't be surprised when you stand before God and He tells you that these graven images and idols have always been an abomination to Him and have served as a stumbling block for others. I had a friend to give me a "black angel" for Christmas one year. I got rid of it. I always wondered why didn't he give me a "white" one or Asian or Hispanic?

"Religion" has gotten so far away from God's blueprint that many can't even see it much less read it. What the world has done is to fall in love with themselves and the *pride* of their culture. What has happened is that many have gone right back to the ways of the Pharisees. We have too many Pastors, teachers, and "religious" leaders who have taken educational opportunities and advanced learning to a level that subtly takes them outside of the will of God. What do you mean, Gregory? Well, I'll tell you straight up what I mean. We have people leading God's people who spend more time admiring their diplomas and certificates hanging on the wall, and not hearing God, than leaders who actually are in touch with God so they can *relate* to *other* people. Notice that I didn't say, "relate to everyday people." See, to say "everyday people" would be to exalt one person over another because of their choice to study under *someone else* who evidently has convinced them that they have the *answers* to a better world and a better life. I don't care who we are, say we are, think we are, or claim we are. If all we have is book sense, which involves your absorption, comprehension, and retention skills and no spiritual relationship with God then we need to leave God's people *alone.* What you know and what you feel is acceptable to God may just be from man and his *beliefs.* What comes from *God* is *Spirit* and cannot be *condemned* by man. It is *truth.* It will always be the *truth* that you receive from the Spirit whether you accept it or not.

Too many modern churches have gotten so far outside of God's blueprint that it finds itself searching for answers in everything but God. The apostle Paul spoke on these things in Rom 15:21. "To whom He was not spoken of, they shall understand." Go ahead and read the entire chapter for yourself. Paul goes on to say in 16:17-18, "Now I beseech you brethren, mark them which cause divisions and offenses *contrary* to the doctrine which ye have learned; and avoid them.18: For they that are such serve not our Lord Jesus Christ, but their own belly; and by good words and fair speeches deceive the hearts of the *simple.* AMEN

What we now have are too many people in the hierarchy of the church who think that any person not in their circle of hierarchy can't think, study, or understand the precepts of God without them *cramming their* views and *limited* understanding of what Christ like means down simple folks throats. What God has given to us to *manage, under* the leadership of Christ, has now turned into a place where we go to exalt *ourselves* and pat *one another* on the back while offering up some superficial praise to God.

The statistics say that more churches are *closing* than opening in the U.S.A. People are choosing more and more to divide into little study groups at home and to forsake assembly with *all* God's people. Or on the other end of the spectrum, people are joining these huge mega-churches so that they can get lost in a crowd without having to do anything for the Kingdom of God. Just go in, listen to the famous charismatic preacher, and go home and brag on the preacher. Not on God, but on the preacher! That's one reason why Paul never forced the Gentiles on the Jews nor the law of the Jews on the Gentiles. He taught that everyone has strengths and weaknesses and are imperfect except through Christ.

But everyone can change from their way of thinking of others by accepting the power of God's blueprint in Isaiah 43:18-19. "Remember ye not the former things, neither consider the things of old.[19] Behold, I will do a new thing; now it shall spring forth; shall ye not know it? I will even make a way in the wilderness, and rivers in the desert." It's called restoration!

So know that Jesus has already forgiven you. Know that you are indeed a new creature in Christ. You are God's child. You were chosen deep in the womb and will be God's child no matter what the world or religion thinks of you. *Know that* you don't have to be like everyone else. You are created in the Masters image. Don't quit just because some men don't want you saying anything to them or their children. I've watched people, even kids, die without ever seeing or accepting the truth of our Lord's blueprint and although it may grieve me, still I press on for God's name's sake. There are too many of Christ's creation still out there in the wilderness with no hope in their lives for us to hang around the gate of some wall hoping to get in with "religious" Christians in order to get busy. We must be about our Father's business. Never forget, even before the beginning, the Spirit of God *moved* and He *moves* in your life.

Jesus doesn't call folks from the wilderness to accessorize. He calls for folks to *testify!* Jesus brought you through wilderness to give evidence of His life changing power. Jesus brought you through the wilderness to make a solemn declaration that He *can* and that He *will* take that needle out of your arm. Jesus brought you through the wilderness to give affirmation that, yes, He does love you and He cares about you. He comes to see about you and He hears your cries and He delivers you even in jail. Jesus brought you through the wilderness to openly give evidence that He will bring you through a childhood where your hope was lost.

You are no scared little kid anymore. You know what God *can* do. You know what God *will* do for His children. You know that when the Spirit of God *moved* upon the water that it *was good!* So no, don't be giving that serpent, more *subtle* than any beast of the field, anything that belongs to you.

You have to go through these storms so that God knows that you will be faithful to *Him* and obedient to His Word. That's why we pray to our Lord to show us and to put us where *He wants* us to be. We know that the Spirit *moves* according to the blueprint of the Lord, so for a season we must just be still. For now we will listen. For now we will study. For now we will endure. We don't want to give Satan anything which *is good* and from God. I know that God has a *season* for everything in His blueprint. Acts 16:6-7 tells us," Now when they had gone throughout Phrygia and the region of Galatia, and were *forbidden* of the Holy Ghost *to preach* the word in Asia.[7] After they were come to Mysia, they assayed to go into Bithynia but the Spirit *suffered them not."* There's a storm a comin'!!

The problem and solution for the church today is the same as it was for Paul. Some folks want to walk in the Word and some folks don't. Some folks have a *true desire* to learn of the teachings of Jesus in order to develop a closer relationship with Him and to keep all of His commandments. Others are so blinded by the world, sin, and iniquity that their only desires are of the flesh. What happens is that no matter which group of people they are from, once the scales are removed from their eyes and they can see the truth then they have to make a choice of either to follow the teachings of worldly doctrine, ideas, or philosophy or to *follow* the blueprint of God.

What happens too often is that God's children go to church only to learn that the Preacher or the teachers have this spirit of "religion" wrapped around *them* and *can't see* God's blueprint. The solution is to believe only God. Adam and Eve let that old serpent in and gave away *their* inheritance. Don't give away *your* inheritance. That is *your* covenant promise. Don't let any person bring that spirit of religion into your life! In the mighty name of the Lion of Judah, *rebuke* that spirit in your life for *God's* name's sake. As the Spirit of God *moves* in your life I *know* that unclean spirits must move out of *His* path! You must claim it in the name of Jesus, your Warrior. Claim it in the name of the Author and the Finisher of our faith! You must *know Jesus is y*our Life! Know *Jesus is* your Strength! Know *Jesus is* the Way! Know the Lord is Alpha and Omega, the Beginning and the End!

It's time for our churches to stop *giving* to the Enemy that which is holy and of God! If God created it, don't *twist* it into something obscene. Instead of *giving* what is God's to the Enemy we ought to be *taking back* that which belongs to Jesus! There are junkies out there in the world. There is hunger out there in the world. There are wars out there in the world. There are babies dying out there in the world. There is sickness and disease out there in the world. There are child molesters out there in the world. There is child pornography out there in the world. There is domestic violence out there in the world. There is loneliness and homelessness out there in the world. There is hopelessness and grief out there in the world. There are all kinds of false gods out there in the world and all the "religious" folks seem to do is have another powerless meeting.

Instead of standing on the Word, what far too many religious leaders want to decide at far too many meetings is what *part* of the Word of God's blueprint is acceptable and which *part* of the Word from God's blueprint is unmentionable. Can you believe God's Word is *taboo*? It's God's Word which keeps your boundaries! It is God's Word which is the standard!

"That part about the destruction of the houses of the Sodomites we *won't mention*. Men laying with men and women laying with women we will have to *skip* over. [Lev. 20:13, Rom.1:26-27] We surely *can't mention* false teachers and false prophets because the congregation may begin to look at our fruit. [Matt.15:14] We can't tell them that they can *claim* deliverance in Jesus' name because Satan may begin to act up. [Lev. 18:22] Let's just not *proclaim* that victory. And surely we had *better not* preach out of or even mention The Song of Solomon. That is just *too* obscene. And surely we must say donkey, not ass." What is obscene is twisting the Word of God!

Again taking what is *good* and *twisting* it into whatever *carnal* minds conceive, never seeing the purpose of our Lord's blueprint. It's hard to see God's purpose walking in darkness. That is why He says to walk by faith and not by sight. Have a little faith that other people aren't as stupid and ignorant and unlearned as we may think they are. You will find out that the same Spirit that guides you is guiding them. Quit spending so much time trying to *protect* God's children from the truths of God's creation and let them grow. They may stumble sometime. They may fall sometime. They may cry sometime. They must be in the wilderness sometime. They may be *in* the world but they don't have to be part *of* the world. I don't know about you city folks but where I'm from, here in East Tennessee, we know our farm animals by name and there *ain't* no misconceptions or obscenity in what God created, Adam named, and Papaw called them. Maybe if we spend more time out in nature and less time in front of the television we all can *appreciate* the God who we claim to know. The truth is you can take an ass, call it a donkey, paint it baby blue, and stamp Ford on its hind-end, and it's still a jackass!

My prayer is that church leaders become more aware of the spiritual storms the Enemy places in their lives. My prayer is that church leaders finally put their faith in God's blueprint. My prayer is that church leaders pray before they instruct or discipline others. My prayer is that church leaders stop acting just like Balaam. My prayer is that we, as a church, come to the place in trusting God's Word that we trust Him to bring His promises to pass. My prayer is for church leaders and families to realize that we don't help God. He helps us to help others to help others. My prayer is that when the church understands the importance of teaching baby Christians the precepts of the Lord, we stop tearing each other down.

God is telling you the same thing He told Balaam. God says that I am blessed and to curse me not. He tells me that all of His children who hear His voice, turn from their wickedness and idols are blessed and I am not to curse them! What we have to learn to do is keep our peace . . . and watch. We meditate . . . and watch. We read God's Word . . . and watch. We ask Jesus to search our hearts . . . and watch. We love each other . . . and watch. We treat everyone we meet as a child of God . . . and watch.

There is no call for any of us to smile in someone's face while lurking in the shadows, waiting to pounce on them over God's Word. We cannot continue to go on praising God with our tongue and cursing our very own brothers and sisters with that same tongue.

Leaders cannot continue to "look for evidence" of another person's calling when they are blind themselves. The leaders cannot continue to exalt themselves and not give glory to God. Leaders cannot continue to call for public prayer vigils and not show up! Neither can Pastors encourage ministries within the church and not show support to the very one they have told to "step out" and begin this ministry. The point is Pastors and leaders have got to support future leaders and not desert them.

Trusting the Architect

[I John 2:20-27] But ye have an unction from the Holy One, and ye know all things.[21] I have not written unto you because ye know not the truth, but because you know it and that no lie is of the truth.[22] Who is a liar but he that denies that Jesus is the Christ? He is antichrist that denies the Father and the Son.[23] He that denies the Son, the same hath not the Father: but he that acknowledges the Son, the same hath the Father also.[24] Let that therefore abide in you which you have heard from the beginning. If that which you have heard from the beginning shall remain in you, ye also shall continue in the Son, and in the Father.[25] And this is the promise that He hath promised you, even eternal life.[26] These things have I written unto you concerning them that seduce you.[27] But the anointing which you have received of Him abides in you and ye need not that any man teach you, but as the same anointing teaches you of all things, and is truth, and is no lie and even as it hath taught you, ye shall abide in Him. Amen

The questions I have been led to ask are, do you trust the Architect? Do you believe His Word? Do you know for yourself that God is *all-powerful*? Do you know that Satan has always been defeated with no chance for error on God's part? Did God create it all, everything for His purpose? Is any power greater? Do you trust or do you rationalize? Who is your faith in? Are you afraid? Do you ponder on "what ifs" and give Satan power over you that he doesn't have a chance of having over God's *promises* to you?

I hate the Devil! I have no fear of him or any of his demons. God is greater! I am greater! God loves me. God is my Architect, even in the womb. In the mighty name of Jesus is Satan rebuked. He was rebuked before Christ died, and he is certainly rebuked now, for God's name's sake! How powerful and wise is our God? I pray, I sincerely do, that you too can fully understand just how defeated Satan has always been, for there's a storm a comin'.

"But ye have an unction from the Holy One, and ye know all things." These few words from God's holy scriptures let us know that all we need for truth begins and ends in the Word of God through the divine inspiration of God Himself. Any other commentary or revelation may or may not be from God. All Satan needs is to take part of the truth and add to or take away from the truth, using basic quotes from the Word to lead you away from believing in the holy sovereign power of God. This can come from listening to or studying from the books written by people who have no understanding of the sovereign power of God Almighty. It can come from radio or television or Bible study groups also.

I was in a Bible study once when the subject of Jesus going into hell to free the captives after he died on the cross was the lesson for the week. One thing led to another and then the question was asked, "Why didn't God go and personally bring Jesus out from there?" It was also asked and discussed, "Did Jesus have to fight with demons while He was there alone?" Then some folks said, "Yes, because God was still in heaven because God couldn't leave His throne unprotected." Now remember that nowhere in the Bible does it say that God is afraid of anything. Nowhere! So for anyone to conclude that God is controlled by some outside demonic force, determining Gods actions, or causing God to now *react* is a lie straight from the Devil!

My Word tells me that God is omnipresent. God is everywhere at the same time. God can show up anywhere, anytime, and however He wants to reveal His glory. When we look to Exodus 33:11 we find that, "The Lord spake unto Moses face to face, as a man speaks unto his friend." Now, if God told Moses to take off his shoes because he was on holy ground, then where was God? If God came in a cloud at the door of the tabernacle, then where was God? If the Spirit of God comes as a dove, then where is God? If God is love and we carry love in our hearts, where is God? I'll tell you where God is found my friend. God is in heaven and God is found wherever he wants to be found through mercy, grace, and His glory! Just study Moses if you don't believe me. Better yet study Jesus who said, "I and My Father are One."

[Exodus 33:18-23] And He said, I beseech thee shew me thy glory.[19] And He said, I will make all My goodness pass before thee, and I will proclaim the name of the Lord before thee; and will be gracious to whom I will be gracious, and will shew mercy on whom I will shew mercy.[20] And He said, Thou canst not see my face: For there shall no man see me, and live.[21] And the Lord said, Behold there is a place by me, and thou shalt stand upon a rock.[22] And it shall come to pass, while my glory passes by that I will put thee in a cleft of the rock, and will cover thee with my hand while I pass by.[23] And I will take away my hand. And thou shalt see my back parts: But my face shall not be seen. Amen

2 Tim.1:7 tells us, "For God has not given us the spirit of fear; but of power, and of love, and of a sound mind." Now since God says that He has not given us a spirit of fear, why would He be afraid? Is God afraid to walk around his own Heaven and earth? Is God afraid of hell? Is God afraid of Satan? If God leaves His throne and Satan ran to claim it would God have to *race* Satan back to the throne? If Satan was sitting on God's throne would that mean "checkmate"? Have you faith in God? Do you know the power of God? All power is God's! Then God gives that same power to Jesus who then gives that same power to you! Jesus tells us how powerful we are in St. Luke 10:18-19 when He says, "I beheld Satan as lightning fall from heaven. Behold I give unto you power to tread on serpents and scorpions, and over all the power of the enemy; and nothing by any means shall hurt you."

In order to walk in His power you must get rid of fear and fearful thinking! Fear, according to the Word of God is a spirit. So now, since we know that fear is a spirit and that spirit is not from God, we know that fear is a spirit from our Enemy. Yeah, Satan has a seat, but it sure ain't God's seat! Revelation 2:12 says, "I know thy works and where thou dwells, even where *Satan's seat* is." Wake up church! Your works and your eternal dwelling place will be directly influenced and determined by whether or not you are fearful minded. There's a storm a comin'!

[Prov. 3:5-6] Our success in life doesn't depend on and isn't determined by *our carnal* understanding. It is your failures which depend on carnal understanding of fear and doubt. The Word says, "In all thy ways acknowledge Him, and He shall direct thy paths." See, your success flows from far above any man or any thought or gift that man can give to you. When you have unction from the Holy One, what that means is that you have an anointing. What you speak and the voice that you follow comes from God. There is no guessing or figuring or doubt about His truth! There is no doubt when you are walking in the unction, or anointing of God because God will speak plainly and clearly to you. All of that other stuff that you *think* you hear and think you know is not from God. You can trust God as your Architect because Jesus said in John 10:27, "My sheep hear My voice, and I know them, and they follow Me." God speaks to His people in a direct way!

The reason why I trust in the Lord is because I know the anointing on my life. I know this anointing comes through my belief that Jesus died on the cross, arose on the third day, and Satan is defeated. I know that the unction, or anointing, comes from an omniscient, omnipotent, and omnipresent God! He is El-Shaddai, God Almighty! He is El-Elyon. "The Most High God! He is El-Roi, "The Strong One who sees"!

[Rev 2:13] It was the Alpha and the Omega who said, "I know thy works, and where thou dwells, even where Satan's seat is: and thou holds fast My name, and hast not denied My faith, even in those days wherein Antipas was My faithful martyr, who was slain among you where Satan dwells." So, whenever you find yourself in doubt and not sure which way to go or who to trust you should seek out your first love. Ignore Satan and man and ask Jesus for a fresh anointing.

There are always going to be books and more books. There are always going to be scholars on top of scholars. There are the wise and more wise. On and on it goes. But we must go forward in Christ and what the Word of God tells us. God is mighty. God is Spirit. God is the great I Am. God is God without help or favors or protection from anyone or anything that He created.

How can even the angels protect God when He is the One who created angels in the first place? When did He fall weak? Can we fight God's battles by speaking from our own understanding instead of standing on His Word? If we or the angels are who God depends on to fight His battle then what does that make Him? How much more powerful than God does this train of thought make anything that God created in the first place? The truth is when Michael the archangel was contending with Satan in a dispute about the body of Moses, Michael simply said, "The Lord rebuke thee." [Jude 1:9] See, Michael needs Christ! Christ doesn't depend on Michael! When Moses trusted in God to lead him then the Architect wrote the Ten Commandments on stone for His children with His own finger. [Ex. 31:18] If God can reach the earth with His powerful hand, then I know that He can reach the Son, no matter where Jesus may have been.

Acts 2:24-28 tells us, "Whom God hath raised up, having loosed the pains of death: Because it was not possible that He should be holden of it.[25] For David speaks concerning Him, I foresaw the Lord always before my face, for He is on my right hand, That I should not be moved:[26] Therefore did my heart rejoice; and my tongue was glad; Moreover also my flesh shall rest in hope: Because Thou wilt not leave My soul in Hell, neither wilt Thou suffer thine Holy One to see corruption.[28] Thou hast made known to me the ways of life; Thou shalt make me full of joy with thy countenance."

Even in our weakness we can trust in God through the unction of the Holy Spirit. Our faith isn't in ourselves or in faith itself. We often say that we have faith. We often claim to believe. We often know what is God's truth. Then we quit listening to His voice and *seeking His face* when we are facing spiritual storms in our lives! When we need the Lord the most is when we seem to turn to family, ignorant friends, and those claiming to be God's messengers. But the Word tells me, "The anointing which ye have received of Him abides *in you,* and ye need not that any man teach you, but as the same anointing teaches you of all things, and is truth, and is no lie, and even as it hath taught you, ye shall abide in Him."

Our sustenance and our strength come from God. Just as the children of Israel angered the Lord by worshiping idols and strange new gods, and following false prophets, know that God will put up with your weaknesses for a while as you seek a knowledge, understanding, and wisdom about His purpose in your life. But He expects you to mature as a Christian! Have no misunderstanding about what I now tell you. Watch who you associate with. Watch who you listen to. Watch what you read. Watch who you pray with. Watch what you say. Watch who you agree with. Watch who smiles at you. Watch what you find comfort in. Watch who you let so called "anoint" you. Watch and wait on the Lord! There is no power in the throne for Satan to take. Only in God, the Great Architect, is there power! There is nothing on earth or in heaven that Satan can or ever could take from our God! God's will shall be done on earth as it is in Heaven!

The question still is, "Will it be done through you?"[2 Pet. 3:10-12] "But the day of the Lord will come as a thief in the night; in which the heavens shall pass away with a great noise, and the elements shall melt with a great heat, the earth also and the works that are therein shall be burned up. Seeing then that all these things shall be dissolved, what manner of persons ought ye to be in all holy conversation and godliness.[12] Looking for and hosting unto the coming of the day of God, wherein the heavens being on fire shall be dissolved, and the element shall melt with fervent heat?"

"What manner of persons ought you to be?"

Before I move on in the mighty name of our Lord and Savior, Jesus Christ, I have been led to first tell and warn you about the Devil and his evil spirits for they are real. Only in recognizing these evil spirits and rebuking them in the name of Jesus will you and your church thrive. We bless and worship only an all-powerful God. We bless and worship the God of Abraham, of Isaac, and of Jacob. The saved need to pray fervently for a discerning spirit. A discerning spirit is a tool from God to give you power in recognizing the Enemy.

Acts 16:16-[18] And it came to pass as we went to prayer, a certain damsel possessed with a spirit of divination, or Python, met us. Which brought her masters much gain by soothsaying.[17] The same followed Paul and us, and cried saying, These men are the servants of the Most High God. Which shew unto us the way of salvation.[18] And she did this many days, but Paul, being grieved, turned and said to the spirit, I command thee in the name of Jesus Christ to come out of her, And he came out the same hour.

Now, know that Python was the Greek name for this spirit of divination. There are many poisonous and often-deadly snakes in the world but only a few kill by wrapping itself around its victim and slowly squeezing the life flow out of its victim. Just as Satan was more subtle than any beast of the field, from Genesis 3:1 to the book of Revelation, so is this spirit of divination or Python. Satan is a liar and is in fact the Father of all Lies. He doesn't want you to know the truth that you have the victory.

Being a predator and a wily hunter, the python will coil itself around you without you even knowing that he has you in his trap. This python will wait until you relax or let your guard down. He will wait until you exhale before tightening his grip on you. By waiting until it's victim exhales before tightening its grip, it forces its prey to draw in less and less air when the victim actually needs more and more air. You see, as a child of God, you need Jesus and the Word of God more and more as you feed your spirit, which is from God.

The python is in no hurry or in any rush to finish off its prey while it has its victim in its grasp. Coiled around and around your body, mind, and soul its massive size and the strength of its constricting muscles are all but impossible to escape from. I say, "All but impossible."

I say "all but impossible" because of the Spirit of God, which lives within you. I say I say "all but impossible" because my Word tells me, and I know deep down in my soul, that all things are possible when you call on the everlasting mighty name of Jesus! I know for myself that all things are possible through Christ who strengthens me! My spirit came from God so only God can have it.

I remember working for an older, wiser, and far more experienced mason while in my early twenties who taught me more about masonry work than I could have imagined. He was a great teacher of masonry. But the thing that I remember the most about those three of four years of my life was that although he taught me immensely about masonry, he still carried a deep-seated disrespect and bitterness towards me. I always sensed that he ultimately had a worldly plan for me in his heart. Although I knew there was a wickedness in him, just below the surface, I still needed the job. I couldn't just walk off and leave him because I had a family to support. And for some strange reason, although I knew that he would openly turn on me, I just felt sorry for him. I could not believe the things that he said to me.

He liked me in a way which he could not help. But this, at the same time is what he hated the most about me. See, to like me as a person, as God's child was for him to have to let go of everything that his ignorant upbringing had taught him. The only way that a person, maybe even you, can be set free from this lying spirit is to recognize and admit that their parents, uncles, teachers, friends or whoever planted that seed of judgment in them are wrong. You have to deny that ungodly spirit and be cleansed from its curse and be filled with the Holy Ghost, which is love.

A lot of people mistake their toleration of other people as love, when in fact that attitude in itself is one based upon their feeling of supremacy over the very person they claim to love. Then they never consider the other person is tolerating them also. See, you don't have to hate the people who taught you to hate. You should hate the sin. So just simply go back to them and tell them, "You are wrong because this is what the Word of God says. "Then *stand* on the commandment of God, which says to "Love thy neighbor as thyself." We can't ignore hatred and hateful speech and think it is going to just go away without us fighting back with the Word of God!

We acted like good friends because I kept quiet while truly just learning to master bricklaying. He was always smiling in my face with his jokes and comments. Just rude or hurtful enough to try and destroy my self-esteem or self worth without completely running me off for good. I was a darn good bricklayer by now; as good as him and he knew it. At one time he had about fifteen masons working for him and I was the baby of the bunch. Some were better than me and some were worse. The funny thing was that he fired them all and kept me.

We would work from sun up until it was pitch dark seven days a week. The only time we didn't work was when it came a thunderstorm. We spent more time together than either of us spent with our families. When I got home from work it was time for dinner, maybe some television or cards, then bed to sleep.

During this time my wife became pregnant. This was really a time for me to prepare for an unknown future. It was also kind of exciting, knowing that I would be a daddy. I liked the thought of being a provider, protector, and teacher. I could hardly wait. After months of doctor visits and buying baby stuff I came home from work one evening and my neighbor told me "Your wife is in the hospital having the baby!" I rushed over to the hospital and ran up to her room where my wife was resting. I was met by a nurse who told me "Sorry, but this is only for family."

"I am family! I'm the husband!" I said. She had a shocked look on her face then I noticed that the doctor turned to look at me, Just in that split second I knew what he was thinking. It showed in his eyes. I will never forget it. I looked at my wife expecting to see joy or tiredness in her eyes but I saw neither. No, what I saw was dread. Her worst nightmare had now come true. I looked in the baby's crib and immediately knew why.

Being born three months early, she only weighed three pounds, two ounces. Then she lost weight down to two pounds, ten ounces. Well, to make a long story short, after six weeks in the hospital we brought the baby home. My wife was so ashamed of herself that she ran off and left me with the baby. I don't know where she went and didn't know if she would come back. All I knew was that I had to take care of this child.

Since we worked from sun up until sundown I had my neighbor to babysit until the baby was old enough to go to day care. I would wake her up. Bath her, change her, and feed her, and then drop her off at daycare on my way to work. I felt so sorry for her. I also loved her more than anything. By the time I got to work I would be about ten or fifteen minutes late every day, but I explained to my boss that this was the best that I could do because the daycare opened at 6:00 a.m., so I couldn't be at work 6:00, but I never left early or ever complained of working overtime. Then, out of the blue, one morning I came in and he told me I had to make other arrangements. His worst mistake!

He thought that he finally had me where he wanted me. After over three years of putting up with him, one day I simply gathered up my tools, climbed down off the scaffolds and left, never to return. Through it all, I was always loyal and faithful in showing up for work, but he thought that I had to put up with him treating me any kind of way. I knew that he had lost the best worker and friend that he would ever have.

I then went to work for another masonry outfit that I had met while working for my former boss. Actually this guy had months earlier offered me two more dollars on the hour to come and lay brick for him right in my old bosses face. But I still stayed because I kind of felt sorry for him. But sometimes it's just time to move on so that you can grow.

Before long I was sent out on jobs acting as lead mason or foreman. We built everything from stores, to churches, schools, etc. By now I was confident in my skills. I was good and I knew it. No bragging, just fact. One night my boss called me and asked "What do you think about working with your old boss?"

"What do you mean?" I asked

"Well, he called me and asked me for a job and I told him that I could use another mason but that Gregory works for me and that you are my foreman on the job," he told me.

"I have no problem with it," I responded.

The thing was that I had pulled off the job in Knoxville to start the brick on a nursing home in Maryville and it would be a couple days before I could return to the first job. My boss called me both nights to tell me that sure enough my old boss was working for him now. He had told him that I would be back to Knoxville tomorrow and that I would be his foreman. I now fully understand what the Word means in Romans 8:28 when it says, "And we know that all things work together for good for those who love God and are the called according to His purpose."

He never came back to work again. He never even came to pick up his check. I've never seen him since the day that I walked away. What he meant for my harm, God turned around for my good, for God knew how to quiet the storm.

This same spirit of divination is exactly what is in our churches today. This same spirit of divination is in many of the people that you worship with every Sunday. This spirit of divination, or Python, will literally choke the life out of your ability to worship, pray, praise, or speak to others about Jesus unless you rebuke this unholy spirit in the name of Jesus, just as Paul did. This spirit is real and it will *slowly* choke its victim until there is no life left unless you take action by your faithful confessions and decreeing God's Word over your life.

When you run around church gossiping about people or talking bad or telling outright lies on a person while smiling in their face and calling them "brother" or "sister" in Christ you are being led by this spirit of divination, or Python. You see, this woman walked around with Paul and Silas, introduced them as the servants of God, while at the same time telling her masters that Paul and Silas were preaching and doing what was against their laws. She stayed close enough, smiled enough, and patted them on the back enough to where she thought they would never even notice that she was indeed a Python set out to destroy them. But Paul recognized that something wasn't right in her and *in boldness* called this spirit by its *specific* name and ordered it to come out.

Some folks in churches today come to church only for the purpose of choking the life out of someone else's worship. You know why you have so much trouble with the choirs? You're having trouble because Satan doesn't want you to sing praises to the Lord or exalt His name above all the earth in gladness and in joy. This spirit of divination will coil itself around certain members of your church body. They in turn will coil themselves around you.

They will tell you that "You can't sing." They will tell you that "You ain't got no business clapping like that. They will tell you, "You ain't supposed to be dancing in church." They will tell you, "You are making too much noise." They will tell you, "Drums ain't got no business in church." They will tell you, "Be quiet." They will tell you, "You preach too long." They will tell you, "I remember *you* back when . . ." They will tell you, "You don't dress right." They will tell you, "You don't talk right." They will tell you, "You ain't living right." They will tell you, "You don't belong here with us in this house of the Lord."

Well, let me tell you what *God* would have for *you* to know. That is that you should worship him in spirit *and* in truth. That you can call that spirit of divination by name and command it to leave your presence. When the Holy Spirit is indwelling in your heart and mind and soul then you have power! When your enemies rise against you, then you have power in Jesus.

This spirit of divination is of Satan and this spirit can be defeated in your life! Don't *let* anybody hang around you that you know means you harm. Don't hang *around* nobody that means you harm. When somebody brings gossip to you simply leave or hang up the phone. When somebody wants to put you down in church, pray for them. If they still refuse to heal then worship and praise God anyway. Don't let anybody coil themselves around you until there is no life left in your spiritual being. There are a whole lot of folks in a whole lot of places that are being slowly suffocated to death because they are either oppressed by this spirit of divination, or they are choking the life out of others. The more you abuse others, the more Satan abuses you, because you have broken your covenant with God!

The very life of our churches is at stake, for make no mistake about it, if we continue on *exalting ourselves*, arguing over doctrines, living any kind of way, allowing perverted sexual acts and marriages to be passed off as blessed, then a lot of churches will surely slowly falter. When you look around you and see less and less people in church every Sunday then you need to look at yourself and ask, "Is this spirit of divination running my church?"

See, I learned all of these things the hard way. My prayer for you is that you seek God early while He still can be found. I learned that at the lowest point in my life that no one would be there to lift me up. Now looking back over twenty-five years, I can see what Jeremiah 29:11-13 means. "For I know the thoughts that I have toward you, saith the Lord, thoughts of peace, and not of evil, to give you an expected end.[12] Then shall ye call upon me, and ye shall go and pray unto me, and I will hearken unto you.[13] And ye shall seek me. And find me. And when ye shall search for me with all your heart."

Only in God, trusting the Architect of your life, will you be given peace from day to day in order to reach an expected end. You can expect a lot from a lot of people who you consider to have your feelings and your interests at heart. But what you may find is that more often than not, the very person that you turn to may turn against you. I learned this lesson when I had to move from Knoxville back to Maryville in order to turn to my family to help me take care of my little girl. She was still in diapers and so precious to me. I never knew where her mother was or when or if she was coming home. All I knew was that I was hurt and needing help.

Well, everybody just stared at the baby and me when I brought her into the family home. It was the first time that they had seen her even though she had laid in the hospital for six weeks clinging to life. No one had come to check on her or me. I will never forget for the rest of my life standing there alone with a family member and asking her if they would help me by watching this child while I was at work. She looked straight at me and said, "No, you need to take her right back to her mother! She doesn't belong here so take her away from here right now!" I remember a family member on Thanksgiving looking at everybody, mockingly, right in my face and saying, "She's cute. What color are her eyes, blue?" I took her and left, living with her in my car, until they sent me to prison. I hated everyone of them for that and instead of trusting in God's promises and provision I tried to fight the battle with my flesh instead of with the Spirit. Now I know we ought to be spiritual persons.

Building God's Kingdom Brick by Brick

[2 Kings 5:10, 14] And Elisha sent a messenger unto him, saying, Go and wash in Jordan seven times and thy flesh shall come again to thee, and thou shall be clean.

[14]: Then went he down and dipped himself seven times in Jordan, according to the man of God: and his flesh came again like unto the flesh of a little child, and he was clean.

It is *true* that we have victory in Jesus. It is also true that part of this victory comes through deliverance. *Deliverance* from these things which separate us from the *full* power of God. *Deliverance* from iniquity, which keeps us from walking in, talking in, and living in the *full* power of God.

What is deliverance and how can we receive it? Is it a gift from the Lamb of God? I believe that it is truly a gift from Jesus, but it doesn't come easy. It wasn't easy for Jesus to die for us either. Jesus had the victory with Him because He was the Father's perfect Son who lived and died without sin. But he still had to feel the pain of sin before being resurrected from the tomb to die no more. Deliverance comes to those who believe that Christ died and arose again and that He has *separated* them from *whatever* binds them from living as Christians should live.

Looking back on the days when I was preparing to get out of prison, I can see the similarities between parole and deliverance. They both freed me from bondage. But upon studying these similarities I also noticed more clearly the differences between freedom and true freedom.

You see, when you meet the parole board and they grant you parole, you don't just get up and head out of the prison doors or gates. It doesn't work like that. What you get is a *release* date, which is months or years away. Just because you have been granted parole doesn't mean that you are "home free." No, you have GED classes to take, counseling, drug screens, AA meetings, job training, etc. All the while you must be a model prisoner. At anytime your parole can be denied or revoked for not obeying the guidelines set forth by the parole board. There is more than one step in this process, which is called *rehabilitation.* In other words just because you have been "delivered" from lockup doesn't mean that you are truly free *yet.*

Now, "He whom the Son sets free is free indeed!" When Jesus sets you free you have *true* freedom. The parole board may have *given* me freedom but it was Jesus who *set* me free. It was Jesus who *delivered* my soul from damnation unto a *right* relationship with God. When Jesus delivered me from my sins, though I didn't realize it at the time, all I needed to do was to *claim* deliverance and to *walk* in it. See this is where so many people stumble or turn back, often times *right at* their breakthrough. Jesus doesn't rehabilitate or rebuild or cover up something old, He *restores* it to something new. He makes us *new creatures in Him*! He said "I am the true Vine and you are the branches . . . Every branch that is in me and doesn't bring forth fruit is taken away and every branch that brings forth fruit is purged that it brings forth more fruit. [John 15:1-8]

So what happens is that on the days that our prayers are answered and our deliverance is granted by the Lord we expect to *not* have to go through anything *hard*. But the truth is that this "pruning" process is what Jesus uses to take away all of the uncleanliness from our hearts, souls, and minds. This is our *sanctification* or "being made holy" process. The deliverance is there when you claim it but it may take a while to become *truly released* from whatever binds you. You just have to walk in faith and not *rebel* against the Lord!

Going to Jesus and singing songs of deliverance is the easy part, especially when we have *nowhere else* to turn. What is hard is to obey because of the flesh. Obeying His *every* command is what our flesh doesn't want to do. We want Jesus to deliver us from bondage but we want to do like Naaman and tell Him where, when, and how to do it.

See, Naaman was told by Elisha to go and wash in *Jordan seven* times and his flesh would become clean. Not one time. Not two times. Not three times. Not four times. Not five times. Not six times. But *seven* times in Jordan. In the river Jordan! Not the river Abama. Not the river Pharpar, but the river Jordan! Why?

Don't worry about why Jesus tells you to do something, just do it! Sometimes Jesus tells us something simple to do and we want to rebel and make a big production out of it. We want to be in *control*. We want to run the whole show. Well, if you can run the whole show then what are you calling on Jesus for? Because you *can't* run the whole show.

We, like Naaman, learn that there is true healing in our lives when we obey the commands of God. Like Naaman, that first "dip" that we take in Jordan just wakes us up. We need to be woken up sometimes so that we can see what is around us. We need to wake up and look towards the heavens from which our strength comes.

We need to wake up and look at ourselves. We need to wake up to what is truth. We need to wake up and see who and what there is that keeps us in bondage and powerless. We need to wake up and *seriously* seek *God's will* and *purpose* for our lives. We've been asleep for too long. We've been weak too long. We've been afflicted too long. We have been sick for too long. We've been poor for too long. We have to take that *first* dip into the river Jordan!

The thing about it is that when we take that first dip into the river Jordan we're still angry with the Lord. We're still upset with the Lord. We still are rebellious with the Lord. We still don't want to obey the Lord. So what we need is another dip in the river Jordan, just to learn that God is the authority in our lives. You can choose not to believe if you want to, but He *has* something for you. He *has* just what you need. He *has* what you asked Him for, to do just what it takes, to get you where you need to be.

That's why we need a second dip. You see one dip would have sufficed and got the job done, but no, we have to go before the Lord with the *nerve* to tell Him what we are and what we aren't going to do! But God is God and He will be God all by Himself. So have another dip.

"Well," you say, "I may have to be in this river Jordan twice but that doesn't mean that I like it." Still rebellious? That's alright, He knew you would be, that's why He told you to go and wash seven times in the river Jordan. You see, this isn't for God, it's for you.

Now you find yourself, just like Naaman, in the river Jordan for a third time. Only this time you notice that something has washed off of you. You don't quite know what it is. but you know that something is gone. Whatever it is that is gone is *not sorely missed* for you can feel a change coming on. You don't know what it is, but you feel just a little better. "Maybe this ain't so bad."

So you get out of the river to warm up only to realize that it's now colder out of the river than in the water. Funny how the "world" seems different once Jesus enters into your life. Only you don't understand that it is Jesus *sanctifying* you. You think that all you need now are some warm clothes and maybe a small fire built. But you see, Jesus knows exactly what is going on and Jesus knows exactly what you need. So Jesus puts you right back in the river Jordan for a fourth time. By now you know what to expect, so the rebellion is gone. Now you don't mind being in the river for a fourth time. Now you realize that a change is coming. It is a change in your heart. You feel the anger is gone. The arrogance is gone. The jealousy is gone. The doubt is gone. You feel a whole lot lighter than you did. A great weight is being lifted off your heart. When you get out of the river Jordan you realize that somebody has taken all your old garments. "Well, that's alright because I trust going back into the river Jordan." You now have your garment of praise! Now this fifth time feels better than the fourth time. "Trusting Jesus is alright with me! Maybe I'll just stay right where I am. I am satisfied with what I have."

But, know that Jesus is not satisfied with where you are. Jesus is calling you to become holy. Jesus is not satisfied with emptying you of uncleanliness. Jesus doesn't just want to wash away your sins. No, Jesus wants to fill you up! Jesus wants to put in your heart those things of a heavenly realm. Jesus wants to restore you. Jesus wants to see the manifestation of the fruit of the Spirit in you. Jesus wants to restore you to righteous fellowship with a *clean* heart that you may *serve* Him. Now you notice that your face is wet but it's not water from the river Jordan, but tears of joy that streak your face as you cry out towards the heavens, "Holy is the Lamb!!"

You see, you've almost made it through. You have *almost* run the good race. You have *almost* learned obedience. You have *almost* learned to let go and let God. But what you haven't learned *yet* is that you must *endure* until the end. It doesn't matter who is the strongest. It doesn't matter who is the swiftest. It doesn't matter who is the smartest. It doesn't matter about how pretty or how handsome you *think* that you are. For, you see, God measures the heart of a man.

When Samuel was sent by the Lord to anoint unto the Lord a king from the sons of Jesse, Samuel looked upon Eliab and said "Surely the Lord's anointed is before him." [1 Sam.16:6]

[7:] But the Lord said unto Samuel "Look not on his countenance, or on the height of his stature; for I have refused him: for the Lord sees not as man sees; for man looks on the outward appearance, but the Lord looks on the heart."

[13:] Then Samuel took the horn of oil and anointed him in the midst of his brethren: and the Spirit of the Lord came upon David from that day forward.

He is the Spirit of the Lord whom God puts in you when you have been restored. He is the Spirit of the Lord who gives you that *conviction* of wrongdoing. He is the Spirit of the Lord who tells you what is right. He is the Spirit of the Lord who orders your steps in the righteousness. He is the Spirit of the Lord who gives you your connection to Jesus when you don't know how to pray. [Rom 8:26] The Spirit himself bears witness with our spirit, that we are the children of God. [Rom.8:16]

I told you that Jesus knows just what you need. I told you that Jesus will look out for you when you don't know how to look out for yourself. So, you see, this sixth dip is just for you. This sixth dip is just what you need. This sixth dip has given you the Holy Spirit to *indwell* within you. All you have to do is *surrender* to His will. You cannot *endure* life's trials, temptations and heartaches without the Spirit of the Living God. It *is* going to be alright! Our Word tells us in Romans 8:28 that, "And we know that *all things* work together for good to them that love God, to them who are called to *His* purpose." So now we know that we can *endure* and we know that God will put *no more* on us than we can bear.

Now you are right on the eve of your breakthrough. You have been washed as white as snow by the Blood of the Lamb. You have been redeemed. You have been set free by salvation. The penalty of your past sins are cast away, never again to be remembered by God. Now you have a Friend and a Comforter! What you have is power over sin. God always will leave you a way out, no matter how great the temptation. Don't worry about tomorrow for tomorrow will take care of itself. God is the same yesterday, today, and tomorrow. So now what you need is that seventh dip. That same seventh dip that Naaman needed in order to *complete* the holy commands of God. You see. This seventh dip is a sign of completion or a sign of *coming into* perfection. But first we had to come through Jesus. Jesus is the foundation of our faith. Without Jesus we are still lost. Without Jesus we are not saved. Without Jesus we are powerless against sickness and disease. Without Jesus we are powerless against Satan and all other forces of evil. Without Jesus surely darkness will come and overtake you. You will be defenseless against the Devil. But *take heart* little children because God has a plan and a *purpose* for you. For you and you alone. His eye is on the sparrow and if His eye is on the sparrow then surely He watches over you. "So fear not for I have overcome the world!!"

Just as Naaman was healed, through his obedience to the Word from Elisha, so are we healed from our sinful nature and restored into a right relationship with God *by our faith.* When you put *all* of your trust in Jesus then He will carry you through. When you put all of your faith in Jesus then the *power inside of you rises up*! Power to stand *up* in these perilous times! Power to carry on in those times of doubt. Power is what makes our relationship with Jesus, the Holy Spirit and God complete. *Power* comes through believing God. *Power* comes through reading God's Word. *Power* comes through faithfully confessing the Holy Word. *Power* comes after you *seek* and *find* God's *purpose* for your life. No, it's not all about you because this *power* from the Holy Spirit is working God's ultimate goal . . . that *all* should be saved and made whole. Keep *walking* and keep on *seeking* your *purpose* until you have that blessed assurance that you have *found* your *purpose* in God and that you will carry out your *purpose* without letting laziness or fear stop you from obeying His Word. Tell somebody so that they learn granted and released are two different things.

I remember watching Gilligan's Island one day. The castaways were trying to formulate a plan to protect themselves from headhunters who were headed to the island. Mr. Howell said, "I know, we'll blow up their bridge!" The Skipper said, "Mr. Howell, they don't have a bridge!" Mr. Howell then replied, "The crafty devils, they've outsmarted us already." How funny! Don't you give up! Your breakthrough is right around the corner and it *will come* through your obedience to God's Word.

When you are building God's kingdom brick by brick you need to be ever watchful as to who is handing you the brick. As a bricklayer I can tell you that the faster I can get a brick in my hand, the faster I lay the brick in the wall, the faster the wall goes up. The faster the wall goes up the sooner I am finished with the job. So, a lot of times a laborer will jump over there in front of me and start grabbing brick and handing them to me. This shortens the distance that my hand has to travel to pick up a brick which eliminates wasted motion and effort on my part. It amounts to less work with more production for me. Now remember, it is my job to lay the brick. It is his job just to carry the brick to me and stock them on the scaffolds. Although he may intend on being extra helpful and I may feel thankful for not having to break my back bending over to get the brick, there is a problem.

See, all brick are not the same. On one building the brick may be two, three, or four different colors. What the bricklayer must do is to spread them out evenly in the wall so that he doesn't end up with all the same color brick in one spot. This is called color range. Have you ever seen a brick job that is all nice and neat throughout the entire wall and then here is this big spot with all the same colored brick? It is one of the worst things a mason can do. It is also the easiest thing to mess up. Especially when you have someone other than yourself picking out your brick. There is a certain way to un-stack the brick when they come from the brickyard. There is a certain way to stack them on the scaffolds and there is a certain way to lay them. Each step must be mindfully performed because each step determines the end result. When my job or reputation is on the line, I know that I have to be at my best. If you handing me brick causes me to be less of a mason, or my work to be less than excellent, then I don't need you to be handing me brick! See, what you have to do as a brick mason is to train yourself to watch the line you lay the brick to, the color range, the bond, and the height of your brick all within a split second. Pow! Just like that. That is how fast a master mason can lay brick.

Now, notice that I switched from saying bricklayer to saying brick mason. A bricklayer can lay brick. He may be the best at actually laying the brick. He may be the fastest. He may be the strongest, But that does not make him a mason. See, a mason can do it all! A mason may not actually be the fastest at laying brick. A mason may not be the strongest and work from daylight until dark. But what a mason will do is work *steady*!! And I guarantee you that if you put a bricklayer on one job and a real mason on another, exactly the same, the mason will get done first and do a better job. Why? Because a brick mason knows a whole lot more than speed in and of itself. What is faster now may slow you down later. What shortcuts you take now may come back to haunt you and cause all of your work to be rejected! What a master mason will do is to first study the blueprints. Then he builds according to the architect's plans. If he has questions he will have to trust the architect enough to ask for directions or clarity. A master mason will recognize and admit that although he has years of experience, sometimes you just can't fully see the desired end result wanted by the architect. In other words don't let pride get in your way. You may find immense satisfaction over the things you have accomplished in the past and that's alright. But you can never forget that it was all accomplished brick by brick. Lots of masons will brag on how fast they are or how many brick they can lay in a day. But what they won't brag on is the fact that another master mason had to lay out the job for them!

Now, I have seen and done this myself. Just trust anybody. Just let somebody hand me brick. Just let anybody who calls themselves helping me, help me. What I came to realize is that the very ones that I let hand me brick or that I let lead me were the first ones to step back and deny any involvement when the job blows up. The crazy thing is that I knew better in the first place.

This is exactly how the Devil works against you as you try to build up God's Kingdom. He knows you have limited time. He knows that you have a lot on your mind. So what does he do? He sends someone with a smile on their face to "help" you. The Devil will send you advice that you didn't even ask for. The Devil will tell you that you are overwhelmed. The Devil will tell you that he or she knows more than you do about what God called you to do. The Devil will send someone into your life to tell you, "We have the same vision." The Devil will send someone into your life to tell you, "That's good enough!" The Devil will send someone into your life to discourage you. The Devil will tell you, "There ain't enough time to do all that, so you might as well quit." The Devil will send your best friend, husband, or wife to tell you, "When you do get done, it won't even be worth what you put into it." The Devil will use anything and anybody to confound your work for God's Kingdom!

What you can never forget is that all that you do for God's Kingdom is done brick by brick. Here's the secret. If one brick is wrong don't go on and lay the next brick. I don't care if you have ten thousand brick laid in the wall. If the ten thousand and one brick is wrong then stop! Take up that brick and fix it! Then move on. You may hide it for a while but somebody someday will find it and throw it up in your face. And I can guarantee you that nine times out of ten it will be the very one who saw you messing up and never said a word at the time! That is how the Devil works. He cannot stand to see you steady. He cannot stand to see you patient. He cannot stand to see you study the blueprint. He cannot stand to see you endure! He wants you to use chipped and cracked brick.

See, what the Devil wants you to use are faulty materials. The Devil knows that by now you are steadfast and determined to stand on the Word of God. He knows by now that you are on alert. He knows by now that you are seriously dedicated to completing what God has chosen you to build up in His kingdom. So what does he do now? Well, we already know that he, that serpent, is more subtle than any beast in the field. So now he tries to slip you faulty materials to build with. He tries to mix in faulty material in with the appropriate material.

If the Devil can't get you to trust your enemies so they can confound you, he will tempt you not to inspect the material you are building with. He wants you to take everything that a friend brings you and use it in whatever you have been chosen to do. What he wants ultimately is for you to compromise on just the smallest of details. He knows that to slip you faulty material and for you to use them will not only weaken what you are building up but will cause delay when you have to start over. This is what he wants. He wants you going around and around in circles like a fly with one wing. The materials that Satan gives you are temporal. Like cars, homes, jewelry, clothes, and cell phones. The things, or materials that God gives you are eternal. Like the helmet of salvation, loincloth of truth, breastplate of righteousness, shoes prepared to spread the gospel of peace. And above all, the shield of faith. There is one true material that you need that will never be found with fault. It is the Word of God! It is the Holy Bible! Build your faith brick by brick. Faith comes by hearing. And hearing, by the Word of God. Then you will know how to defeat the Enemy.

When I was about eleven or twelve, two friends and myself walked over to the department store in town. It was after dark. On the way back home a man passing by all of a sudden ran over to us and grabbed a hold of me. He said "Yeah, boy, I'm gonna throw you off of this bridge!" I couldn't get away from him! He was a lot older and stronger than me, since I was just a kid. I fought him with all that I had. But the next thing I knew, he had me up on the rail of the bridge trying to throw me onto the boulders thirty feet below. The creek also flowed through there. I was scared to death to see my sissified friends take off running while this man was trying to kill me saying over and over, "Yeah boy, I got you now!" The next thing that I knew was a power rose up inside of me and I mean to tell you he could not hold me! I went straight off on that man. I got away from him and ran all the way home. I just couldn't wait to grow up. I couldn't wait to get big.

I was at vacation Bible school about thirty years later. I was on the church van going around picking up children. We pulled up in front of a house here in town and who do you think was standing on the front porch? I could never forget that face. I will never forget that night. It was him! As I stared at him an anger rose up in me and all I wanted to do was to get out of that church van and stomp that man to death. Then I looked at those two little children. It was all out spiritual warfare! I hated him but I could not hate those children. I just kept my mouth shut. I opened the door for these children and helped them into the van. One was only three years old. The little rascal got off the van and raised her arms up for me to carry her into the church. And I did just that. I've seen him since then and even then I honestly wanted to beat him to death. Then God asked me, "Are you going to build my Kingdom brick by brick or not?" I let it go.

Torn Down to Build Up

When we first started out on the text of this book we were dealing with the spiritual storms in our lives and with God's help we will not deviate from it. There are storms in my life. There are storms in your life. There are storms in the Pastor's life. There are spiritual storms in the very life of the church body. But there are no spiritual storms in the life of the Head of the body. The Head being Jesus, the Lamb of God. The battle was finished on Calvary, though it was actually won in the garden of Gethsemane when Jesus said, "Not My will, but Your will be done." Too often people forget that Jesus not only is our Savior and Christ but is set up as the Head of the church. [Col.1:18] In order to follow Jesus, we should be following Him to church. Church is what God gave to Jesus. Church is what Jesus is building up. Church is what is being torn down.

[Joshua 6:26] And Joshua adjured them at that time saying Cursed be the man before the Lord, that rises up and builds this city Jericho: he shall lay the foundation thereof in his firstborn, and in his youngest son shall he set up the gates of it.

What I first noticed about this scripture was that Joshua, as the leader, spoke to the people concerning the consequences of any disobedience to God's command. As the person in authority, Joshua imposed the obligations of an oath upon the children of Israel. In order to stay within the boundaries of the oath from God, Joshua, as leader had to relay to the people the *exact* message from God.

What he was doing in effect was saying, "The anointing flows from the top on down." What he was saying was that "I am telling you *exactly* what I received from the Head." This is strengthened by the fact that he said, "Cursed be the man before the Lord, that rises up." Understand that God desires us to rise up, but the God does not desire us to rise above doing anything that He says not do. No matter what your intentions may be, if God says don't do it, then don't do it.

The city of Jericho was in the land of Canaan, which was the Promised Land to the children of Israel. The land was to be given as an inheritance from God to the Israelites. Joshua, as successor to Moses, was given strict orders by God to totally destroy the Canaanites because of their pagan religious practices and worship of false gods. God wanted these people destroyed so He could build up the Israelites without His chosen people being tempted by the Canaanites immoral religious practices. God wanted walls torn down so that the Israelites would remain holy and faithful to the covenant given to Abraham and delivered by Moses and entered into under the leadership of Joshua.

[Joshua 1:5] There shall not any man be able to stand before thee all the days of thy life; as I was with Moses, so I will be with thee; I will not fail thee, nor forsake thee.

[I Kings 16:34] In his days did Hiel the Bethelite build Jericho; he laid the foundation thereof in Abirem his firstborn son Segul, according to the word of the Lord, which he spake by Joshua the son of Nun.

[Malachi 1:4] Whereas Edom saith, we are impoverished, but we will return and rebuild the desolate places; thus saith the Lord of hosts: they shall build but I will throw down; and they shall call them the border of wickedness, and the people against whom the Lord has indignation forever.

When you go right on ahead to do and to rebuild whatever you choose, not only do your actions affect you, but your children as well as your children's children. Both Abiram and Segul, sons of Hiel, died at Jericho when the walls were destroyed and their father wanted to build them again. When God says that He is angry at the disobedience and the unholiness in your life He will either put a stop to your rebellion in order to use you for His glory or allow you to perish in your own sin. The battle is in the choice of who you are going to follow. Choose you this day, is he the Lord or Satan?

As a bricklayer with over thirty years of experience in building walls I can tell you that walls are designed to join one thing to another or to separate one thing from another. Walls also are used as structures to hold nature back, such as dirt, water, or wind. These are called retaining walls. They are designed to keep one thing as it is while keeping another thing from intruding upon it. Walls are used as the main source of strength or foundation for a structure. Or walls may be used purely for aesthetic purposes. Remember this last one!

No matter what the intended purpose of building these walls, and although these walls are part of one unit, they nonetheless have two sides. And we can all attest to the fact that we can't see both sides at the same time. But there is One who is able to see all sides at the same time. There is One who sees and knows all. There is one and only One who sees and knows all. There is only One who is everywhere at the same time. He is our Almighty God! Jesus is our load bearing wall and the One who helps us keep the Enemy from intruding into our lives.

When God tears walls down in our lives it is for His purpose. When God restores something in our lives it is for His glory. A lot of times we don't even realize there are walls in our lives until God begins to tear them down. Once God begins to tear down these walls we are able to see more clearly. We are able to see the other side of things. Without God tearing down these walls the only way for *us* to see the other side of these walls is to go around these walls ourselves to see what is there. By the time *we* get to the other side we may not even see what originally was there. It may not be as we envisioned.

It could appear a whole lot worse. Then by the time we get back to the side where we were it may not look the same as before we left.

But by God showing you both sides at once you are now able to compare the two according to His Word. One side may please God while the other side seems undesirable. One side may pass inspection while the other side may need more work or fail inspection. One side may be right and the other side wrong. The craziest thing is that when a lot of masons know the only way to correct a problem is to tear it down and start over they will leave things as they are and convince themselves it's alright. The truth is both sides should be the same in that both should be in excellence.

A lot of Christian folks try to do the same thing whether in church, at home or at work or at school. The act of convincing yourself that what you are doing is alright when it is not is called justification. You want to live your life without being held accountable to anyone except for yourself. But what you forget is that your actions are the values and morals and ethics that your children learn. The very ungodly speech or actions that your child sees in you is what shapes their outlook on life, the world, and God. To know to do right and not to do it is sin! Too many of God's children are being mentally and spiritually crippled at far too young an age by so-called Christian teachers and leaders whose actions are not ordained by God. If you want to put today's youth down and talk about their behavioral problems, I suggest that you first take a look at yourself. Ask yourself, "Did I help build these walls of rebellion, indifference, defiance, laziness, hatred, intolerance, irreverence, and ungodliness in their lives by rebuilding walls God tore down with the Blood of Jesus. No one is free behind these walls that Jesus redeemed mankind from. We are only free by standing on the foundation that Jesus laid, for "He whom the Son sets free is free indeed."

You see, it was Jesus who set me free! Not Abraham Lincoln. Not Martin Luther King Jr. Not the parole board or turning twenty-one. It was nothing but the Blood of Jesus. I was covered by the Blood because I found Christ at an early age and although the world, through Satan, tried to destroy me Jesus never forgot about me. Jesus never let me go. It was Jesus who kept me secure in the knowledge that I am His child no matter what anyone says to me to try to make me doubt His love for me.

The point is that we are all God's creation, but we are *known as His children* by our salvation and love for each other. Let me make one thing perfectly clear right now. Tolerance for people is only a *part* of *showing* love. Tolerance in and of itself is not love at all. You can, and Christians do, far too often "tolerate" ungodly behavior in themselves while at the same time claiming to be Christ-like. People far too often think that they are doing someone else a favor by saying in effect, "I'm not that much better than you" when the lost show up at church. If you really want to see this world change for the better and your worship explode then get that agape love in your heart. Then these walls of division will fall in praise to the Lord of Heaven and Earth!

I learned a very valuable lesson on the topic of tolerance versus agape love while in school. I was in building trades class learning masonry. Part of the curriculum involved going to the Vocational Industrial Clubs of America convention. Not only were our hands-on skills evaluated through competition, but our parliamentary procedure and social skills as well. Part of my school's presentation was to build a complete model of the school with all the different classes being represented. Along with each class represented we cut out little figures of people from *wood* to represent each class. Sounds simple enough until we got to the part where it was time to paint the *wooden* people. The first thing I heard as I was painting the little wooden bricklayer was, "I'm not black, I'm white!" It was my friend who I would later go into business with after graduation. And he was mad! I mean mad! The next thing I know he stomps off and then here comes a teacher.

First of all, let me tell you that there were only three or four black kids out of the entire class. Every day that we came to class some of the other kids had painted the people as jet black as they could get them, with big red lips, bulging white eyes, and holding watermelon. They all, including teachers, found this extremely amusing. But what I noticed most was that when they painted the people white, they didn't choose white as the color to paint with. No, they always chose peach, tan, or an olive color. In other words, they wanted to present themselves as what they *perceived* themselves to be. They wanted to present themselves as something they weren't, but evidently considered as more desirable than what they actually were. They wanted to present themselves in what they considered as the best possible light to the world. But in all of their actions the darkness that ruled their hearts was plain for me to see. They wanted to make us out to be monkeys or just some caricature of a man, a mistake of God, while lifting themselves up to a position equal to God at most or favored of God in the least. They were using old racist stereotypes against us just like their parents and grandparents before them. They were an ignorant people. So what did I do?

Well, here comes one teacher like a coward. Grinning. "Uh, boys, you're doing a good job. You really are. The only thing is you have painted too many of them black." It wasn't too many of them black when the other kids were painting them as buffoons! "Uh, boys, why don't you paint the majority, maybe fifteen or twenty white and you know, two or three black." You know? All I know is that what we were dealing with was little *wooden* figures of people! How crazy! If you can't deal with seeing little wooden black people as equal then how in the name of Jesus can you see a real, living, breathing person such as myself as equal?

This is exactly what I thought as I studied this man who was supposed to be a teacher. Believe it or not those little wooden blocks of people not only exposed the wall of racism that existed but deepened the division. By the end of class I painted *all* of them as white as I could! Then I laughed.

Sometimes all you need to do is laugh. "A merry heart doeth good like a medicine." Don't let nobody steal your joy! If a man be ignorant let him be ignorant [I Cor. 14:38]. Don't give any man power over your mind to make you hate him. You have the victory! Nobody can take your praise. Nobody can take your joy. Nobody can take your salvation. Nobody can take God's love away from you. Nobody can rebuild anything in your life that you have freely turned over to Jesus. Just give everything to Him and watch and see if He doesn't start tearing down those walls and strongholds from hell. You could choose to be bitter or you can choose to forgive and move on in life with a closer walk with Jesus. Your journey through this world will not be dictated by this world. The Word tells you that you are in the world, but not of the world. You can make the world a better place by leaving the tearing down and building up to the Lord. All you need to do is to get your own personal relationship right with God. Stay in his Word. Stay in prayer. Stay under the umbrella of protection by following every instruction of God. Put on the whole armor of God so that you will be able to stand against the evil day. Then you are prepared for battle.

It's strange how these walls once torn down, keep popping right back up in our lives. For a nation that was supposedly built on Christian values, America's history includes fighting between the English and pilgrims. Fighting also between the Spanish and the Americans, as they called themselves. Fighting between the whites and the Native Americans. Then divisions between whites and African slaves, and later freedmen. Then the whites and the Mexicans. At one point even the slaves were hunting and killing Indians while Indians were being paid to hunt and kill slaves at the same time. We see this same division in the church today, which we claim, is open to all who claim Christ as their personal Savior. I am truly convinced that Satan has a brick dolly. I am sure that he follows us around loading up those same stones that Jesus has torn down from the walls of division. When we give Satan the "mortar" he needs we allow these walls of division to be rebuilt. What is the "mortar" that Satan uses to rebuild the walls that God has torn down?

Proverbs 6:17. "A proud look, a lying tongue, and hands that shed innocent blood.18. An heart that devises wicked imaginations; feet that be swift in running to mischief.19. A false witness that speaks lies; and he that sows discord among brethren." It is the same "mortar" which is given to man by the Holy Spirit to build the

Kingdom of God, which Satan takes and perverts, to use men to do the very evil which God doesn't want done.

If the Lord hates these things then don't you think that once He tears those walls down that He intends for them to *remain torn down?* Not only can you curse some other person's life, but yours as well. Discord affects everybody. God operates in unity. Discord and division come from Satan and once in your heart must be torn down in order for God's "being made holy" or sanctification process to begin to take root in our lives. I say "our lives" because we are all connected through Jesus Christ our Lord and our Savior.

So when someone new is appointed to the board or organization that you've been on the last thirty years, don't ignore them or their insight into matters of the church. Don't separate yourself from them just because they don't look like you, act like you, or agree with every belief you have, because our commonality is in the Lord that we serve and worship. Offer that person *gentle* correction in love and a spirit of meekness and expect the same if you are "off the mark" for Christ's sake.

When someone new joins the choir that we have been in for thirty years we should welcome them as another "praise warrior." It's supposed to be all about praising God, right? It's not supposed to be about being praised by the congregation or the Pastor for our "performance." If it is all about praise being a *part* of our worship of God, then we can't praise God by talking about someone else! Who are we to get angry and talk about the new choir members for not knowing the songs or singing them right when we ourselves show up for rehearsal twenty minutes late? If we are on time, or even early, do we take the time to *teach* them the songs instead of staying within the walls we and a few others have built right in the church choir? If we are *serious* about God and *serious* about praising Him then *teaching* a new member would be our *priority* instead of running to spread gossip about them when rehearsal is over.

I once had a person come to me and ask, "What key do you sing in?" I told him "off" key. He had no choice but to laugh. At that moment I had a choice of whether to build, or rather to help Satan build a wall between us or to let God tear it down. I didn't know whether or not he was trying to be smart, repeating what he had heard through gossip, in a way that he thought would let me know that I wasn't wanted in the choir without tipping me off about who had said it to him or not. But the thing is, that by him opening his mouth *at all*, I already knew that it wasn't from God and I wasn't going to give up my joy. I also knew that I always felt just as joyful *before* I joined the choir as *after* I joined the choir. He or the choir didn't change me one way or the other. My mind was already made up to follow Jesus.

There's a storm a comin'.

Now that Satan had his stones from walls torn down by the blood of the Lamb, along with *his* freshly provided "mortar", he could and would save this "mortar" for another opportune time. I say another opportune time because Satan is a crafty strategist. Satan builds these walls not only where he tries to separate us from each other, but from the church. And ultimately from God. In other words Satan hates Christian *relationships*. Satan knows that to break down communications is the forerunner to the breaking down of relationships. If you don't believe me, stop talking to your spouse or significant other and see what happens. I guarantee you that you won't have a relationship for long! To think that you can love someone and not relate to or communicate with them is to disobey God's commission to assemble and to spread and share the Good News.

What Satan wants you to do is shut up. He wants you to stop singing, stop praising, and stop sharing God's Word with others, whether or not they know Christ as their personal Savior. Satan will use this "mortar" where he feels it will be most effective in damming up the flow of God's peace in your life.

In one instance, a person came up to me after one particular Bible study. Now this was an open study where we were encouraged to participate with different input and scriptural references. I was only one of many gathered who vocally shared God's Word. When it was over this person comes to me with a "smile" and let me know they felt I need to just be quiet and let the "old saints" do the talking. Smiling.

Again, I was faced with the choice of whether to allow Satan to use unkind words to build a wall of discord or to allow God to tear down this wall of contempt. I chose the latter, saying, "God calls all His people together to share the Word." Then all that was left for the person to do was to try and joke it all off. Although I knew that the person was seriously telling me to be quiet from now on, I really couldn't get angry with the person because I realized that the person had been coming to church for longer than I had and still didn't know how Jesus operates. This person thought I hadn't been in church long enough to be speaking. I also realized that I don't have to *even give* it a second thought because there were several others whom I didn't *even know* come up to me and say, "I really enjoy your insight."

God had another plan for this Bible study. God had a plan that would have included this person with the "proud look" if only this person would have let the walls of discord and mischief stay torn down. I would have missed my blessing if at anytime I would have given Satan the "mortar" of discord that he needs. The story would not have ended with me finding out that I have a real desire to spread the Word and to spread love among people.

What I learned was that I cannot be rebellious towards a rebellious person because God does not ordain rebellious messengers to bring God's message. So, all in all, I remain unchanged in my purpose of spreading unity and not discord among God's children. I've willingly given it all to Christ who has given me freedom to worship and freedom to share the Good News with anyone who has faith enough to believe and praise God. The victory is only one praise away!.

[Joshua 16:16] "And it came to pass at the seventh time, when the priests blew with the trumpets, Joshua said unto the people, Shout; for the Lord has given you the city."

Shout! Shout! Shout!! That's what you need to do! You need to shout because the Lord told you to shout. You need to shout because the Lord has told you that you *could* shout! The Lord told you to shout because He has given you the city. You can shout because ain't nobody going to build any walls in your life to separate you from the Lord. Ain't nobody going to stop your praise. Ain't nobody going to shut you up. Ain't nobody going to run you out of your *Father's House*!

You see, our Father has *already* given you the "city." So you have to do just what Joshua did among his enemies. You have to step out. You must walk in faith in God's promises. Then you need to shout till the power of the Lord comes down! You can shout hallelujah, praise His Holy name! And as you step out, you are going to keep walking and keep walking and keep walking. You are going to walk through these walls. You are going to speak to these walls and they shall be cast into the sea!

You see, God doesn't want these walls of racism, ageism, and sexism. I'm talking about these walls of division among God's people. You are a mountain mover! You are an overcomer! You are victorious! You are a child of God and any wall that God tears down, let no man rebuild. Don't you let anyone take your shout, your praise, or your sharing in the Lord's promises. You just go ahead and shout and these walls will come down!

From the Ground Up

[Nehemiah 2:12] ". . . neither told I any man what my God had put in my heart to do at Jerusalem."

[Nehemiah 2:20] "The God of Heaven, he will prosper us; therefore we his servants will arise and build;"

[Nehemiah 13:8] "And it grieved me sore; therefore I cast forth all the household stuff of Tobiah out of the chamber."

[Nehemiah 13:21] ". . . Why lodge ye about the wall? If you do so again I will lay hands on you. From that time on they came no more on the Sabbath."

"I will lay hands on you!" Now that is what I call *serious. Serious* about building, guarding, and protecting that which God has ordained. Don't get me wrong here. I'm not suggesting that we should go around beating people up for God's sake (remember Peter) but that we need to get *serious* about what we allow to go on in the church and in our homes. You see, that's where it all starts. What we allow at home inevitably ends up in church because we bring it to church. That is why Nehemiah laid Jerusalem's "groundwork" by first securing the walls and the gates. He wanted to make sure that the enemies of his people couldn't just walk in and confound the builders. He wanted to make sure that no one was in his people's midst that did not serve the One and Living God. He wanted to make sure that no one would lead his people astray. He wanted to make sure that God's house, God's kingdom, or holy city and God's chosen people were pure and undefiled.

Though Nehemiah was *serious* about doing what God had anointed him to do, he didn't start building the city or temple until he *first secured* his *perimeter.* We in turn must *first* secure our walls and gates for there's a storm a comin'.

When God gives you something to do or a people to lead, you don't have to tell *everybody everything.* (Study Joseph) A lot of times you need to just keep it to yourself until the time that God sets for you to reveal your mission. What happens a lot of the time, when you tell everybody everything is that they (1) become jealous, (2) try to talk you out of it, (3) try to hinder you, or (4) try to sow discord among your flock. They will say that you are either rising above your church or your denomination's rules, or that you are going against what society embraces as correct. And ultimately they, your enemies, will challenge your very relationship with God. In other words, watch who you associate with and who you confide in. Watch who is appointed to positions of leadership in your church. I'm sorry that I have to say this but ain't nothing worse than a person whom the Pastor has appointed to a leadership position in the church to stand up and announce, "The Lord has laid it on my heart to do this or that every Sunday from now on . . ." and then never mention it again. I've seen it done far too many times and the sad part is it's usually when the Pastor's not in the room. Pastors, make sure that those around you, as *God's messenger,* are bringing *God's message!!* These type of people will undermine your ministry whether they intend to or not. It is confusing to your congregation to see someone *not* do what they claim the Lord "laid on my heart" *to* do!

If you are *serious* about the Lord and want to see your church *seriously* prosper then you will get *serious* about who is right in your face doing what is against building your church. The problems most of the time don't come from the Pastor's, but from the people that hold leadership positions and can't be monitored twenty-four hours a day, seven days a week. So if you notice or if the Holy Spirit convicts you about one of your officers behavior not being in unity and love for the rest of the congregation don't be shy about telling them to shut up. Again, secure your walls and gates against the enemy.

When Eliashib prepared Tobias a great chamber in the house of the Lord behind Nehemiah's back, Nehemiah got *serious* enough about God's chambers being defiled that he threw Tobias' stuff out and him too! That's what I call *serious* about Gods house.

Far too often we want to look the other way or to make excuses for people. Why? They aren't a people of a hard language or a strange speech [Ezekiel 3:6]. They know exactly what they are doing and they know that it is not what their Pastor asked them to say or do. They don't care! If they are bold enough to sow seeds of discord then you need to be bold enough to show them God's discipline for the church. It sure ain't about their money or their stature because God's Word tells us, "The God of heaven, He will prosper us; therefore we *His* servants will arise and build."[Nehemiah 2:20].

I'm not saying that you need to *act* out anger but that a lot of behavior should make you angry enough *to act* instead of saying, "Well, we will pray for them" and letting the same stuff go on day after day, year after year, and wondering why your ministry or church isn't growing. It's not growing because you haven't secured your perimeters and let Satan in and he has dragged everyone down in the mud with him! When you *stay* down in the mud like *swine* you can't be blessed because God can't give *pearls* to the swine because they will only trample the *pearls* into the mud also. So stand on God's Word and get *serious*.

We've got people in church, husbands and wives that mistreat each other at home either by words or deeds and then try to assume leadership positions in church. If a person won't treat their own spouse right what makes you think that they are going to treat anyone else right? If a man can't run *his home* in a Christian manner then how can he run the church? If a woman cheats on her husband how is she going to lead in the church?

We can't stress enough the importance of a stable and loving Christian home. The *home* is the perimeter of the church. If a Pastor is a crook at home and it doesn't bother him to cheat, lie, and swindle people at work then that Pastor will do the same thing in the church, bringing shame on the church and shame on any other Pastor associating with them. [Heb. 6:6-9] You can always spot these people because they always say one thing while preaching and then *act* like the rest of the world. Always living above reproach. Always deserving to *receive* more than they give. Always *comfortable at home* while God's house lays in waste.

Now, you see, I learned this lesson the hard way. I, myself, found out that I was not guarding my perimeters and let the Devil come into my life and have his way. He was able to get in by me not having the courage to walk away from old girlfriends, old hangouts, and old habits. I never *spoke* up and said, "Thus saith the Lord." I never *walked* in, "Thus saith the Lord." I never ran the Enemy away from my walls and gates saying, "Thus saith the Lord." I never said, "I trust in the Lord and God only" until I got *serious.* I'm *serious* when I say *build from* God's foundation and guard your walls and gates for there's a storm a comin'!!

The main purpose in building is to build something that lasts. My Word tells me that it is foolish to build on the sand. My Word tells me to build on Christ the Solid Rock. All other ground is sinking sand. Christ is the foundation on which Christians are commanded to stand. God doesn't just give us commandments to boss us around in order to feel that He is important. He gives us instruction in the form of commandments because He knows that the imaginations of a man's heart are evil from his youth. We need guidelines, instruction, and boundaries to have consistency in our day-to-day lives. The book of Proverbs reminds us repeatedly that God loves an equal balance and a just weight. Only through obeying God should we arise and build. To build any other way than through God shows that we're not His at all. The sheep obey the shepherd and follow the shepherd's commands.

When God says to build here and you decide to go build over there, you are building on the sand. When God says he has joined you together in holiness with this person and you run off to build a relationship with that person then you are building on the sand. When God says this is your purpose in ministry and you want to go out and "do your own thing" then you are surely building on the sand. You can build all you want to no matter what comes up against you if you are stubborn enough not to listen to wise instruction. God will even let you do it. God will not make you do anything. You and I have been granted free will. But by not following God's instructions you will find yourself building sandcastles that are washed away in the storm and there is a storm a comin'.

[Matt. 13:3-8] Behold a sower went forth to sow; [4]And when he sowed, some seeds fell by the wayside, and the fowls came and ate them up;[5] Some fell upon stony places, where they had not much earth; and forthwith they sprung up, because they had no deepness of earth;[6] and when the sun was up, they were scorched; and because they had no root, they withered away.[7] And some fell among the thorns; and the thorns sprung up and choked them.[8] But others fell into good ground, and brought forth fruit, some an hundredfold, some sixty-fold, some thirty-fold.

In order to have fruit at harvest time you have got to sow in good ground. A grain of wheat is but a grain of wheat until it is planted in good ground. Then it brings forth more wheat. Everything grows on Earth from the ground up. Your faith works the same way. Jesus is the good ground. When your faith is in Jesus and His righteousness you are able to build on your faith in Him and His righteousness.

We have all been given a measure of faith but in order for your faith to grow you must consistently keep your faith in good ground. To get sidetracked by leeches who want to latch onto your ministry and advise you to go against what God has told you do is to doubt God. You can't get caught up in what Brother So and So says God told him to tell you to do. Don't get caught up in what Sister So and So says is how, "We did it at my old church." Don't allow yourself to get caught up in that "confirmation" crap (I meant trap). Some people live for that mess. You hear it all the time. "Uh-huh girl, confirmation!" Well my question is, "If I know I heard from God then what do I need confirmation from you for?" Either I heard from God or I didn't! I can't allow you to be my spiritual barometer. You can't tell me whether or not I heard from God if you weren't there any more than I can tell you whether or not you heard from God if I'm not there. We could both be agreeing with each other in error. You should know His voice for yourself just like I should know His voice for myself. That's when it should be confirmed! The confirmation is that what we hear is lined up with God's Word!

You have to consistently remind yourself, and them, that your vision, your passion, and your faith didn't just begin when you met them. You have got to remember that your desire, like Nehemiah's desire, began with a seed in your heart to serve the Lord by doing what He blessed you to do. Whether you have a burden to build, sow, or rebuild from the ashes, remember that it all begins from the ground up. Remember that just because you are on good ground doesn't mean that you don't have to clear the ground first. Just because you are on good ground doesn't mean that there are no rocks or stones beneath the surface.

It doesn't mean that there aren't any roots under the good ground that can hinder your progress. It sure doesn't mean that the Enemy won't come in and sow tares among your wheat. Just remember that whether it's stumbling stones of racism, sexism, or ageism, you are standing on good ground. Whether there are roots of bitterness, degradation, and jealousy, you are standing on good ground. Whether the Enemy comes in to sow tares of supremacy, division, and lies, you can do all things in Christ who strengthens you.

Remember that greater is He who is in you than he that is in the world. Remember that if God be for you who can be against you! Remember I John 3:22. "And whatsoever we ask, we receive of Him, because we keep His commandments, and do those things that are pleasing in His sight.[23] And this is His commandment, that we should believe on the name of His Son Jesus Christ, and love one another, as He gave us commandment.[24] "And he that keeps His commandments dwells in Him, and He in him. And hereby we know that He abides in us, by the Spirit which He hath given us."

I can tell you as a bricklayer that when you are building from the ground up, it gets a little muddy sometimes. It gets dirty sometimes. People who don't understand why I'm doing what I'm doing may want to criticize me and pass judgment on me without even bothering to remember all of the work I've done in the past which has stood the test of time. People don't always understand why sometimes I just have to get down there in that muddy ditch alone. People don't always understand why when they want to question me while I'm busy alone in that ditch, that I don't give them a straight answer. And they don't ever understand how I can accomplish my job without their praise.

See, what they don't understand is a thing called *urgency.* What they don't understand is a thing called consistency. What they don't understand is that thing called faithful. What they don't understand is that thing called experience. What they ultimately don't understand is Who I put my faith in when I *started out*!

My confidence in my skills came from the consistency in which my faith in Jesus allowed me to experience life with Jesus *carrying* me through *every time. That* is the key to knowing how to come up out of the ground, no matter how deep or slippery the ditch. It is by remembering the awesome power of the Lord in times past that allow me to live without fear *today*! I know what the Lord has delivered me through when I wasn't even trying to please Him. I also know that it is impossible to please God without faith. I never said that I have faith in my skills, just confidence. My faith is in the Lord's power! My faith is in His Word. My faith is in His promise never to leave me nor forsake me. My faith is in the Holy Spirit to guide me and correct me if I fall.

That is why I am not afraid to go out after God's lost sheep no matter where they may be or who they are. If I see someone who is on the ground and the Spirit convicts me to go bring them back into the pasture, or good ground, then I will go out after them. I am not discounting the threefold cord principle but I would rather go after a lost child of God and fall, and have faith in Jesus to pick both of us up, than to sit back in my own comfort zone worrying about what the church thinks of me or in fear, than to face God and God say, "And they were scattered, because there is no shepherd; and they became meat to all the beasts of the field, when they were scattered.[6] My sheep wandered throughout all the mountains, and upon every high hill; yea my sheep was scattered upon all the face of the earth, and none did search or seek after them." [Ezekiel 34:5-6]

[34:16] I will seek that which was lost, and bring again that which was driven away and will bind up that which was broken, and will strengthen that which was sick; but I will destroy the fat and the strong; I will feed them with judgment.[29] Therefore will I save my flock and they shall no more be a prey; and I will judge between cattle and cattle.

You must understand this point! When Nehemiah heard the news about the Jews that escaped captivity it moved his spirit. The news about the Jew's great affliction and reproach, with the walls and gates of the city broken and burned with fire, lit a passion inside of him! Nehemiah bitterly wept, mourned, fasted, and prayed for forgiveness for his family and all Israel. He then reminded God of His promises to restore the children of Israel. Then the most important part was that Nehemiah *acted* on his request to rebuild the city walls and gates. He went back to Jerusalem, *leaving* his position serving the king in the king's palace. He was willing to give up *everything* in order to get down in ditches to save a remnant of his people. That is love.

I spent twenty-five years with a woman who I was married to for about four years. I didn't know when I married her that she had a drug addiction. This addiction sent her to prison about three times and to jail dozens of times. She was absolutely the most pitiful little thing that I had ever seen. She could be my best friend and dutiful wife one day and then I would drop her off at college and not see her for a month. But still I vowed not to desert her even after six straight years in prison.

Many times all she could do was break down and cry like a baby. I used to pray to God so hard for her. No matter how much I prayed for her to get better, she never acted on any of my prayers. She came into and out of my life for years. Each time we always shared our dreams of starting a ministry to teach youth and convicts about the hell of drug addiction. Then she would disappear until I read about her arrest in the newspaper or she showed up at the door broken and too weak to go on any further. I would pet her and listen to her heartaches and just pray God would show her the way. She should have known the way. Her daddy was a preacher. I'm not going to run her down in the dirt here, because I still love her that much. Besides, some things you just keep to yourself when it only serves to glorify the power of Satan in someone's life.

I will say this, though. She had a real heart for God but she could never let go of her past and get up from the ditch. She never gained the inner strength to give it all to Jesus and allow the Blood to cleanse her from her bondage. Of all the mess that she pulled, she only ended up destroying herself. Nobody, especially my family and friends, understood how I let her do the things she did to me and never move on past her. I tell you the truth. I never wanted to marry her. I didn't love her as a man loves a wife in the beginning. Then one day I looked at her and saw her as a child of God. A child who at too young an age, instead of getting the help that she needed, was sent to a women's prison. I thought I could help her in my strength. We went down many a road together, just two lost kids. Then one day the Holy Spirit said, "No more!" I told her this. I couldn't live with her in sin any longer. She cursed me out and left. God told me, "The next time you see her she will be dead." Every day after that for almost two years, I would grab the newspaper and head straight for the obituaries. I never questioned that I heard God's voice. Never! Then one day I opened the paper and there she was.

I had a friend who stood by me through all of this. She talked me into going to the burial. I had to see the ending. I finally got to see my baby that I hadn't seen in seventeen years. Her mama, my wife, had been found in a motel room dead of an overdose. As I watched them lower her body into her grave I couldn't help but wonder where she is now. I pray that her last words were, "Jesus forgive me." But I just don't know. All I know is that she walked out the door and I never went after her like I had so many times before.

That is why I would gladly give up any position in church if that position hindered me from going after one of God's own, which has lost their way. If serving the Lord doesn't save the lost souls, who are just exactly like her, then what am I doing calling myself having faith in Jesus to carry me while I'm out there in the wilderness alone because no one else is willing to risk failure. I am willing to put my very life on the line before I sit back and do nothing but *talk* about how Jesus restores. I know better. There are times when you have to get up off of your knees, come on down from that pulpit, and go out there yourself and lead your flock out of the bars and crack houses by the nape of their neck kicking and screaming if necessary! When your flock is in the wilderness in the lion's mouth, how long will you continue to call yourselves leaders while doing nothing but hiding in church without ever talking to the persons you have vowed to harvest? Faith without works is dead!

When I Labor for God's Kingdom

[John 3:3-5, 6] "Unless one is born again, he cannot enter the Kingdom of God . . . Unless one is born of water and the Spirit, he cannot enter into the Kingdom of God. That which is born of flesh is flesh, and that which is born of Spirit is Spirit."

[I John 2:6] "He that saith he abides in Him ought himself also to walk, even as He walked."

[2 Pet. 2:20-22] For if after they have escaped the pollution of the world through the knowledge of the Lord and savior Jesus Christ, they are again entangled therein, and overcome, the latter and is worse with them than the beginning.[21] For it had been better for them not known the way of righteousness, than after they had known it, to turn from the holy commandment delivered unto them.[22] But it is happened unto them according to the true proverb, the dog is turned to his own vomit again; and the sow that was washed to her wallowing in the mire.

The phrase "When I labor for God's Kingdom" seems to bring to mind connotations of hard work. Visions of going places and dealing with people whom we don't know without knowing the outcome of such a venture can be overwhelming to lots of folks. It is hard to leave what we know and to walk into the unknown. It is hard to do what we don't want to do. It is hard to approach a person that we don't know. It is hard to speak up about Jesus to a people that don't seem to care to hear about Jesus. It is especially hard to witness for the Lord when we are too preoccupied with what other Christians will think about us associating with drug addicts, alcoholics, prostitutes, or anyone else who has either lost their way or haven't ever found the Lord. That's why the harvest is plentiful but the laborers are few.

Why are the laborers so few when so many folks say that they are saved and are living a Christian life? Remember, "He that saith he abides in Him ought himself also to *walk*, even as He walked." I believe that this is the problem of so few laborers. We are not walking as Jesus walked! I, for sure, have too many times returned right back to the same sinful lifestyle that I had given up just as a dog returns to his own vomit. The funny thing is that it is *normal* for a dog to eat its own vomit. It comes *natural*, I should say, for the dog, especially when it's sick. I, on the other hand, must be sick in my mind to turn back to that which separates myself from God. It just doesn't make sense. I am supposed to rule over the animals, not act like one. I am also supposed to rule over *my* spirit and practice self-control. The Devil didn't make me do anything in my life. I chose to do what I did in my life and I take full responsibility for my sin. But of all that I have sinned I really don't want to have to face God and have God to tell me that I *didn't use the gifts* that He gave to me, in order for me to tell a dying world about the love of our Savior. That is our commission. Why can't we carry it our? Well, it's not so much that we can't carry out our commission, as it is we just don't carry our commission because far too often we are just like the lost souls we're supposed to witness to.

I have seen and heard for myself, many lost persons, who haven't found their way, quote scripture concerning behavior, lifestyles, or language, which is unacceptable to God, but which I was practicing. Are you beginning to get the picture? How can I carry God's Word to a dying world when I am dead myself? How can I be a light to others while I am living in darkness? You see, it doesn't matter that I *know* the Word. It doesn't matter that I *understand* God's precepts. It doesn't even matter that I have gifts from God to carry out His purpose in my life. If I don't have the wisdom to seek Christ daily in order for me to *do exactly* those things that He has commanded of me and has equipped me for then I have done *nothing*! Not only have I done nothing, but also many times have been a stumbling block for those who are lost if they are looking up to me as a living *example* of the *power* of Christ to change lives. I can't tell a drug addict that Christ will change their life while we are sharing drugs or information on where to "cop." I can't tell an alcoholic that Christ will remove alcohol from their lips while sitting around drinking with them. I can't tell a prostitute that Christ will deliver her from a life of fornication while she's watching me hop from bed to bed while unmarried. I can't tell a rebellious or hardhearted person that Christ will deliver them from blaspheme and a froward mouth while they hear me "go off" on someone and curse them out on Monday, right after leaving church on Sunday. See, I have been guilty of all of this stuff and upon studying myself I realized that I would keep my mouth shut when I knew that Jesus wanted me to tell someone about His amazing grace, but I was afraid to speak up because I knew that they would say "You have got your nerve. You are just like me!"

Once I understood how *imperative* it is for myself to live a holy and righteous life, acceptable unto God, I realized that I had to make a change in *my* life for *His* name's sake. This was harder for myself to *want* to change than to *actually* change. To be perfectly honest with you, I've never cared if anybody liked me or not. If you like me, fine. If not, that's fine too. But then Jesus turned on a light in my mind that it matters to Him. Yes, Jesus considered me and my ways. I could no longer have it both ways. I could no longer just take my one talent and bury it, live any kind of way and then present that same one talent back to Him when He comes to harvest His people. I had no "free pass" when it came to serving the Lord. The thing is that I really liked my life with all the craziness and sinfulness that came along with it. It was fun. So why change? Surely I can change just right before I die and that way I won't miss any parties on earth and still make it into heaven.

How wrong I was. See, God doesn't have to let you die. God will love you when you wish you were dead. God will let you do what you want to do, including sin, but you will have to face the consequences. [Ezk. 20:25-26] I found myself polluted in my own sin and right back in the fire until the point of desolation. Then I realized how far I had strayed from when Christ had *first* forgiven my sins and *called* me into *His* pasture and into *His* flock. The choice to change was mine to make. I chased after the *world* until I couldn't go any further down that road, for all that was left before me was *death.* I knew that I wasn't ready to die that far away from God. So I made another choice. *This time* to put my hands to the plow and *not* to look back or ever let go. I now realize that I was always serious about other people's souls but I never understood that I had to change my *lifestyle* to receive the *power* to help others to seek Jesus. What *Jesus* calls this changing of lifestyles is repentance. When you repent you turn away from sin and live according to God's Holy Word. I can't say that I have *repented* when I still have one foot in sin and the other foot in Jesus' pasture. No, that is still serving the flesh and the flesh is against God. The flesh is lost without the Holy Spirit guiding it. There is an old Indian proverb: "It is the spirit that dances, not the man."

Well, you better make sure that your spirit is first in unity with the Holy Spirit before you start dancing at all. You may just be dancing with the Devil. Genesis 3:1 says, "Now the serpent was more subtle than any beast in the field which the Lord God had made." That should let you know to be ever vigilant about what you do, where you go, and who your friends or associates are. You cannot make it in this world alone. Find yourself a good church home and praying people to associate with. Satan preys on those whom he can separate from the body of Christ. It's called *temptation.* Ecclesiastes 4:9-10 says, "Two are better than one; because they have a good reward for their labor. For if they fall, the one will lift up his fellow: But woe to him that be alone when he falls; for he hath not another to lift him up. [12:] And if one prevails against him, two shall withstand him; and a threefold cord is not quickly broken.

You see, your spirit without the Holy Spirit is still prone to go astray. Your spirit without the Holy Spirit is still separated from that *indwelling* of holiness which convicts us when we are not living as God has commanded us to live. No, we're not perfect, but we can be obedient to His Word and strive to be Christ like. Jesus was obedient to the Father and walked in His precepts. That is why Jesus was bold in harvesting God's lost, sick, and wounded people. He knew that He had *power* over the storm.

When I labor for God's Kingdom I cannot do those things that I used to do. When I labor for God's Kingdom I can't say the things I used to say. When I labor for God's Kingdom, as Jesus commands, then any darkness in my life will show up and contradict the very words that I speak. It is the light of the Word which brings my darkness into evidence.

Lots of times people don't even realize that what they are doing or saying is against the Lord's precepts until you show them God's Word. Now, once told, they can see the light. Then the problem can be that they are also able to see more clearly the life that the messenger is leading. This is what too many "would be" laborers are afraid of today. This is the point where these "would be" laborers stop and become complacent in our duties. This is where these "would be" laborers try to justify our behavior even when we know deep down inside that our own behavior is not Christ like. This is where we try to stay out of the light and just try to blend into the background. We just want to sit on "our pew" every Sunday and look around trying to find someone just a little bit worse off than we are. But my Word says in Numbers 8:2-4: ". . . When thou lightest the lamps, the seven lamps, shall give light over against the candlestick.[3] And Aaron did so; he lighted the lamps thereof over against the candlestick, as the Lord commanded Moses."

[4:] "And this work of the candlestick was of beaten gold, unto the shaft thereof, unto the flowers thereof, was beaten work: according to the pattern which the Lord has shewed Moses, so he made the candlestick."

First there was darkness until the lamps were lit. Then there was light against the candlestick. What Jesus is telling you is that, "My *Word* is a lamp unto your feet and a light unto your path." And with you being the candlestick your *intricate details* will be made clear to those whom are watching you. See, Aaron could see the candlestick in the dimly lit tent. He could see the shape of the candlestick, so he knew that it was indeed a candlestick. But when the light of the seven lamps were cast upon the candlestick not only did he see the candlestick but also the work of *craftsmanship* which *marked* the candlestick. Once the seven lamps were lit Aaron could plainly see that this was no *ordinary* candlestick! This candlestick was of beaten gold, unto the shaft thereof.

Has the Word of God ever convicted you to the point that you say "I heal, I heal, I can hold out no longer!" And when you spoke these words did you notice that Jesus began to shape you and to mold you into just what He wants you to be? If not, then you aren't *receiving* the Word. You see, to *hear* the Word doesn't mean that you have *received* the Word, for to receive the Word involves the *heart* and not the ears. I have always heard the Word but it just went in my *ear* and not into my spirit like so many "would be" laborers today. The Word must become alive and real to you through your spirit. You must *own* that Word!

What we have to do is to listen to the Word and to take the Word deep down inside our heart, or inner man. We need to write God's Word on our hearts and to hide His Holy commands deep down in our spirit to the point that God's Word pierces us so deeply that it separates our soul, or our will, from our spirit, or God's will, which is in us through the Holy Spirit. Then when the lamps are lit and the candlestick is clearly seen as one of beaten gold and fine craftsmanship even unto the flowers thereof, it is evident to everyone that all of the glory belongs to Jesus! Jesus is willing and Jesus is able to do a mighty work in your life if only you will call upon His name, turn from your wicked ways, and submit to His authority. Then the flesh dies so that the Spirit may live. Then we won't have to be ashamed to step out and tell a dying world about a Savior who is gathering up His people, for there is a storm a comin'.

God didn't begin a work in you for you to just give up, give in, or to quit obeying Him. God would not have brought you this far just to leave you open to shame. No, we bring shame on ourselves. That is why God sent His only begotten Son into the world to carry the burdens that we can't seem to let go. And that's all that this *junk* is that we *insist* on not letting go. Burdens! These burdens keep us in bondage and keep us held down and held back from having the courage and the boldness to *speak out* without fear of reproach.

It's these little secrets that we hope no one sees and these little secrets that we hope no one hears about or reads about that keep us from doing our labor for Christ's harvest. We say that one little drink won't hurt anything until someone who is having a problem getting off of alcohol sees us in Wal-Mart buying beer. Then guess what? You've just lost your witness with them. When you get on that telephone and gossip all over town until the persons that you've been gossiping about hears what you've said, then guess what? You've lost your witness with them. When you cheat someone in the church out of some money outside of the church when you are a leader then guess what? You have just sold your witness for that dollar amount and Satan is the one that redeemed it. Satan, that serpent, more subtle than any beast in the field. That is why Christ said, "Seek ye first the kingdom of God, *and His righteousness . . ."* Amen

When you seek the kingdom of God *and His righteousness*, then the lamps or Word of God are lit. You don't have to worry about people throwing it up in your face that your feet are on the *wrong* path. You will no longer have to try to justify your relationship with the Father, because you see, Jesus will personally "handcraft" the *intricate details* of your character into what the Lord originally intended it to be. The "flowers" on your candlestick will be *exactly* what God commands them to look like. You may think that you look good now, but just wait until Jesus is through with you! See, when Jesus is through with His *holy* craftsmanship concerning those *intricate details* in your character you will be *able* to stand in the light. When God's Word is shining all through you then you too will *be able* to let your light, which *Jesus* has *anointed* you with, shine for a dying world to see. For it is written that, "No man lights a candle and then hides that candle in a secret place but he sets that candle on the table for all to see its light." [Luke 11:33]

It is time to wake up, church!! There is a great work and a great commission to be fulfilled. We have been too comfortable for too long! Jesus is calling for laborers in the world which is lost. Jesus is calling His children home soon. The harvest is plentiful but the laborers are few. So if you feel in your heart, a calling on your life to tell someone lost in sin about our Savior don't let *your* unrepentance stand in your way. I'll be honest with you just as I have been with Jesus. If you know that you are saved and you still are living in the flesh and from a carnal mind, then all you need to do is to stop right now, right where you are and ask Jesus for forgiveness, repent, and confess with your mouth that He is the Lord of your life. Then *you* let it go! Renew your mind! Let it go and walk in the newness of your restoration.

It is from the heart that the mouth speaks, whether praise or evil. So when you get a taste of Jesus in your heart then your mouth can confess also. When you believe for yourself what Jesus has done in your life then surely there is *no way* that you will be able to keep it to yourself. The grace and mercies of Jesus are *not intended* to be kept to ourselves. His grace and His mercies are to be *shouted* from the highest mountains unto the lowest valleys for it is the Blood that gives us strength from day to day and it will never lose its power!!

When I labor for God's Kingdom I realize that all labor doesn't include a hammer and a nail. All labor doesn't include fixing plumbing. All labor doesn't include mowing the church lawn or cleaning the sanctuary. All labor doesn't include printing the bulletins or working in the kitchen. No, the true labor involves getting outside of the church and being a *living testimony* as to the power of Jesus to turn lives around. All of the maintenance, building, daily tasks, and work of church officers are service unto God to keep the church up and running and are important to the church, but the truth is that even without the building God is going to have "church" anyway. So, it's not *all* about the building, the church grounds, or any of that other stuff that we too often try to offer as our *only* labor to God, but is *all* about saving lives. We can't save anybody, not even ourselves, but we have been commissioned to tell a dying world "Thus saith the Lord." When you labor for God's Kingdom there is no turning back once you put your hands to the plow. There is absolutely *nothing* to turn back for. There is no joy for you in *this* world except in Jesus. I do pray that you find it for there's a storm a comin'.

[John17:13] The joy we receive is the joy we operate in as we labor for God's Kingdom. This joy is the joy Jesus gave to us with our salvation. To operate in this joy we must remain in Him as we labor for God's Kingdom. We must abide in Him and walk as He walked. We are co-laborers. When we labor for God's Kingdom we must first accept and acknowledge that it is indeed His Kingdom! We have no vote to remove Him from office and we cannot campaign to set any other man up as King! We therefore must accept and acknowledge that our labor is all about Him.

Here's where we often mess up in one of two ways. [1] We either act like the rest of the world or the unsaved until they see no reason to come to church and be taught Kingdom principles. [2] Or we act like the rest of the world and they see us in church and still living in the same sin the world commits and then decide *to come* to church because they see us do this craziness and think it's alright for Christians to behave this way!

The only thing worse than running people off from the church or turning them against attending church is for them to attend because we give them this false image of God!! When we live and act like the rest of the world while inviting them to church, we are saying that God tolerates sin. I'd hate to think someone started coming to church because I am showing them, "You don't have to even repent or change or be sorry for your sin." My actions are saying that we can approach a Holy God any kind of way we want to. We have no rules from God. We have no precepts of God. We don't have any boundaries set forth by God. We have no commandments to obey from God and holiness and righteousness aren't even expected of us from God.

We must never give the world and the lost a false image of God's holiness. We must let the world know that God is Spirit and those that worship Him must worship Him in Spirit and in truth!

There is no room for anything less in God's Kingdom. And there is a storm a 'comin!

I Set My Kingdom Upon This Rock

[2 Kings 15:3-5] And he did that which was right in the sight of the Lord, according to all that his father Amaziah had done;

[4:] Saved that the high places were not removed; the people sacrificed and burnt incense still on the high places.[5] And the Lord smote the king so that he was a leper unto the day of his death, and dwelt in a several house.

"Thy Kingdom come, Thy will be done." How many times have we said these very words in prayer? These very words that Christ taught the multitude at the Sermon on the Mount. These words come from our Lord, as a model prayer, so that we can come to God through our Lord giving honor and praise to God while confessing our sins, asking for His forgiveness and His blessings for His *name's sake.* We open up our prayers by acknowledging *Him* for who He is. We praise Him. We offer up our petitions. We close our prayers by acknowledging *Him* for who He is. Again praising Him. Then for some *reason* we nod off to sleep. To sleep!

Well, there's a storm a comin' and we had better *wake up*! We need to wake up at home. We need to wake up on our jobs. We need to wake up at our schools. We need to wake up in our government. And we need to wake up in our churches. Wake up and take a good hard look at yourself. Who are you trying to please . . . yourself, your friends, the world, or God? Who are you going to serve . . . yourself, your friends, the world, or God? Who are you going to follow . . . your friends, the world, or Jesus? Choose you this day whom you will serve. Wake up church and meditate on these Kingdom principles.

Fulfillment: N. The act of consummating something. N. A feeling of satisfaction at having achieved your *desire.*

Freedom: N. The condition of being free; the *power* to act or speak of think without externally *imposed restraints.* N. Immunity from an obligation or duty.

Azariah did what was right in the sight of the Lord according to all that his *father* Amaziah had done. But sometimes *daddy* just can't carry you through. Azariah, the son, seemed to be looking too much towards *daddy* and not enough towards God. For you see, he did right in the sight of God . . . "saved that the high places were not removed." He must have slept that one.

God's will must be done! God's Kingdom will come! There will be nothing sitting upon the high places except the Kingdom of God! Do you think that Jesus taught us how to pray only for us to go to sleep and God's Kingdom not be fulfilled? When something is fulfilled then it has been consummated, or brought together. When God's plan for His Kingdom is fulfilled then His children are brought together with Him. The Kingdom is in you! Jesus brought you the Kingdom![Luke 17:20-21]

His Heavenly *Kingdom* is already together with Him! The way that *we get* to Him is following Jesus, who died on the cross and was resurrected on the third day. Only when we "get right" or saved in Jesus are we right with our Father. With Jesus being our consummation with the Father we are now presented as perfect or complete before our Father. The way that we move on into perfection is to be obedient to Christ's teaching and His instruction. If you are not following Christ's instruction then you aren't being obedient. Is it imperative that you are obedient? Let's see.

Azariah did right in the sight of God, but only up to a *certain point.* What Azariah did was all that his father Amaziah had done. Then he went to sleep. For the high places remained and the people still sacrificed and burnt incense on these high places. Does this sound like, "Thy Kingdom come, Thy will be done?" When God has something that He wants you do, do it. When God says that what you are doing is an abomination in His sight then stop it. Just stop!! Ain't no use in trying to explain why you are doing what you are doing or why you haven't done what is commanded of you to do by Him. God desires mercy and not sacrifice; and the knowledge of God more than burnt offerings. So the Lord smote Azariah with leprosy and he was a leper until his death. There are consequences to pay for your disobedience. You cannot go through life and not obey the Lord *without paying* for your disobedience. In sin and disobedience we are actually in an *intimate* relationship with Satan and he always destroys and devours. He is not and will not ever be your friend! There will be no truce! There's a storm a comin'.

When you are faithful and obedient to the teaching and instruction of Jesus, then you are in an *intimate* relationship with your Savior. When you have an intimate relationship with your Savior, then you have fulfillment. What you have is a feeling of *satisfaction* at having *reached* your *desire*! When you reach your desire then our Savior will give you *freedom* because freedom is *His desire* for you! Freedom from alcohol. Freedom from cocaine. Freedom from smoking. Freedom from pornography. Freedom from homosexuality. Freedom from oppression. Freedom from a promiscuous lifestyle. Freedom from anger. Freedom from loneliness. Freedom from bitterness. Freedom from depression. Freedom from anything that holds you in bondage and separates you from God.

Freedom with Jesus Christ our Lord gives you the power to act or think or speak without *externally* imposed *restraints.* In other words there is no longer anything in the world that can hold you down. In plain language, Satan has to turn you loose by you confessing the Word!! He no longer has *any* power over you! When you have finally reached or found *fulfillment* in Jesus you are *now* unleashed from the chains of bondage that sin had on your soul. You are free!!

Shout it!! "I'm free, for he whom the Son sets free is free indeed!!"

You no longer have to walk like the rest of the world. You no longer have to talk like the rest of the world. You no longer have to think like the rest of the world. You no longer have to do what daddy did. You no longer have to do what mama did. You no longer have to be what you used to be. You are no longer all alone in this world because you *are* a *child* of God Almighty who says, "I set my Kingdom upon this rock." You see, on *this* rock there is no room for any other kingdom. On *this* rock there are no sacrifices or burnt offerings. Upon this rock "My Kingdom has come." Upon this rock "My will *is* done!" Exodus 6:8 and Matthew 16:17-19 has confirmed this.

It doesn't matter what your family thinks about you. It doesn't matter what your boss thinks about you. It doesn't matter what your teachers say about you. It doesn't even matter if the system is designed to keep you down, because I know it is my Father's Kingdom that I belong to and I know that you are welcome too. So wake up and follow the voice of the Shepherd. He won't lead you astray. You now have the *power* to rise up from your despair. I know, you didn't realize that you had despair until . . . you woke up. I know you thought, "Well, that's just the way that things are." You thought, "Well, that's just the way that I am." It's easy to feel like, "That's the way things are gonna be." But you can now see that God has a calling on your life. Jesus has a purpose for you. Daddy can't find it for you. Mamma can't find it for you. Your Pastor can't find it for you. Your purpose in *this* life is something that you must *seek* for yourself. You now have the *power* to act the way Christ acted on earth.

You don't have to be a follower of men. Be a follower of Christ. There is *no* temptation of the Devil that you can't overcome. God says that He always leaves a way out no matter what the temptation.[1Cor.10:13] If you are watching TV and something comes on that causes you to lust, you have the power to turn it off. If you meet some woman that is trying to seduce you, you have the *power* to walk away. If your old running partners offer you alcohol or a shot of dope, you have the *power* to say no. If Jesus tells you to go left and Satan says go right you have the *power* to tell him, "NO, Jesus said go left!!"

That's the kind of freedom that our Savior gives us. We have immunity from any obligation or any duty that Satan sends our way. God's Word tells us that we do. I don't know about you, but I *am* going to *continue* to *walk* in it. My Word tells me to *continue* to *walk* in it. My Word tells me that, "Greater is *He* that is in *me* than *he* that is in *the world*." Isaiah 54:14 tells me that "In righteousness shalt though be *established*: thou shalt be far from oppression: for thou shalt not fear: and from terror; for it shall not come near to thee." What I *really* like though, is this part on down in verse [17] . . . "No weapon that is formed against thee shall prosper; and every tongue that shall rise against thee in judgment thou shalt condemn. *This is* the heritage of the servants of the Lord, and their righteousness is of me," saith the Lord. Notice that the Lord says, "this *is*" not "this was" or "this will be," but that "this *is* yours right *now!*"

Now I am free to think the way that Jesus thinks. My mind is no longer *bound* to the satisfying of the flesh but to the perfecting of the spirit. I'm no longer *bound* by paranoia, *thinking* that folks are talking about me behind my back. I *know* you are. (Just kidding) I no longer have to tell a lie. I no longer have to curse people out for getting on my nerves. I have *power* over my mind being polluted by blaspheme and thoughts of revenge. I have power over my mind leading me into diver's lusts. I have *power* over my mind telling me to put aside following Lord "just one more time." This *power* over my mind is what sets me truly free to meditate on, "Whatever things are true, whatsoever things are honest, whatsoever things are just, whatsoever things are pure, whatsoever things are lovely, whatsoever things are of good report; if there be any virtue, and if there be any praise, think on these things." [Philippians 4:8].

Once your mind has been *released* from all externally imposed restraints then you *will* have that joy and that peace of spirit that only comes through the indwelling of the Holy Ghost. "For God has not given us the spirit of fear; but of *power*, and of love, and of a sound mind." [2 Tim. 1:7] Once your mind is free from the bondage of sinful *thought* you receive the Word with all *readiness* of mind and search the scriptures daily to gain knowledge in those things of the Kingdom realm. You are no longer caught up in worldly doctrine or worldly thinking. You are now able to discern what is of God and what are fiery darts of the Enemy.[Eph.6:16] You now understand that what your mind thinks is acceptable unto God may not be acceptable to Him at all.

Once your mind is *released* from all externally *imposed* restraints you won't be silent anymore about these fashion designers who think nothing of exploiting our young girls with outfits on the store shelves aimed at them but more fit for a hooker. You will no longer keep silent about our teenagers engaging in sex before they are married. Once your mind has been released from all externally imposed restraints you will tell your daughters that *it is alright* to remain a virgin until marriage no matter what the world is telling them is okay. You can tell your young sons it is not okay for boys to think and act like they are girls. You *see* it's *not okay* with God!![Rom.1:27] You have to wake up! You now have the *power* of Christ to change our children's direction. *You* have the *power* of mind in Christ to live a holy and righteous life in front of our children and to *speak* holiness and to *speak* righteous values into *their* minds! I'm tired of seeing our youth walking around with no direction and purpose and with no goals in their lives other than to satisfy their flesh and carnal lusts. We have got to take our children *back*, for there's a storm a comin'!

Who is this Kingdom upon this rock? This Kingdom is none other than Jesus the Christ who now lives inside you! He is the Rock. He is more than a conqueror, which makes you more than a conqueror in Him. Not only did He overcome the sins of the world, but he provides us *daily* with the *power* to resist temptation as the Lord of our life and to turn away from sin. Christ lives in those who believe and follow His voice. Christ lives in those who have a renewing of the mind through the Spirit. Christ lives in those who read, pray, study, fast, and meditate on His Word. You need *all* of His Word not just part of it. You need to do *all* that His Word tells you to do, not just part of it. You see, that is what got Azariah in trouble. Azariah slept through the part of the scripture that tells us, "Ye shall observe to do therefore as the Lord your God hath commanded you: ye shall not turn aside to the right hand or to the left." [Deut 5:32]

In your fulfillment you have achieved *His desire* of freedom for you to speak up for His Kingdom on earth. There is *power* in your tongue! There is *power to speak life* in another person's life. Your freedom gives you the *power* to speak without any externally *imposed* restraints. You can now speak those things which aren't as if they are! Once you reach your *desire* you are in an intimate relationship with the Lord. Have you ever noticed that when you are in an intimate relationship with someone that everything else is blocked out? The whole world can pass you by and you don't even notice. Folks at the green light blowing their horns because you are so involved in your conversation with your spouse or significant other, that you don't even realize the light has changed. They are cussing you out and you're waving at them, talking about, "Hi!" Folks hate your guts and you don't even care.

Now why would God, in His sovereignty tell you, "I set my Kingdom upon this rock?" [John 17:20-21] The point is that God's will shall be done. How do I know that God's Kingdom has come? Because His Holy Word tells me so. How do I that His will shall be done? Because His Holy Word tells me so. Numbers 23:19-20 tells me, "God is not a man, that He should lie; neither the son of man that He should repent: hath He said and shall He not do it? Or hath He spoken, and shall He not make good of it." [20] "Behold, I have received commandment to bless: and He hath blessed; and I cannot reverse it."

Boy, don't you know that makes the Devil mad! He can't stand you knowing God's Word. The Word of God tells you things about the God that you serve that Satan doesn't want you *to know.* He doesn't want you to know that the Word of God is a lamp unto your feet and a light unto your path. [Neh. 8:10] He doesn't want you to know that the joy of the Lord is your strength. [Jer. 1:5] He doesn't want you to know that even "Before you were formed in the womb, I knew you." [Mat. 28:20] He, that serpent, sure doesn't want you to know that Jesus says, "I will *never* leave you, nor forsake you and I will be with you even till the end of the world." He doesn't want you to know, "In my Father's house there are many mansions; if it were not so, I would have told you, I go to prepare a place for you. And if

I go and prepare a place for you, I will come again, and receive you unto myself; that where I am, there ye may be also. And whither I go ye know, and the *way* ye know." [John 14:2-4]

Satan doesn't want you to know these things because once you take God's Word into your mind then God's Word takes root in your heart and once God's Word takes root in your heart then you start speaking it and when you start speaking it then you start living it and when you start living it you have *power*!

The Word says that we can speak with the *authority* of Christ. In *Christ's* authority you can speak any good thing into someone's life. In speaking in *Christ's* authority, what you are doing is speaking hope into the conscience of a dying world. We grow up hearing all these stories about a man called Jesus from long ago. But as time goes by, from the time we were children, we tend to go astray if that fire is not fed. We tend to lose hope. We tend to lose our way when we lose our *focus* on Jesus. We become fixated on material wealth and those things of the flesh. We inevitably end up searching for peace, for joy and for comfort in all the wrong places and in all the wrong people and in all the wrong things. We search for answers to what is keeping us from reaching our *desires*. The truth is that the problems in your life are not going away because your desires aren't Christ's desires. Ask Jesus to search your heart and for Him to show you those things in your character and heart that are holding you in bondage. Then you have to lay them down. Y-O-U!!

For instance, are your priorities in order? Quit waiting on Jesus to do something which He has already given you power to do! If Jesus, and seeking the Kingdom of God first are not your priorities then you need a shift in priorities. If Jesus in not your priority then you are living without *freedom*. What you are doing is living for the flesh. When you live in the flesh and for the world you have far too many externally imposed restraints. You are in bondage to your very *lifestyle.*

"Well," you say, "I know the Lord. I go to church. I pay my tithes. I hug my kids and treat people like I want to be treated but I still can't seem to break free. I'm faithful to my wife. I don' t drink, smoke, cuss or do drugs but I just can't seem to reach that *fulfillment* in my life. I seem to always end up going around in circles and never growing. I've read my Bible more times than most folks I know and they have a lot more joy and a lot more understanding than I do. I've been in the church since I was a baby. I was brought up in the church. I even used to sing in the choir and taught Sunday school."

If this is you then what you need is deliverance. What you need is deliverance from whatever is holding you back from seeking and finding your *purpose.* What you need is that *clarity* from On High to break those chains that have been keeping your soul and your spirit from being receptive and able to *receive* your gifts from God and *using* these gifts to all of your abilities. That is why it is so important to be in the church home which Christ *wants* you to be in. You can't just say, "I don't like them folks," and move around from church to church. You cannot be listening to just anybody who comes along trying to "preach" to you or trying to tell you what your gifts are and what "God" has told them to tell you to do.

Only you can look at your own heart. The thing is that you don't *always* know what these things are that are hidden in your heart and are *not* acceptable to God, so you must ask Jesus to *deliver* you from them. You may not drink but may be bitter. You may take good care of your kids but maybe you gossip. You may put more money in church than God asks but maybe it's from haughtiness. Maybe you study your Bible but you still judge others. Maybe you *are* faithful to your wife but you still sneak around watching movies, looking at magazines or secretly lusting after *another* man's wife. Whatever it is that is keeping you from walking in the *power* of the Holy Ghost, you need deliverance from its grip. If you've prayed about it and can't seem to break free of whatever is holding you in bondage you need to *keep your eyes* on Jesus for your breakthrough is just around the corner!

You see, God inhabits the *praises* of his people. If you want that deliverance right now then you have got to *expect* it right now! If you want that deliverance right now then you have to *claim* it right now! If you want that deliverance, then you have to *walk* in it right now! If you want that deliverance then you had better begin to *shout* in it right now! If you want that deliverance then you had better begin to *worship* God right now! If you want that deliverance then *don't wait* 'till the victory is over, shout *now*! If you are in prison *don't wait* till you meet the parole board, shout now! If you are fired from your job *don't wait* 'till you find another job, shout now! If your kids are running around and acting like you ain't taught them anything, *don't wait*, shout now! If you haven't gotten your results back from the doctor, *don't wait*, shout now! If you can't seem to lose all that extra weight that is keeping you in bondage, *look up* to Jesus and shout now!

What we need in our churches, in our homes, in our schools, and in our government are some folks who aren't afraid to step up and *speak* with *boldness* about the *power* of *Christ*! You see, we're getting a whole bunch of *information* without any *message*. The message may be *strengthened* by giving information, but information without a *clear-cut message* is confusion. Wake up church!

You see, Azariah was only sixteen years old when he began to reign as king of Judah. He had what *we* call bad habits. He did just what his daddy did. He did that which he saw his daddy do. He doesn't see it as evil that his daddy did before the Lord by worshiping strange gods. At least he seems to not take it *seriously*, for he too never removed the high places and continued to burn incense and make sacrifices on these high places. Azariah just "*slept through*" that command from God, it seems. But God wasn't sleeping. And He's not sleeping now. He is a God who never sleeps nor slumbers. God's message to Azariah was one of *self-accountability*. God's message to Azariah was that as king he was *held responsible* and *accountable* for his *leadership* of the people.

Have you ever noticed that throughout the Bible, God always goes straight to the *top*? Whenever God is judging the actions or lack thereof, or the behavior of the people, He always seems to go straight to the king or ruler or judges or prophets or the high priests. Do you think that it is coincidence that God looks upon and judges the high places first? I personally don't believe that God does anything by coincidence. Everything that God does serves *His divine* purpose. When the leaders of these high places aren't obedient to the commands of God and don't get *serious* enough to *do* the things that God has commanded them to do, or to teach, the people have no direction. When God sets you up on the high places, there comes a responsibility to holiness.[Luke 12:48] What God trusts leaders of people to do is to serve these people by giving them the *direction* they need in order to serve *Him.* The way to get these directions is by asking Him through prayer and fasting.

What I'm talking about here is *serious* prayer and *serious* fasting. God holds you *accountable* but that doesn't leave church members *unaccountable* for their actions. The thing is that you, as a Pastor or church leader have been chosen or called to a *higher* calling. As a Pastor you have to keep a watchful eye out for anything that stops the flow of the Holy Spirit in your church whether it is the Trustees, Stewards, Elders, Deacons, Teachers, or any other member. It doesn't matter who or what is stopping the flow of the Holy Spirit in your church, you as the Pastor must put a stop to it.

I know . . . you've preached until you are blue in the face. You've gotten on them from the pulpit about their gossiping. From the pulpit you've warned them about their pride. From that same pulpit you've told them that the wages of sin is death. You've told them all about love thy neighbor as thyself and you've told them to forgive one another, comfort one another, help one another, and to lift each other up. And still this infighting and division and complaining goes on. "Brother So and So got caught drunk driving with a hooker in his car on the wrong side of town. Sister So and So got the nerve to be up front waving her arms like she's so sanctified while she's creeping too. Plus she be singing all out of key looking at folks like she's better than us. With that wig on and her run over shoes."

Before long the joy of the Lord is gone. The praise of the Lord is gone. The worship of the Lord is gone. The uplifting of His Kingdom is gone. The blessings from the Lord are gone. [Ps. 18:13]

The consuming fire of the Lord is here! Wake up! If they won't act right, get *serious*. There's a storm a comin!

It doesn't matter if you are a *young* Pastor. It doesn't matter if you are a *new* Pastor. It doesn't matter if you have been leading this particular congregation for *twenty* years. If your congregation isn't *walking* in the *ways* and on the *path* that you have been directing them by telling them "Thus saith the Lord!" then what you need to do is to get *serious* with them and *serious* about your duty.

For your church to have fulfillment with God you have got to get serious enough to call everybody together and say, "Look, *this* is what we *are* going to do!" See, sometimes you have got to *stand up*!! Sometimes you have got to come out of that robe, suit and tie and put on your own sackcloth. Sometimes you've got to *get down* in the ashes *with* your flock. Sometimes you've got to *send out* a decree *throughout* the land. Sometimes you've got to let it be *heard*, "Let neither man nor *beast, herd* nor *flock,* taste anything: let them *not* feed, *nor* drink water: But let man and *beast* be covered with sackcloth, and cry *mightily* unto God!"

You see, what that king of Nineveh did was to get *serious*. What that king did was to *wake up*! What he did was to *look* around his kingdom. What he *realized* was that his kingdom would *not* be allowed to supersede God's Kingdom. Surely, he knew about all of his peoples' evil ways and the violence in their hands, and he as a king should have put a stop to it a *long* time ago. But no, he sat up there on his throne in the high palace like he doesn't even know that there is a storm right in his midst. Stand up Pastors and set your people free!

You see, what happens a lot of times is that your flock, like Azariah are victims of old habits. Sometimes the church itself can be a hindrance. What do I mean? Well, some people have grown up in the church listening to and being taught that there are lines that they just shouldn't cross. Women becoming Pastors, for instance. But the Word says that on the day of the Pentecost, "that God poured out His Spirit on all flesh: and your sons and *your daughters* shall prophesy . . . and on my servants and on my *handmaidens* I will pour out in those days of my *Spirit*; and they shall prophesy." Some people have been raised in the church to believe that you don't speak up or *claim total victory* in Jesus because that is *boasting* of tomorrow. These people have been convinced that "you don't make Satan mad."

They have been led to believe that when things go wrong that Satan has the power and is punishing them for standing up and *claiming* the power of Jesus when in fact God lets them or has them, or even better, is *leading* them *through* these tests in order to *strengthen* them *against* the Enemy and to draw them *closer* to Him. The strength God equips you with today prepares you to stand tomorrow.

In plain English a lot of your flock are *superstitious*! Their grandmother was superstitious. Their granddaddy was superstitious, so all of these old habits must be addressed before they can be set free in the Spirit. "You better be careful of the boogeyman will get you." The boogeyman can't get *anything* that belongs to God! These are the people who stay in their seats *scared* to death when they hear speaking in tongues, or see folks slain in the Spirit. Others are thinking that you are crazy and that it's all an act while still others are just plain *scared* of anything unknown, or either *afraid* that they may *lose control* of their manly emotions or professional elegance in front of others. So they *elect* to stay in bondage.

What they don't understand and what they don't see is that you, as their spiritual leader, are *leading* them to a higher spiritual realm and into an intimate relationship with the Holy Spirit who will grant them what their hearts, minds, and souls desire in order for them to dwell in God's higher places which are places of a spiritual *identity*. What they are not accepting is the *fact* that there are no old wives tales in God's higher places. There are no fables in God's higher places. There is no superstition in God's higher places. There is no fear in God's higher places, and no one has *control* except for God on His higher places. The problem is that your flock thinks that they have *control* on earth or here in the lower places, if you will, but the truth is that our *control* is all in our tongue by speaking God's covenant promises, for all we truly have in reality are *choices*. Only God is in control from On High, to the high places, all the way to *wherever* our feet are *standing*!

I set *My* Kingdom upon this Rock! What happens is that a lot of your flock are just *barely* hanging on where they *are* standing and can hardly keep a toehold. They don't know why they can't seem to reach any higher. All that they know is that they can't seem to reach any higher. All that they know is that they feel their feet slipping out from under them. All that they know is they are praying but they still can't seem to keep going forward. They are not quite to God's higher places yet and the *next Revival* is months away. That's why David prayed to the Lord for hinds *feet,* that he could *dwell* in high places.

In other words, "Lord, grant me now what I *need* now to stay near to You." For myself a Revival is too far away when I need help now. We must listen to the Holy Spirit always and with the invitation to accept Christ as their personal Savior be prepared to offer an invitation for repentance and baptism of the Holy Ghost for those needing to let go of some things such as bitterness, hatred, fear, or covetousness. The folk honest with themselves will be set free.

About fifteen years ago I worked for a construction company that was remodeling K-Marts. I started here in Maryville on the local store. I knew masonry and the construction part, such as setting doors, pouring concrete, hanging pegboard, etc. But there was a whole lot more that I had to learn, such as building displays, hanging department signs, and the layout of the floor design. All of the design of the store had to be exactly like the design of all the other K-Marts in other cities. And the corporate offices in Michigan are dead serious about it, too. I used to laugh at how serious they looked and acted when they came to inspect the progress of construction. Even funnier to me was the way everybody who was a manager, assistant manager, or department head would run to grab their suit coats and straighten their clothes when these folks form headquarters showed up. I mean everything had to look perfect in the midst of all the construction. When we knew they were going to be there, cleanup was highly stressed, to say the least.

The problem is that while you are renovating these stores, the stores are open for business. People are coming in shopping, and people are pushing buggies out to their cars. Kids everywhere. Old folks poking up and down the aisles in no kind of a hurry. In the parking lot nobody is paying attention to me on this big forklift, backup bell ringing, with counters, displays, big boxes, or whatever, blocking my view while I'm trying my best to maneuver through this maze of confusion in order to get these materials into the store without anyone getting *killed*. At this point, I'm sorry, but *hurt* does not count! What a mess. All day long. Are we making progress? Sure. Is progress slow? Yes. Can you tell? Barely.

We are behind schedule and everybody from the K-Mart corporate offices are complaining to the owner of my construction company who then tells my boss, his job superintendent, who now tells me that we will be fined thousands of dollars for each day that we go beyond our completion date. We are talking a lot of money. Time to get *serious*!

Now all of this time I had been noticing that when the dumpster pickup and new dumpster delivery was on time I could haul the old stuff out of the store faster because I would always have someplace to dump it. The faster that I could dump the old stuff, the faster I could bring in the new displays and new stuff. The faster that I brought in the new material, the faster the guys could get it assembled. The faster that they got it assembled, the faster we made progress. The faster that we made progress, the more time we made up. The more time that we made up, the more we caught up to being on schedule. Finally! Now everybody is happy and smiling at each other, helping one another, encouraging one another, working in unity for one common goal.

The point is that a lot of the time our spiritual lives are just like those stores. We can't *see* progress and we can't *make* progress because we have too much stuff, too much personal garbage in our hearts. Paul said, "I die daily . . ." Not when the next Revival is on the calendar, but *daily*. See, what I did was to tell the man that picked up the full dumpster that one dumpster just wasn't enough and that I needed a second dumpster to keep the job going. Only when we could get rid of that old stuff would we bring in the new stuff because other than that, there was no room for new stuff. The confusion brought on not getting done those things which we were hired to do. All that it took was for someone to give me an outlet to let go of old stuff.

Jesus is My Laborer

[Num. 9:15] And on the day that the tabernacle was reared up the cloud *covered* the tabernacle, namely, the *tent of testimony*: and at even there was upon the tabernacle as it were the appearance of fire, until the morning.

[Num. 9:21-23] . . . whether it was by day or by night that the cloud was *taken up* they journeyed. [22:] Or *whether* it were two days, or a month, or a year that the cloud tarried upon the tabernacle, remaining thereon, the children of Israel abode in their tents; and journeyed *not*: but when it was *taken up*, they journeyed. [23:] And at the commandment of the Lord they *rested* in the tents, and at the commandment of the Lord they *journeyed*: They *kept* the charge of the Lord, at the commandment of the Lord by the *hand* of Moses.

Blessed be the name of the God and His Word will go forward! Blessed be the Lamb of God who *takes* away the sins of the world. Blessed be the Word of God which leads each man in truth and righteousness for His name's sake. Blessed be the Holy Spirit who dwells in us as our Comforter and Intercessor. Blessed be the name of Jesus who gives us our commission and strengthens us day by day.

You see, what God was telling Moses concerning the Levites and all of Israel is the same charge that He is giving us today. What He is saying is that there is a time to journey. There is a time to pitch tent. There is a time to rest. And that *always* is the time to keep His commandments. It is in *keeping* His commandments that we are able to do what He has commissioned us to do. Study means study. Listen means listen. Speak means speak. Stop means stop. Be still means be still. Go means go. Pray means pray. Fast means to fast. Wait upon the Lord means wait upon the Lord.

There is a season for everything according to *His* will and judgment. God will *light* the flame bringing *to light* His Word. His Word is not my word in my timing. It's not your word in your timing. Not the preacher's word in their timing, but His Word in His timing. My word may get someone in a whole big mess. A mess worse than the mess they may already may be in. Your word may lead someone astray or down the wrong path. Only God knows w*hat* God wants done and *when* He wants it done and *how* He wants it done. Our charge is to *study* the Word, not just read through it. Our charge is to stay *prepared* to do His will whenever and wherever He says we should. Our charge is to humble ourselves before Him. If we can't humble ourselves before Him then we can't humble ourselves when *speaking* His Word to others for the simple reason that we just *aren't* humble.

I know that you have heard this because I've heard it a million times. God tells some "Christian" to witness to the lost soul on the corner and invite them to church or to Bible study. This "Christian," maybe even you, has to "take time out of *my* busy day" and go down on the corner with "God's Word." The first thing out of their mouth is, "You need to quit that drinking and get off this corner. You need to find you some new friends. You need to get in church." Does it stop there? Shoot no! "I'm on a mission for the Lord, so just come whenever you want to but you need to put on a belt and pull those pants up."

Does this sound Christ like to you? Do you think that this person pitched tent and waited on the Lord? Did this person journey in the paths of righteousness? Did they keep God's commission? Since Jesus is our laborer, all that we need to say to people is that, "After Christ died on the cross, laid in the tomb, arose on the third day and ascended into Heaven, there was, we have, and we will always have a new testament. Jesus loves you." So, you have the testimony. You have a living testimony in Jesus. This new tabernacle dwells not in a tent, but in the very hearts of you and I. This new tabernacle isn't written on scrolls or chiseled in stone. This new tabernacle is the *new covenant*, which we receive through the Blood of the Lamb. He *is* our pillar of cloud by day and our pillar of fire by night when you believe in your heart and confess it with your mouth.

You should be able to look anybody straight in the eye and say, "I don't know about you, but as for me and my house, we will wait upon the Lord. I don't know about you, but as for me and my house, we will follow only the Lord God Almighty. I don't know about you, but for me and my house, we will praise His holy name. I can see the cloud that tarries over me by day. I can *feel* the pillar of fire, which leads me in darkness, in my spirit. I don't know about you, but this fire deep down in my soul allows me to *rest* with peace tarrying over me at night. And I know that all is well because I know that He is the Holy One of Israel!"

So whether it be two days, a month, or a year, *however long* our Lord decides, we should rest in our tent and at the commandment of the Lord, journey to wherever He leads us. In knowing that the cloud of the Lord tarries over us, we will not fear. In knowing that the cloud of the Lord tarries over us, we will not worry about tomorrow. We will not worry about our enemies for the cloud of the Lord tarries over us. What is man that God should consider us? Who I am that He should be concerned about me? Who I am that He should provide for me? Who I am that He should die for me? Not just for me, but for the sins of the world. So I will serve our God all the days of my life. God sent His Son that we are a living testimony as to the power of the Blood, which washes us white as snow. In Christ we can do all things. Not some things. Not most things, but *all things* in Christ who strengthens us!

So when God says, "Journey and do My good works" we don't have to worry about how we are going to get there, what we are going to eat, what we will have to wear, or how we are going to pay for it. What we do is seek first the Lord, listen to His voice, and step out in *faith.* What I am gonna do is like that certain widow with the two sons. I'm gonna take my little pot of oil. I'm gonna ask for God's anointing. I'm gonna ask for His blessing. I'm gonna ask for His mercy. I'm gonna ask for His grace. I'm going to ask for His increase. I am going to ask all these things according to His covenant with me. [II Kings 4:1-7]

Then I'm gonna start out on my journey pouring the oil from my little pot on my car payment. I'm gonna pour oil from my little pot on my insurance payment. I'm gonna pour oil from my little pot on my house payment. I'm gonna pour oil from my little pot on my grocery bill. I'm gonna pour oil from my little pot against sickness and disease. I'm gonna pour oil from my little pot against poverty. I'm gonna pour oil from my little pot for tithes. I'm gonna pour oil from my little pot for my offerings, seed offerings, and church fundraisers. And I'm gonna pour oil from my little pot into the lives of the children, elderly, and the sick. I am pouring the oil of the very anointing of God Himself out against all the works of the Devil! And I know there will be oil left over . . . for Jesus in my laborer.

[Rom 8:14-17] You see, faith is good. Hope is good. Humility is good, Honesty is good. Patience is good. Repentance is good. Forgiveness is good. Joy is good. Praising God is good. All of these things are good and are the foundation of any "good Christian." We learn these and all the fruit of the Spirit through our study and through our *walk* with Christ. As we *walk* with Christ we give Christ the authority in our lives. When we give Christ authority in our lives then He is able to keep us in a right fellowship with God. In Him keeping us in a right fellowship with God we are now being joint heirs. Once Christ *has* restored us to a right relationship with God then we have *power through our fellowship.* Holy Ghost *power*! *Power* from On High! *Power* from the One and Living God! *Power* to do all things that Jesus has commissioned. *Power* over all evil. *Power* over sin for we have now seen and received the *power* of resisting temptation. All we have to do is have faith in the name of Jesus whenever we are *serious* about staying the course. There's *power* in your *speaking* for Christ.

There is no physical battle for us to fight. "Not by might, nor by power, but by my spirit, saith the Lord of hosts." The Lord gives us His Word, which is the "sword of our mouth." So you must speak your decree openly. We have the power to step out and to take back that which the Devil has corrupted. I'm sick and tired of hearing Christians just repeat anything from anybody. A lot of it is so beautiful and poetic . . . but powerless!!

[Gen.1:3,6,9,11,14,20,24,26,29] God *spoke* all creation into existence and I don't know about you, but I ain't gonna let nobody water down God's power in my life. I understand that God's power in us is greater than mediocrity. All God does is speak a Word and whatsoever He speaks springs forth. What He expects us to do is speak what He has already spoken, in faith.

Being *good* isn't good enough. As we all learned in English class, after good comes better, and after better comes best. So God calls us not to just to be *good*, but to be the *best* in what He calls us to do. When we reach to be the best then we are *moving* on into perfection. This is how God saw us when He created us. Perfect. Made in His very image. Perfect in His eyes. Perfect in likeness. The best we can speak is always going to be what God has already said!

[I Pet. 2:19] So when you look at it like that it is easy to understand why we are not of this world but a chosen generation passing through. And if we are royal priests passing through here then that lets us know that we have a higher calling. If we are an holy nation and peculiar people, then we know that this is only a place of preparation. If we know that this is only a place of preparation then we also know that it is God who prepares our way. If we know that it is God who prepares our way then we need to shout of His *power* which brings about change in peoples lives. Everybody has heard of Jesus. A bunch of people know about Jesus. A lot of people have a relationship with Jesus. Very few people understand that there is *power* in shouting about Jesus' power. This gives the glory to the One who is our source of power. This power is unleashed and glorified by our *faith* in speaking of Jesus' power which He has given to us.

We are called out of darkness into His marvelous light. It is our shout of God's power that brings about change to a dying world and into peoples lives.[Num: 20:8] We don't, and I'm not going to be beating twice on any rocks for water to come forth when God says *speak* to that rock and *tell* water to come forth. When God says to go down to the river, step in and dry up the flow of the river so that we can cross over, I'm not going to turn back in doubt and fear. I'm going to step out at His command because it is the Blood that gives me strength and it will never require anything less than faith!

When Jesus is my laborer I don't have a whole bunch of stuff to carry around with me. When I am covered by the "cloud of the new tabernacle" I can wake up in the morning knowing that for the entire day ahead of me that I am favored because Jesus has carried all of my old worn out baggage to the cross and cleansed me. And He didn't even throw it up in my face and talk back. He cleansed us without saying a word. You ever asked your husband or wife to do anything for you the first thing in the morning? The only thing that is covered is their head when they look at you like you're crazy for asking them to get out of a warm bed. You are on your own, Jack!

You know that you are covered with favor when you get on up to fix breakfast and the phone rings with someone offering you a good opportunity to make more money. You know you are covered when you open the stack of bills on the table and realize that you don't owe on any of them. You know you are covered when you realize that by paying your tithes first you have opened up the floodgates of heaven in your finances. When Jesus is my laborer, all I have to do is praise Him instead of pay Him. See, our tithes belong to Him in the first place [Mal.3:10-11]. When Jesus is my laborer I don't have to worry about whether or not I will have seed money to sow because when He wants me to sow only He can provide the seed to the sower anyway.[2 Cor.9:10] Not only that, but He will rebuke the devourer for my sake, and he shall not destroy the fruits of the ground; neither shall the vine cast her fruit before the time in the field.

Jesus is your laborer because He never sleeps and you are always on His mind. Jesus is your laborer for He is constantly making intercession to God for you. When Jesus is your laborer it isn't like any other relationship that you have. Most relationships work like this: The one telling the other what to do reaps the rewards. Who else but Jesus will tell you what to do and if you do it will give you all of the profit except for a dime on the dollar? Jesus doesn't mind giving you the better half because He has already given you His best when he was nailed to the cross. All He expects from you is your best. That's all, just your best. What is your best? Is it showing up for church once a month? Is it praising His name *after* He does something for you? Is it spending more time watching the television than studying the Word? Is it looking at your brothers and sisters in need and saying, "I got mine, you get yours?" Is your best getting on the telephone or running around the church talking about people behind their backs? Or is your best living your life to be a mirror image of Christ?

When Jesus is my laborer I can rest. I'm not talking about a physical rest from not having to ever do anything for myself. I'm talking about a spiritual rest. I'm talking about the rest that comes from peace in God that surpasses all man's understanding. Resting in Jesus means that I don't need to worry about fighting battles that He has already won. I don't have to lay awake at night with thoughts of fear running through my head. The new tabernacle of the Blood of Jesus covers my life throughout the darkest hours. I don't have any need to pollute my mind with plots of revenge. I no longer have to harbor bitterness in my heart. When Jesus is my laborer I now have my mind free to think of things eternal. Jesus has placed His pillar of fire over me to guide me through trials and temptations. Jesus never gets tired of loving me.

Jesus never turns His back on me even when I do mess up. Jesus offers me the best gifts of all. Salvation and repentance! Jesus is my laborer and my Justifier before God and men. Jesus knows that I am only a man and sometimes fall weak. He also knows that I need a Comforter. So He sent me the Holy Spirit to indwell within me for the rest of my life. As my laborer, Jesus does not leave me to the liars and selfish wolves that smile in my face while trying to use me to further their self-centered ambitions in the church. I have found that there are actually quite a few similarities between church and prison.

In both church and prison you can find Jesus if you seek Him. Both are full of sinners. Both have a Pastor on hand. Both have good people and bad people. Some will be there for life while others leave. Some complete their duty and some don't. Some people repent and never look back and some spend a lifetime there and never change. Some spend a lifetime in both and change for the for the worse. Some people beg forgiveness and some people carry bitterness to their grave. Both the Warden and the Pastor have a Higher Authority to answer to. Church and prison both allow visitors. In both someone always manages to run the visitors off. Both have at least one person who runs to the Warden or Pastor to snitch. Both church and prison may punish you beyond what God intended if you don't adhere to man's rules. But most of all whether in church or prison you get to see the best and the worst out of people. Whether you are in church or prison most of the time you are dealing with broken lives. There is also a deep-rooted desire to clique in both. There is division in both. And in both, prison and church, you also find a desire to stay away from attending as much as possible. I crack me up.

I have found out that Jesus carries me as my own personal laborer no matter where I am. The point I'm making is that life is all one big journey. So don't get too high or too low. Just trust in the Lord with all your mind, heart, soul, and strength. You have to get to the point in your life where it does not matter if people are patting you on the back saying, "You can make it," or if they are kicking you in the face saying, "I'm gonna destroy you!" Just remember that we can do nothing without Jesus. And Jesus is not cosigning anyone's mess! So ask Jesus to be your laborer. He gives you rest in the midst of the storm. It all boils down to choice. We have no control, only the choice to give all our battles to Jesus or to try to control what we can't fight in our power anyway. The closest we come to control is speaking God's promises.

I'll never forget the look on the parole boards' faces when I went up for a parole hearing when I was at Brushy Mountain State Penitentiary. The only thing they asked me was, "Tell us why you should get parole?" I looked straight at them and said, "I don't care if you give me parole or not. I ain't got but four years. If you give it to me, fine. If not, fine. I was watching television and you called me up here. I didn't ask you for nothing." They just stared at me and then said, "You can go." A few months later they sent me to the work release center and then home in about a year without ever saying another word to me!

See, When Jesus is your laborer the words from your mouth bring you favor from the top that you don't even expect. One day while still in prison, my cellmate and I said to the captain, a no-nonsense man, "Let us out of our cell tonight so we can go out in the yard and use the phone." To our surprise, he did! Not only that night, but about four or five times a week while six hundred other inmates were on lock-down! I wouldn't even use the phone. I would just go out there and walk around. How funny!

Using the Right Tools

[Isaiah 55:8-9] "For My thoughts are not your thoughts, neither are your ways My ways; saith the Lord.[9] For as the heavens are higher than the earth, so are My ways higher than your ways. And My thoughts than your thoughts."

[II Cor. 3:5-6] "Not that we are sufficient of ourselves to think anything as of ourselves; but our sufficiency is of God.[6] Who also hath made us able ministers of the new testament; not of the letter, but of the spirit: for the letter kills, but the spirit gives life."

[17:] "Now the Lord is that Spirit, and where the Spirit of the Lord is, there is liberty. 18: But we all, with open face beholding as in a glass the glory of the Lord, are changed into the same image from glory to glory even as by the Spirit of the Lord."

Now let's wrap this thing up with this question. What does man need to build up God's Kingdom? God the Father, God the Son, and God the Holy Ghost!! These are who you need. Notice that I switched from "what you need" to "who you need." What implies that you are still requesting information about the character, origin, identity, worth, usefulness, force, or importance of a person or thing. Who lets us know that we indeed have this needed information and now have an intimate relationship with God through Jesus with the indwelling of the Holy Ghost. The way man communicates with God the Father, God the Son and God the Holy Ghost is through prayer. Prayer is the key which opens up the windows of our hearts in order for us to make our desires known to God and for God to answer. Without prayer we have no power in our lives. Without prayer we cannot understand what God wants us to do. Without prayer we have no direction. Without prayer we don't know God's purpose for our lives. Without daily communication with God, through Jesus, we are lost. Jesus and the Holy Spirit are our Intercessors before God.

Romans 8:26-27 says, "Likewise the Spirit also helps our infirmities; for we know not what to pray for as we ought; but the Spirit itself makes intercession for us with groanings which cannot be uttered. [27] And He that searches the hearts knows what is the mind of the Spirit, because he makes intercession for the saints according to the will of God."

You must first accept Jesus as your personal Savior, repent, and follow Him in faith. You must birth that desire to be filled with the Holy Ghost. You have got to be like Jacob when he wrestled with the angel all night long. You have just got to say, "Lord, I'm not going to let You go until You bless me! I'm not strong enough to do this on my own. Come Holy Spirit, come Holy Spirit, come Holy Spirit and strengthen me. I need You to have Your way in my life."

Now don't think that once you have received the baptism of the Holy Ghost that you have "arrived," because the Word says. "But we all, with open face beholding as in a glass the glory of the Lord, are changed into the same image from glory to glory even as by the Spirit of the Lord." What do you mean, Gregory? What I'm telling you . . . what God is telling you is that the Holy Ghost is your Comforter and your reprover of sin, teacher of righteousness, and of judgment. The Holy Spirit will guide you into all truth, which comes from the Father. All that the Father has are Christ's. So, the Holy Ghost takes what is of Jesus and shows it unto you! The way to find out anything again is through prayer. It's all about prayer. Prayer is what takes you from glory to glory through your faithful acts.

Let me tell you a funny story. I woke up one morning, said my prayers, and began to read my Bible. I was off from work so I just laid in bed and read my Bible, prayed, meditated, and blessed God all day. I finally got hungry, and fixed breakfast that evening and went back to my room and continued reading and praying. This all started around 9 o'clock in the morning and it was now dark. By now, I was lying on my side in bed with the lights off, meditating, when I don't' know what possessed me to ask, "Lord, do I pray enough?" And He answered me. I mean right then, clear as a bell, "Have you fell out of the window yet?" It caught me off guard, you know, so I just burst out laughing. He didn't.

Then I remembered a young man named Eutychus who sat in a window in the upper chamber of the third loft listening to Paul preach all day, even unto midnight when he fell asleep and then fell to the ground killing him. The Lord was serious. What He was saying was, "Your desire to pray to me should be just as strong as that."

Your desire to pray should bring up a passion and a hunger from deep down inside of you that keeps you on your knees and in fervent prayer no matter what the circumstances. When I told my Pastor of this word from God she told me, "What He's saying is that we must continually pray until we die." Now this took me to the realization that I have no problem praying when things go wrong in my life, but when everything seems to be going well I forget all about seeking God's will and direction for my life. Then I end up right back in trouble which could have been avoided.

You have to use the right tools for any job or you or someone else will end up getting hurt. *Prayer is our trust* in the Lord, who has the blueprint and the tools for building His Kingdom. Not you, I, or even the angels can do anything without God. [Job 4:18] "Behold He put no trust in His servants; and His angels He charged with folly. [Job 15:15] Behold He puts no trust in His saints; yea the heavens are not clean in His sight. [II Pet. 2:4] For if God spared not the angels that sinned, but cast them down to hell, and delivered them into chains of darkness, to be reserved into judgment."

Satan was an angel, cast out of heaven by God Almighty! Don't put all your trust or seek all your comfort in such things. [Col. 2:18-22] Get rid of all graven images of such things. They can't see, talk, hear, fly, or walk! And graven images sure won't be who throws Satan in hell! [Rev.20:1-2,10] Seek the Lord with all of your mind, heart, soul, and strength and you find that He alone will take you from glory to glory. [Ezk. 13:3] All Glory is His and His alone. He will not share *His* glory with anyone nor does His glory dwell in images made from man's hands. Seek God in prayer and when He answers you, follow Him. [I John 5:21] When the fruit of the Spirit shine forth in your life, your spiritual gifts will not be *used contrary* to the Word by how you live your life.

It is the fruit of the Spirit which brings the flesh into subjection that you may carry out the perfect will of God. When your flesh is in subjection to the will of God then your flesh or carnal self will not sin against the Spirit. When your flesh or carnal mind is in subjection to the spirit then you, the Spirit, Jesus, and God are as one. [John 17] Now, you find yourself in an intimate relationship and fellowship with God. It takes us to have the mind of Christ in order to edify our spirit to live in the Kingdom of God on earth before we reach the destiny of our desire.

All of our sufficiency is of God and we learn of His will through the Word of God. The new testament of our Savior is taught in the Word of God. You have got to read the Word to even learn how to pray. Read God's Word everyday! Don't wait on your study leaders to read it to you or for them to explain it to you. Their interpretation of the Word may or may not be correct. Read and pray for yourself! Your Pastor should know the Word, but it may be weeks or months or even years before they preach the Word you need. As bad as I hate to say it, some teachers spend more time changing or challenging the Word and its percepts than they do delivering God's message.

[Jer. 7:4] "Trust not in lying words saying the temple of the Lord, the temple of the Lord, the temple of the Lord are these. [Jer. 7:8] Behold ye trust in lying words which cannot profit.[10] And come and stand before me, in this house, which is called by My name. And say, We are delivered to do all these abominations? [19] Do they provoke me to anger saith the Lord: do they not provoke themselves to the confusion of their own faces?"

[I Cor. 4:19-20] "But I will come to you shortly, if the Lord will, and will know, not the speech of them which are puffed up, but the power.[20] For the Kingdom of God is not in word, but in power."

What started as a prayer and a burning desire in my heart a long time ago when I was just a little boy has been nurtured along by the most caring, concerned, and loving person that I have ever known. I have now birthed a new creature in Christ who has found the True and Living God, been filled with the Holy Ghost and I am excited to share Christ's goodness towards me with anyone with the heart and desire to hear the truth of His love. Without my little Pastor I would still be lost and I know it. But see, she loved God *first* and came to do *His* will and good works and to bring His Word and power into my life. Who would have thought that this little woman could be a tool from God? I for one! You see, there's something about an *anointed* disciple of God that even a person or people like me will have enough sense to listen to and to follow. No matter how hard or cold-hearted a person is, or how long a person has been on drugs, alcohol, the streets, prostitution, or in prison, we *cannot deny* the *power* of God's love when we see it lived out and practiced by His shepherds. She never exalts herself and has always been reverent in giving God all of the praise, honor, and glory in all that He does through her. For me it's all about *trust,* plain and simple. I trust her with my spiritual growth because she trusts God to lead.

This is what she first instilled in me. "Obey my voice, and I will be your God, and ye shall be my people and walk ye in all the ways that I have commanded you, that it may be well unto you." [Jer.7:23] I recite lessons she taught me to drug addicts, drunks, and anyone else lost all the time and *they* understand it. Many even repent. I can't even count the number saved.

Don't get me wrong and run around saying, "He's' witnessing in the name of Reverend Estell, like the sons of Sceva," because I'm not and that's not what I'm saying at all. What I'm saying is that she was the right tool for the job because she uses the right tools to get the job done which God anointed her to do. Iron sharpens iron. No more, no less, ". . . for the letter kills but the Spirit gives life."

What is the fruit of the Spirit? Love, joy, peace, longsuffering, gentleness, goodness, faith, meekness, and temperance. The same as is the character of Jesus, who walked this earth and experienced the same sorrow, pain, jealousy, hatred, and slander against Him as everyone else.

Why is it so hard to trust someone who died for you? What more could He do? God trusted the Son to live a life without sin in the flesh and Jesus did just that by trusting in the Father to deliver Him and raise Him from the dead. Jesus showed all of His trust in the Father in the garden of Gethsemane when he said, "Oh my Father, if it be possible, let this cup pass from me; nevertheless not as I will but as thou wilt." It was all about trust. *Jesus shed His blood in that garden to give us power to make the right decision to trust God.* You think He just goes around bleeding for nothing? Every drop of blood served its purpose to restore mankind back to God. It is about *trust* that Jesus gives His church to Pastors to lead. It is about *trust* that your Pastor has assigned you to leadership positions within the church body of which Jesus is the Head. See, Jesus didn't just shed His blood for you on the cross, but He shed His blood for you even before the cross! Just as Jesus made the right decision in the garden of Gethsemane, so are we granted the power to make the right decision every time by the shedding of His blood in that garden.

See, it's all about the warning signs of storms in our spiritual lives and how to recognize these warning signs and where to turn and who to turn to in order to quiet these spiritual storms and move *forward* for God's Kingdom. The best way to see if you are headed for a spiritual storm or even already being devoured by this spiritual storm is to "look with open face beholding as in a glass or mirror." [I Cor. 8:18] Now, what is flesh is flesh and what is spirit is spirit. These are contrary the one to the other. If what you see is adultery, fornication, uncleanness, lasciviousness, idolatry, witchcraft, hatred, variance, emulations, wrath, strife, sedition, heresies, envying, murders, drunkenness, reveling, and the such, then you are in big trouble and are bringing division to Christ's place of worship.

When we bring our flesh into a house of worship it should be for cleansing, forgiveness, or deliverance, not to tear down what God is building up. The Word says to, "Enter into His gates with thanksgiving and into His courts with praise." [Ps.100:4] The only way to enter into His gates and courts with thanksgiving and praise is to have the Spirit of God already manifested in your heart. The very word "with" implies that thanksgiving and praise are accompanying you or connected to you before you get to church. Anything else offered up to God as praise or thanksgiving is dead worship. You either bring it with you or you ain't got it. If the Pastor has to plead with us to praise God before we shout then we ain't got no shout. If it takes the choir to get us fired up then we ain't got no fire. If we come in late every week to worship God when in a leadership position then we ain't no leader. If we don't love our brother or sister sitting beside us, then we don't love God and if we say we do love God, we are liars. [I John 4:20]

When we surrender and let the Blood of the Lamb cleanse us then we will have an *authentic* praise and worship and not the same old show each week with some kind of fake joy. God will give you the tools you need, show you how to use them correctly and order your steps. When you receive all the right tools from God, you realize that these tools were already placed within you before you were formed in the womb, by God, and have been birthed anew by your *desire* to be set free.

Those feet that used to run to mischief, now stop, turn and run the other way. Those hands that used to shed innocent blood now are used to lift up in praise to God, to anoint, and to heal. Those ears that used to crave all for the latest gossip, vulgar language, and blaspheme now are burning for the Word of God. Those eyes that used to lust after men, women, children, or anything materialistic and worldly, now long to see God's face. The lips that used to curse God's church and children now praise Him. That old tongue that never could keep from destroying other people's joy now is speaking in a language that hasn't been taught by man. Above all, your mind now seeks the gift of prophecy.

I used to say, "I come in peace, but whether or not we keep the peace is up to you. It doesn't matter to me. If you want peace we'll have peace. If you want to go to war, I'll take you to war." But then Jesus stepped in and gave me a clean heart. That's when I understood that whether or not we kept the peace was too much power to give over to someone else. I have a choice. And if it means *walking away* in order to keep peace in my life or in the church, that's what I'll do.

The Holy Ghost will let you know through prayer . . . "For we wrestle not against flesh and blood, but against principalities, against powers, against rulers of darkness of this world. Against spiritual wickedness in high places.[13] Wherefore take unto you the whole armor of God, that ye be able to stand in the evil day, and having done all to stand.[14] Stand therefore having your loins girt about with truth, and having on the breastplate of righteousness;[15] And your *feet shod* with the *preparation* of the *gospel of peace*;[16] Above all, taking the shield of faith, wherewith ye shall be able to quench all the fiery darts of the wicked.[17] And take the helmet of salvation, and the sword of the Spirit, which is the Word of God."

You *must* learn how to use the Holy Ghost in your prayer life. I don't claim to know all about the Devil. I don't claim to know all the thoughts or ways of the Lord. But what I do know is, "He that does good is of God: but he that does evil hath not seen God." [3 John 11]. I do understand that we are to love one another just as Jesus loved us. I do understand that God gave man freewill in whether or not we would follow His commandments. "This is love, that we walk after His commandments. This is the commandment, That, as you have heard from the beginning, you should walk in it" [2 John 6]. I do understand that, "And from a child you have known the holy scriptures, which are able to make the wise unto salvation through faith which is in Christ Jesus.[16] All scripture is given by *inspiration* of God and is profitable for doctrine, for reproof, for correction, for instruction in righteousness:[17] That the man of God may be perfect, thoroughly furnished unto all good works" [2 Tim.3:15-17]. I do understand in the last days that religious leaders shall be, "Traitors, heady, high-minded, lovers of pleasures more than lovers of God; [5] Having a form of godliness, but denying the power thereof; from such turn away. For of this sort are they which creep into houses, and lead captive silly women laden with sins, led away with divers lusts. Ever learning and never able to come to the knowledge of the truth" [2 Tim.3:4-7].

What has happened through religion is that we have held on to the powers and principalities and rulers of darkness sermon to the point that we don't' want to look at *ourselves* "with open face beholding as in a glass the glory of the Lord." What has happened in the church is we have too many people who find it more convenient to blame all of *their* wrongdoings on the Devil. What has happened in the church is we have too many people that don't want to take responsibility for their actions or lack thereof. [I Tim.6: 1-5] What has happened through religion is we have too many leaders saying, "I've been called, anointed, and set up high by God over you and I don't need to seek His counsel anymore." What has happened through religion is that too many leaders want to take the glory of God's work for themselves. What has happened to the body of Christ is that too many leaders are not praying. And when they do they want to tell God what they're going to do instead of asking, "What is Your will, Lord?" Then when everything falls down around them say that, "It's that old Devil trying to stop us." Some even blame the few righteous among them who try to steer them to the path of righteousness, never once even considering that is in fact God who is putting a halt to their folly. What has happened to the body of Christ today is that we have too many leaders who think that their education "trumps" the baptism of the Holy Ghost. What has happened through religion today is that we have too many leaders trying to lead without the power of the Holy Ghost. What we must have in the body of Christ today are Holy Ghost filled leaders who are not ashamed of, afraid of, or unlearned of the power of the Holy Ghost! The truth is without Holy Ghost power you have no power! There's a storm a comin'.

God gives all leaders in the *church* today His decree of power in Isaiah 42:13-14. "The Lord shall go forth as a mighty man, He shall stir up jealousy like a man of war; He shall cry yea, roar; He shall prevail against His enemies.[14] I have long time holden my peace; I have been still, and refrained myself; now will I cry like a travailing woman; I will destroy and devour at once."

[John 15:5] Jesus said, "Without *Me*, you can do nothing." Luke 1:37 says, "For *with* God nothing shall be impossible." What scripture is telling us is that we are no match against the Enemy in and of ourselves. In Christ and Christ only are we able to overcome the Enemy and are more than conquerors. I said in a previous chapter that we should take back what we have given to the Enemy but don't misunderstand the context of what I'm saying. What I'm trying to get across to you is that you need the rightly divided Word of God, not your *own interpretation* of the Word, to take into the world to share with God's creation. [I Cor. 3:3-7] Only Jesus, God, and the Holy Ghost can manifest themselves in a sinner's life to *take* back anything from Satan.

What I was saying (and I know this is true) is that the problem with the church today is that "religious" folks or teachers spend so much time trying to "clean up" the language of the Bible that children don't even know what is a curse word and what isn't.

What they (children) are subliminally learning from such teachers is that the Bible is miswritten, misinformed, misleading, and that God actually had no inspiration in its conception. They learn man's judgments of what's holy is greater than God's. Above all, that even an Almighty God makes boo-boos, and needs daddy and mommy to correct and chastise Him. Children *learn* more and *react* more to *your anxieties or peace* than to the actual reading of the Word.

I have nothing personal against women Pastors or women in teaching positions in the church. The storms arise when women don't subject themselves to the authority of the men. There is an anointing that flows from the top on down. Just as Christ is subject to the Father, so is the man or husband subject to Christ. Just as the husband is subject to Christ, so is the wife subject to her own husband. [Eph.5:23-24] "For the husband is the head of the wife, even as Christ is head of church: and He is the Savior of the body." [I Timothy 2:12] "But I suffer not a woman to teach, nor to usurp authority over the man, but to be in silence." Far too often what happens is that woman's motherly or wifely instincts rise up to supersede the order of God's Holy Word. Then the Word of God changes precepts from being God's revelation to no more than a battle of wills between men and women. Anytime one's motherly or wifely instincts rise up to supersede God's order of leadership you must bring that spirit into subjection or be silent. The writer of 1Timothy doesn't say women should "stay" silent. Paul doesn't say women should "remain" silent. He says in verse eleven, "Let the woman *learn* in silence with all subjection." I believe this means for women to be silent long enough for men to hear God's voice for themselves. It is hard to hear God's voice and instruction with a bunch of women talking in your ear at the same time. If God says that men are to be the spiritual leaders of the church and home, why wouldn't He want to talk to them?

The answer is God does want to talk to them. The battle is not ours. The battle is the Lord's. We forget it is a battle between holy and unholy, flesh and spirit, or God versus Satan until either man or woman is found lacking. Men are not stepping up and walking into their calling to the point that the duties of the church and in the home have become a point of contention. Men expect women to just move out of the way. Men want to claim leadership with their mouths but don't want to do what it takes to lead. Men just want to be money earners and provide for their families (if even that) at home. Men don't step up as they should and get spiritually involved in their family's church life.

What men aren't fully comprehending is that home and the church each act as and depend on the other as the perimeter for stability. It is all connected by the Holy Spirit and cannot function properly without our desire to serve God's way. Men aren't leading the church today because many aren't even leading their own households. Far too many men have run off on their wife and kids or they just won't stand up and be leaders. Men on drugs, drunk, in prison, selling drugs, at war, whoring, lost, or whatever are taking a toll on the direction of the church. Many women are forced to lead! But because some women have been forced to lead by necessity doesn't negate God's original mandate to Adam and Eve.

Genesis 3:16 says, "Unto the woman He said, I will greatly multiply thy sorrow and thy conception: in sorrow shall thy bring forth children: and thy desire shall be to thy husband, and he shall rule over thee." Now how can a man rule over his wife, kids, and church when he can't even rule over his own flesh? What happens when men don't walk in their anointing? What you have is a dysfunctional family, community, and church. What happens when you have women constantly usurping authority over men? What is the reason Paul cautioned against this in the church? Does this order still hold true today? I have heard some people, even men, say that this is an outdated concept. My question to them would be, "When? A.D.49? 1492? 1856? 2007? When? Does God's Word just slowly fade out of style? Is it about what's in style? Or could it be that He means exactly what He says as much now as He did then? I asked God about this and here is what He showed me through His Word, in which heaven and earth shall pass away before one tittle shall pass till all is fulfilled [Mat.5:18].

The issue is that a man is always in authority somewhere. Even if he is not in authority at church right now, he is still in authority somewhere. That somewhere being his home. Now when a man is set up by God in authority at home that means that he is in authority over his wife. Not her boss! Now since his wife has submitted to her husband's authority over her, what makes you think she is going to sit back and watch another woman strive with her husband in church, when she doesn't even do that herself? That is the problem. Ain't no woman going to put up with another woman telling her husband what he is and isn't going to do in an unkind way. Everybody knows the mess that goes on in churches, so let's not act naive or play stupid here! It won't be long before the wife gets in the woman's face at church to tell her, "You ain't going to be talking to my man like that!" Or the man strives with her and she runs home and tells her husband, who most often ain't even in church,(oops) that some man is rude to her. Now he runs up in the other man's face to defend his wife's honor and you have one big mess. The women aren't speaking to each other and the men are fighting. Or the woman tries to "load up" the ministry with other women, who aren't even anointed for the ministry, in order to pacify her husbands insecurities of his wife being around a bunch of men and him not there to watch over them. I have seen all this crap (I mean trap) before.

The tool men aren't using is their anointing to lead their families. It is imperative that men use their God given anointing to rule over women. This is pleasing to God. There is nothing negative in God's meaning of "rule". As a matter of fact God's charge for men to rule is far from negative. It's casting aside your anointing which isn't pleasing to God. 1 Timothy 5:8 says, "But if any man provide not for his own, and specially those of his own house, he has denied the faith and is worse than an infidel." Then in God's order, we see the woman's place in that, "Likewise, you wives, be in subjection to your own husbands; that, if any obey not the Word, they also may without the Word be won by the conversation of the wives; While they behold your chaste conversation coupled with fear.[1 Pet.3:1-2] So they are equal with the assignment to lead going to the man.

You ever have somebody to just start telling you negative things about their husband or wife which you don't want to hear about? You ever have a person to resent you because they see you doing the things of God that they can't get their husband or sons to do? Or, on the other end of the spectrum are drawn to the anointing and think that they're in love with you?

What has happened to the church is that since the home life is unstable or set up against what God blesses and has ordained as a family (by shacking up, unnatural relationships, cheating, etc) men and women both spend more time and more energy caring about love lost or finding love than they do on how they may please the Lord. It is during or because of this *spiritual* battle between man and woman, fought in the *flesh*, that the church ends up in division or in a constant conflict when it is time to make tough choices about the direction of the church.

[I Cor. 7:32-33] A man operating only in his manhood only does whatever pleases the woman. This becomes a distraction to any man with a higher calling because it is her will, not God's will, that he seeks unless he has a *real* praying and God fearing woman. She knows that when her motherly or wifely instincts are superseding God's plan that she must bring that motherly or wifely spirit into subjection to further edify God's Kingdom; Not edify her womanly idea of a perfect little church and home. Feelings get hurt sometimes when folks don't get their own way. I've heard people say, "Your first ministry is your home" in order to justify their behavior, scheduling, and choices when these actions don't coordinate with anyone else in that ministry. So the truth is, if this is true, then it is obvious that they need to be home ministering! I say this according to the Word of God which I mentioned earlier. So to be trying to minister at church when your home obviously isn't in order is already contradicting your very own words. Whether or not he is saved has nothing to do with the fact that the man has the authority over his wife to tell her when he expects her home, even if his wishes are not best for the others who *are* in that ministry. Whether or not she's there at home is between them, not the church!

The people who like to claim that women are more submissive to God than men, are another example of the division that exist. And yes, I have heard men speak this ignorance too. What we are talking about here has to do with *emotions*, humanly perceived servitude, or humanly perceived level of intimacy, which has nothing to do with the *depth* of a person's relationship with a God whose emotions don't change. If we have not *repented* and *turned* and *walked* the other way by following God's commandments, then we haven't *submitted* to God's authority at all! Any person, whether male or female who lack walking in the fruit of the Spirit *has not submitted* to God and by *talking* about "more submissive" we only give fuel to those women who will try to *pass off* "more submissive" as *actual* submission to the Holy Spirit. Now one certain woman may be more submissive than one certain man but you cannot say this as a general truth about all men and all women! God is Spirit and those that worship Him must worship Him in spirit and in truth! Gender has nothing to do with it. It's all about *God* and whether or not we *do His* will! If we don't do His will then nobody has submitted to God. Should you be proud to miss the mark just because you are told you are "more submissive" and closer to the mark than others? Other than that, who is "more submissive" is a pointless conversation and we are one in the Spirit and one in the Lord just as God says in His Word!

The problem with religion today is "educated" preachers who only serve to exalt their carnal thoughts and to pass this off as insight into spiritual matters, God has not called preachers to take the Word of God and twist the deliverance of God's Word to where the only one receiving glory is themselves. We cannot expound on God's Word then not back it up with scripture and draw from our pride. Many never realize that they are in the middle of this spiritual storm. They will argue with each other over "once saved always saved" instead of telling their flocks to, "Get saved and walk in God's righteousness!" They carry on and on and on about whether you have to be submerged, poured, or sprinkled in order to be baptized. These educated preachers even have the nerve to argue about when Jesus will return.

But my Word tells me in I Corinthians 1:19, "For it is written, I will destroy the wisdom of the wise, and will bring to nothing the understanding of the prudent." [20] Where is the wise? Where is the scribe? Where is the disputer of this world? Hath not God made foolish the wisdom of this world? 21 For after that in the wisdom of God the world by wisdom knew not God, it pleased God by the foolishness of preaching to save them *that believe*." Believe what? Believe the Kingdom is here!

You see, what far too many of these "educated" preachers do is to stand up in front of a crowd and preach everything but *Christ's Kingdom*. [Luke 17:20-21] Have you ever listened to an entire Bible study or sermon and Jesus bringing the Kingdom is never mentioned? This is where the power is!! The point is that all things in the Bible point to or lead to Jesus! Why leave Jesus out and dwell on other names, places, or numbers? What does knowing "some stuff" have to do with whether or not a person is saved and growing? The storm arises when you have different beliefs all under the same umbrella of Christianity. They never agree. Everything is open to debate. These "educated" folks never agree with each other on God's Word. They never even agree with God on God's Word. They are forever learning but never understanding *Christ's* teachings.

The particular area of contention in the church of baptism is just childish. Far too many Pastors want to stand on what they believe instead of what *all* scripture is *telling* us. Luke 3:3 tells us, "And he came into all the country about Jordan, preaching the baptism of repentance for the remission of sins." Verse 7 says, "Then he said to the *multitude* that came forth to be baptized of him . . ." Now we can go on over to St. John 3:23, which says, "And John was baptizing in Aenon near to Salim, *because* there was *much water there*: and they came and were baptized." In plain English, a multitude of people takes a whole lot of water. The point is "much water" is needed, not in volume of water for *one* person, but for a *number of persons*.

Ezekiel 36:25-26 says, "For I will *sprinkle* clean water on you, and you shall be clean. I will cleanse you from all your filthiness and from all your idols. I will give you a clean heart and put a new spirit in you: and I will take away the stony heart out of your flesh, and I will give you an heart of flesh. And I will put my spirit within you, and cause you to walk in my statutes. And you shall keep my judgments. And do them.

Acts 2:17 says, “And it shall come to pass in the last days that I will *pour* out My spirit on all flesh.” Proverbs 1:23 tells us, “Turn at my reproach: behold I will pour out my spirit unto you, I will make known my words unto you.” Amen

John the Baptist says in Matthew 3:11, “I indeed baptize you with water unto repentance; but He that *cometh* after me is mightier than I, whose shoes I am not worthy to bear: He shall baptize you with the Holy Ghost and with fire.” Isaiah says in chapter 4:4, “When the *Lord shall have washed* away the filth of the daughters of Zion, and shall have purged the blood of Jerusalem from the midst thereof by the spirit of judgment, and by the spirit of burning.”

The baptism of water is a dramatic and symbolic sign of a person’s decision to surrender their life to Christ. It is a way we give witness to the world that we are saved and now are celebrating our acceptance into the body of Christ. Romans 6:34 asks each of us, “Know ye not, that so many of us were baptized into Jesus Christ were baptized into His death. Therefore we are buried with Him by baptism unto death; that like as Christ was raised up from the dead by the glory of the Father, even so we also should walk in newness of life.” Amen

See, when Jesus was baptized by John, the Holy Spirit descended upon Him like a dove. Jesus was already God in the flesh, who lay down His divine nature to become like man! What Jesus was doing was showing us the *steps* to follow in order to receive *power* from the Holy Spirit. It doesn’t matter to God whether you are in water over your head or have water sprinkled or poured on top of your head. It is the *act* of obedience and surrender, which God blesses and anoints. This *act* is what gives you the power through the Holy Spirit, to accomplish your purpose in the Kingdom, not the amount of water!

My sincere desire is to take you to a whole new level of revelation of who God is in relation to you being able to live the Kingdom life. I'm not trying to *belittle* anyone's belief, but oftentimes what we believe isn't the revelation God has for us. When we speak on these issues we must be careful not to end up speaking vanity. I've heard "preachers" on television and talked to some in person who insist that if I'm not *immersed* in water, then I'm not baptized. They all have the exact same reasoning that, "Jesus was baptized in the water, just like Momma and me." Here's the revelation for you. Jesus *was* baptized in the water. In the Jordan River! Were you? Not Pistol Creek, not the church pool, not even the Atlantic Ocean, but the river Jordan! I see a contradiction here. There seems to be some lack when I look through spiritual eyes. If the *amount* of water is so important in order to be like Jesus, then why isn't being at the exact same *location* of Jesus' baptism just as important?

The tool these "educated" preachers and teachers need to learn to use correctly is their tongue! I know this is true for myself. I learned the best three words to speak when asked about scripture are "*I don't know.*" If I don't know, then why just guess? Why repeat what Ma-maw said if I haven't read it for myself? Why quote something that sounds scriptural that turns out to be from a famous poet or author? Why count myself as a disciple or teacher of Christ's Kingdom when I can't hear from God? Why talk to or teach others about Jesus when I can't even confess my own shortcomings? You must pray about these things! Prayer is your toolbox. You put all your other tools in your toolbox and carry your toolbox with you, keeping it unlocked, wherever you go. Many people don't know or forget that the toolbox is actually a tool in and of itself. So, all of your spiritual gifts, weapons, fruit, and language are delivered by prayer.

Pray In Faith

The tongue can speak life or death. The tongue should lift people up. The tongue should speak life, not death! The tongue should speak truth! The tongue should speak praises to God, our Creator. The tongue should speak creation and not evolution. The tongue should speak it just as God said it in His Word. I don't care how educated, open minded, or scientific you think that you are, always remember I Corinthians 1:31, "That according as it is written, He that glorieth, let him glory in the Lord."

The glory of the Lord is revealed through the Word of God. The glory of the Lord bears witness in you by the Holy Spirit which lives in you. The glory of the Lord extends to each of us through mercy and grace. The glory of the Lord is upon us because we are created in *His image*. Can't no "educated teacher" convince me that I evolved from some ape! I've been to the zoo. I know, and you know that we are created in God's image and God ain't walking around heaven on all fours, digging in His hind-end! Jesus didn't come into this world looking like a monkey. He wasn't born by an ape in the jungle. His bloodline is the root of Jesse. We aren't saved by any monkey. Even the sacrifice of animals is done away with by the New Testament! How ignorant. But you notice the ones teaching this nonsense are smart enough to not get in front of a crowd and start digging in their hind-end like a monkey. Because they know everyone would laugh at them and get up and leave! 1Timothy 1:15 is from Paul and speaks to *each of us,* "This is a faithful saying and worthy of all acceptance, that Christ Jesus came into the world to save sinners of whom I am chief." Thank God for Kingdom-minded spiritual wisdom!

Jesus spoke of this Kingdom life to the Jewish people. [John 2:19] Jesus answered and said unto them, "Destroy this temple and in three days I will raise it up.[20] Then said the Jews., "Forty and six years was this temple in building, and wilt thou rear it up in three days?[21] But he spake of the temple of His body."

I love this scripture because it shows just how carnal men are and how spiritual the mind of Christ is in contrast. Also, being fifty years old myself, it gives me reflection through the building up of my old wretched self, which the power of Christ has done for me. See, the point is that I am a witness to the fact that God is no respecter of persons. No matter who you are or what you've done, Jesus loves you and is waiting just for you. Jesus loves you. God loves you. [John 3:16] "For God so loved the world that He gave His only begotten Son so that whosoever believes in Him should not perish but have everlasting life." God judges the hearts of men and their faith and surrender of all their flesh for the gifts of the Spirit. God understands that sometimes your fake joy comes from a deep down misery and emptiness that you can't seem to fill. God understands that sometimes you may have to fake it on order to keep coming back to church in order to be around true worship and to see the power of the Spirit working in other people's lives so that one day you too will say, "Let us seek the God that they serve. Let us worship and praise the God that they serve. Let us serve the God that they serve. Let us walk in our purpose for His Kingdom." That's why we should forgive people in their weakness.

Your body just like Jesus' body is a temple. Jesus, being God in the flesh, could rise from a physical death but could never be spiritually dead. [I Cor. 3:16-20] You and I, on the other hand although living, are dead if we are not spiritually filled and living in the Spirit. It takes prayer and surrender to Jesus for you to stay filled with the Holy Spirit. I don't even have to look at men deeply at all to know whether or not they have the Holy Spirit manifest in their life, so how much more so can the Giver of the Spirit see? I cannot stress enough the importance and the urgency for men to seek first the Kingdom of God and His righteousness and *turn* from this lack of wisdom, and *walk* in righteousness for His name's sake. [Ezk. 20:26] You and I are nothing without God, and any person who thinks we are something when in fact we are nothing without God will be left powerless to take care of God's Kingdom agenda. [Gal. 6:3]

God has got to be number one in your life. Not you, your wife, your husband, your kids, or anyone or anything else but God. Any man that doesn't put God first in his life will confide in his wife who may or may not have the discipline to behave in a Christian manner. By the time he can get her home from church and "straighten her out" for running her mouth, because he ran his big mouth, the damage has already been done. Don't let the Christian faith be made to be a mockery of God, and Christian ministers and leaders no more than a bunch of self-righteous hypocrites. There's a storm a comin'!

Remember, I said that God will give you the tools you need, show you how to use them *correctly*, and order your steps. Well, I'm now telling you that there are tools for tearing down, and tools for building up. For me, that person was my Pastor, Reverend Estell. She said, "If you are watching television or reading something that takes your *mind* places and into lusts that shouldn't be there, turn it off or put it down!" The first thing I thought was, "She has went crazy now, telling me to turn off a movie because of some cussing or nudity. That's just life." Until I grew and did just as she said. Then I realized it's all about that seed!

[James 1:13-15] [13] Let no man say when he is tempted. I am tempted of God: For God cannot be tempted with evil, neither tempts He any man: [14] But every man is tempted, when he is drawn away by his own lusts, and enticed, then when lust has conceived, it brings forth sin: and sin, when it is finished, brings forth death.

God doesn't need to tempt man to see whether or not man will sin because He already knows that man will sin. This is what she was teaching me. See, if I continued to be blind to the *truth,* that there were some behavioral *habits* of my flesh that needed tearing down, then I would never have grown past that point in Christ in which I stood. This would have prevented me not only from changing into the image of the Lord, from glory to glory, but actually would have brought forth more sin, which not only kills physically, but spiritually as well. Sin doesn't get less and less on its own. You must lay it down!

This lust and covetousness go hand in hand and are most destructive to your lives. The Holy Spirit has been speaking this to me for a long time and today this is what I believe He is saying, "It all begins with a seed!" This lust and this covetousness bring forth more sin that anything else God commanded not to do. Lust and covetousness will, in fact, cause men to turn from God and to serve other gods. Lust and covetousness causes men to make and to possess graven images for they must see, feel, touch, hear or smell something tangible in order to find comfort. Lust and covetousness will cause a man to blaspheme the name of the Lord in order to follow strange pagan women and be led into unholy faiths or doctrines. Lust and covetousness cause men to forsake the holiness of the Sabbath and to mow lawns, work unnecessarily or hang out at the sports bar instead of attending church services. It is this lust and covetousness which causes teenagers to forsake their parent's instruction and pursue drugs, alcohol, sex, gangs, body mutilation, suicide, and devil worship.

Lust and covetousness will cause men to kill to get what their flesh desires, whether it be a woman, property, money, land, or whatever. Lust and covetousness will cause church leaders to lay up with their flock, rape little boys, and even try to condone same sex relationships. Lust and covetousness will cause men to rob God in tithes and offerings in order to buy himself a new boat or the wife a diamond ring. It is lust and covetousness that causes a person to stand in church and attempt to shut up a messenger of God through a false witness about that messenger's character. Carnal people cannot stand in the light of the Word and righteous judgment so they will slander, mock, ridicule as nonsense any teachings from the Lord which expose *their* dark hearts. Finally, we come to covetousness itself . . . that begins . . . with a seed. Amen. The Devil sure didn't want you to have that.

You see, it was a seed of perversion planted in the hearts of the people in Sodom which took root and conceived the wickedness of the mind to lust after all sorts of sexual perversions to the point that these people had become so possessed by sin that they had the nerve to go to Lot's house and try to rape the angels! [Gen 19:4-11]

It was a seed of doubt sown by Satan in Eve's mind, which then caused her to entice Adam. [Gen 2:16-17] See, God had already told Adam that he could eat freely of every tree of the garden except the tree of knowledge. [Gen 3:1-6] It was Eve who said, "ye shall not eat of it, neither shall ye touch it. Lest ye die." God never said not to touch it. He said not to eat it. So she touched it and didn't die, then got bold and ate it, then gave it to Adam. Adam knew better but still there was a spiritual death because *he chose* to abandon God.

It was a seed of greed, with the promise of eleven hundred pieces of silver from the lords of the Philistines, which caused Delilah to betray Samson and feign sorrow of not being loved in order for him to tell her the secret of his hair being his strength. [Judges 16:5] It was a seed of invincibility and jesting that caused Samson to mock her with silly riddles and lies until he was caught up in a trap, which could have been avoided if only he had avoided the love of beauty and jesting with the anointing.

It was a seed of lust in the eyes of King David, which caused him to look upon Bathsheba and to desire her. [II Sam11: 3] It was that same seed which caused him to lay with her and conceive a child. It was that same seed which caused David to send a letter to Joab, saying to send Bathsheba's husband, Uriah to the forefront of the hottest battle where he would most likely be killed. God's wrath was so great against David for having Uriah killed and then marrying his wife that the child Bathsheba bore David was born sick and died seven days later.

It was a seed of lust for a strange woman that made King Solomon lay with the daughter of Pharaoh, women of the Moabites, Ammonites, Edomites, Zidonians, and Hittites, all of whom the Lord had forbidden the children of Israel to go into, because surely they would turn away their hearts to other gods. [I Kings 11:1-11] Solomon went right ahead and married seven hundred wives and had three hundred concubines who turned away his heart to other gods. The Lord became angry with him after appearing unto him twice and commanding him to stop this wickedness, but Solomon would not do what the Lord commanded of him, so the Lord took all his kingdom from him except one tribe for David's sake and for Jerusalem's sake which was chosen.

The point I'm making is that too many folks want to claim their *actions* are an involuntary reaction to some demonic spiritual *force* when in fact they are *voluntarily* submitting to their own lusts. Satan or his evil spirits or demons can do nothing to any God fearing, righteous, Holy Ghost filled child of God! God's will is for you. Satan's will is against you. And your will makes the difference. Satan can only use what is already in you. Choose you this day who you will serve, period!! Satan needed God's *permission* to even torment Job. [Job 1:12, 2:6]

It's that lust for power in our hearts that make us want control over everything, even spiritual matters, we haven't even prayed about. When God says, "No" we get mad and stubborn with Him and set out to prove to Him we don't need Him anyhow. When we find out we can't have power over God then we want to settle for power over people, who by the way, are disobedient to the same all powerful God that we try to rebel against! But see, you can't rebel against God without giving up your personal, intimate relationship with Jesus. So, what you now have done is to break the yoke that binds your spirit to Jesus. And when that yoke is broken, then whether you know it or not, you are now involuntarily yoked together with Satan, more subtle than any beast of the field, like two jackasses pulling the same wagon.

The thing is though, Satan loaded the wagon with all sorts of envy, strife, jealousies, bitterness, hatred, lust, anger, resentment, heresies, deceit, and lies, adultery, fornication, fear, variance, strife, rebellion, sodomy, lesbianism, cutting, drug addiction, violence, disobedience, uncleanliness, emulation, etc., which keeps your focus on yourself and others instead of on God.

That's why when you focus on yourself to "clean up" or challenge the holiness of God's Word in your carnality, instead of praying about it, children learn subliminally that God isn't so holy and neither is mommy and daddy because, "I saw them make a mistake just like God makes mistakes."

You wonder why they come back home from college pregnant, run around and getting drunk, partying, and living in the flesh, as if you haven't taught them better? The problem may be that they as children have learned that God's Word is to be questioned for its righteousness and that your word is no better. So they set out in life into a world full of danger, lies, and snares disillusioned and trusting *nothing* or no one, especially *anything* Christian. Now they, although having been brought up in church, have broken the yoke which bound them to Jesus and just like you, are yoked together with that Serpent, more subtle than any beast of the field.

When you *use* the Word as the right tool then your job takes a backseat to God, who said, "If *I* be lifted up from the earth, *I* will draw all men unto me," See, the Word of God is Holy and will be understood *as Holy*, even if it's not totally understood. You read the Word, teach, or preach the Word of God and let the Holy Spirit minister God's Holy Word into the minds, spirits, and soul of the hearers of His Word. God's Word will not be tempered, watered down, or added unto by any man. God's Word brings life to anyone who listens and follows, right? If this is true, then ask yourself, "Did I save myself unto eternal life, or did the understanding and acceptance of a Savior from God's holy scriptures *lead* me unto salvation?" The Word of God will stand even when the world is on fire.

Our thoughts without understanding through prayer, bring confusion. [Ezra 3:12-13] "But many of the priests and Levites and chief of the fathers, who were ancient men, that had seen the first house, when the foundation of this house was laid before their eyes, wept with a loud voice; and many shouted aloud for joy: [13] So that the people could not discern the noise of the shout of joy from the noise of the weeping of the people; for the people shouted with a loud shout, and the noise was heard afar off." Amen. Are you just making noise? Or are you using wisdom to rightly divide God's Word to others?

It's not the Word, but skeletons, which hinders us. It's not the Word of God but these mothers who don't know or won't tell their kids who their father is that's confusing these kids. It is not the Word of God, but these mothers who stay in relationships with abusive and violent men who rob these children of their innocence. It is not the Word of God, but these mothers who force their kids to be part of a "family" where her new boyfriend only wants her and not her kids, who make these kids feel unwanted. It is not the Word of God, but these women who don't love their new husband's kids as her own who leave these kids searching for love in all the wrong places. It is not the Word of God, but these mothers who dump their children off on someone else to raise who fill these kid's heads with lies, superstitions, and false myths. It is not the Word of God, but these mothers who dress like hookers and encourage their daughters to do the same, who lead these girls astray. It is not the Word of God but these men who don't claim their children that cause these kids to grow up not knowing they have family roots. It is not the Word of God, but these men who walk out on their kids who cause these kids to grow up bitter. It is not the Word of God, but fathers who think is cute to teach their sons that unless they are having sex they "can't be my boy," who pervert these teenage minds. It is not the Word of God, but the fathers who teach their children to be violent, who cause these kids to grow up not knowing what a real man is like. It's not the Word of God, but these fathers who keep on having babies by every woman in church, who teach young boys ungodliness is tolerated. We should use the Holy Spirit to line up our walk with our talk or just be quiet and pray for our own deliverance!

"A prudent man foresees the evil, and hides himself: but the simple pass on and are punished.[4] By humility and the fear of the Lord are riches, and honor, and life.[5] Thorns and snares are in the way of the forward: he that doth keep his soul shall be far from them. Train up a child in the way he should go and when he is old he will not depart from it." [Prov.22:3-6]

I know that there is something about many folks, who having been blessed with money, a home, nice car, job, and financial security that just draws them away from the Word of God and into a dependence on their own wisdom. [II Cor. 8:2-15] It's like we become so comfortable looking at what we have and what we don't need materialistically that we lose that desire to seek the Lord with all of our heart and now lean on our own understanding of right and wrong. A prudent man will see danger coming or the warning signs of an approaching spiritual storm and turn away, but the froward want to live contrary to Kingdom principles. This teaches disobedience to our children.

I believe that many people have had it so good for so long that we don't believe that we have to answer to anybody in authority. [Proverbs 23:4] Many people believe that they have been sanctified just because we have been so financially successful. We cannot lose our passion just because of this financial success and "good life" many are enjoying. Too many now just kick back and relax, as far as pursing their destiny, which once was the driving force of their desire. [Rev. 3:17-18] Now, slowly, step-by-step, they are losing ground, falling deeper and deeper into carnality without considering the consequences. People actually believe that we can buy our children God's favor by association and having our children to associate with other children whose parents have money and attend a church with a prominent reputation. What they need is a Pastor to stand on the Word of God and tell them they need knowledge of God's way of doing things!

Knowledge is what keeps you focused on God and the Kingdom. It is written in various scriptures, "My people perish because of a lack of knowledge. Rebuke your brother if he sins, but if he repents, forgive him. I desire mercy and not sacrifice. Do unto others as you would have done unto you. Our God is a God of salvation, not of revenge. Knock and it shall be opened unto you. Ask and it shall be given to you. Have faith and you shall be made whole."

It is our carnal self which doesn't allow us to forgive others and to pass judgment against them, which keeps us from being set free. It is your carnal mind that keeps you from forgiving your former boyfriend or husband and trusting any other man to teach your children. Too many women carry around that old hurt, disappointment, and resentment from a past relationship gone bad, which may not have even been ordained by God, to the point that their mind is made up that "I don't need a man for nothing and I'll raise and teach my children by myself." The very man that some can't bring themselves to trust teaching their sons the Word is the very person sent by the Lord *to* teach these boys.

"Don't do this and don't try that" has a lot more effect on teenagers coming from a man who has already lived out in the world, has now repented, and can bring to these teenagers the *Living Word* as it applies to the consequences of bad choices. Not every tool used for revelation is some member of the congregation who has already been saved for the last forty years. Remember, "He who is forgiven much loves much. And he who is forgiven little loves little." [Luke 7:47] Don't get caught up in religiosity, legalistic doctrine, and church tradition. Over-protection is bondage because you never allow your kids to go *through* any test or trials. Then they don't know what power they have in themselves and you don't know what power you have in you either.

Kids today are flooded with information. With television, the media, the music, and the Internet, they are receiving more outside influence in a day than their parents did in a year, according to private and government studies. These kids need *guidance* and someone to *share* their feelings, fears, anxieties, hopes, dreams, peer pressures, emotions, and temptations with. They need someone to listen to *them* first and not someone who wants to do all the talking. When they know that you are honestly interested in their problems they will open up to you. Especially when they know the person they are talking to is going to be *honest* with them and treat them in a manner that says, "I know what you are going through although I don't know exactly how you're feeling right now. I have been through the same thing and here is how I got through that problem."

They will open up a whole lot faster to someone who has lived through the drug, alcohol, rebellion, and prison life than they will to someone who has never experienced life's trials and pitfalls. Life is scary to these kids and they have lots of questions they are afraid to ask because they feel that grownups don't understand them. And it's true: Most adults don't understand where teenagers are coming from, because they have always been too scared to live and too scared to die. [Rev. 3: 15-16] They never have done anything bad but they haven't done anything good, either. They have never done any wrong, but they haven't done anything right. They can tell these kids what they are against, but they can't tell them what they are for. They are never cold, but they are never hot, either. They live in fear of the *truth,* so they hang on to myths and lies of the Enemy, never finding the *faith* in a God who can be *trusted* to speak *power* into the lives of these young people that they shall be *able* to *rise up* above all the temptations of the world and to *stand* on the *Word of God!* It is through the *teaching of faith* in the *Word of God* that kids will grow! Why seek the living amongst the dead?

When God says, "Go," are you even prepared to go? Do you use the tools you need in order to prepare yourself to go anyplace, anytime, and tell a dying world about a mighty Savior? Can you *physically* go in obedience to God's instruction? If my boss tells me to climb up the scaffolds and help those other masons top out that wall forty feet in the air, then that is what I'm needed for. If I can't climb up there then someone else has to do my job. Now the boss sees my shortcomings and I am now deemed expendable or not capable of doing what is required. Jesus doesn't look at any of us as expendable but He knows when and *why* we aren't capable of carrying out our Christian duties.

There is no way to break this to you softly so I'll just start by telling you the statistics. Sixty percent of black men and eighty percent of black women are overweight with fifty percent of black women obese, according to the National Center for Health Statistics. Also seventeen percent of black teens were obese, according to the U.S. Centers for Disease Control and Prevention in 2004. By 2010 over 30% of people in the south are obese. I say all this out of love because I know God wants you made whole and serving to your full potential and, [Rom 12:11] "Not slothful in business; fervent in spirit serving the Lord." [Heb 6:10-12] "For God is not unrighteous to forget your work and labor of love, which ye have shewed toward His name, in that you have ministered to the saints and do minister, And we desire that every one of you do shew the same diligence to the full assurance of hope unto the end: [12] That ye be not slothful, but followers of them who through faith and patience inherit the promises." Amen.

We know from medical studies that fat messes up your blood pressure, sugar, heart, cardiovascular system, hips, knees, feet, and on and on. We know it also affects your mood, personality, self-esteem, and how you view or get to participate with society. Schools are even forced to abandon the very Physical Education classes which give children exercise because some say it is embarrassing to the overweight kids who need to exercise. You have got to start somewhere!

What I have studied in my years of watching people is that people who feel they can't get out and get around and participate or associate with others either watch a lot of television or they gossip on the telephone. Television, is them watching someone else's life, who they don't know or can't interact with, so they just live through these characters lives by daydreaming about how they would react or what they would do if they were these people or in that situation. Then some will actually talk to the television set and curse it out!

The same holds true when many get in church. This may be the only day of the week that some really get to interact with people. Often times this weight keeps us from getting around town to actually participate or associate with people. The way of feeling like we are "in the loop" is to gossip. If we can't go to the world, then we feel that gossiping brings the world to us. We don't think about who we hurt.

Some people would rather (and I've seen it a million times) have another church member to call them up and curse them out for gossiping about them than to sit at home all alone until the next Sunday. Now they feel they have a life because they are the author and finisher of everything that goes on in that particular body of Christ. Not only that body of Christ but several other churches too, because they have buddies in those other churches they share "news" with everyday on the telephone. Then the poor old Pastors have to go back and teach and preach the same old elementary scripture every week because they can't move into the meat without their congregation being in unity and one accord with themselves, the community, and the Holy Spirit. It's sad, [Heb. 5:12-14] "For everyone that uses milk is unskillful in the Word of righteousness: for he is a babe." Amen

With limited understanding we should not even speak. Just because we watch Hollywood women and men cheating, fornicating, and lying all week on television, doesn't give us the right to judge people. Don't assume that everyone else lives in the flesh. We really must understand we have to look past the outward appearance to the inner part of another brother or sister in Christ. We can't just distrust any other person around our husband, wife, or children. Don't be disappointed in yourselves, deep down inside, just because you are overweight. It manifests itself into destroying others you should help. Don't allow someone else to have to do what God called you do. It starts with generational bad eating habits, which begin with a seed. So don't give up on yourself! Just begin to take care of your temple with better, healthier eating habits.

[James 3:14-16] "But if you have bitter envying and strife in your hearts, glory not and lie not against the truth.[15] This wisdom descends not from above, but is earthly, sensual, and devilish,[16] for where envying and strife is, there is confusion and every evil work."

What makes it so sad is when the churches have to deal with men who carry on with the same old gossiping as their parents. Many were raised on this mess, by sitting around listening into grown folks conversations, all through their teenage years into adulthood. It's all they know! The point is too many folks have lived in this bondage for so long that it is normal for them to carry on with it in God's house from generation to generation. They are lost in the storm. They haven't been convicted to take a good long look at themselves and the spiritual storm that has them in bondage. They want to quote scripture that condemns the behavior of a drug addict, drunk, or ex-convict, but hold their own transgressions up in the church as God's plan. See, they don't want anybody to call their child illegitimate, saying, "No one is illegitimate to God! God has a plan from the beginning for my child." And it is true that God has a plan for all children.

Well, if this is true for my child and my Christian walk then why can't it be true for *anyone else* who has sinned and fallen short? Man's gluttony, slothfulness, and gossiping are just as much a sin as drug use, drunkenness, or any other sin. I'm not even going to dwell on whether or not we were married when the child was *conceived*, because that is not the point that the Spirit is leading me to right now. The point is that we are not to judge and condemn another person, but that is exactly what we are doing when we take it upon *ourselves* to decide who is and who is not a child of God, *redeemed* by the Blood of the Lamb and fit for service to the Lord. What we are saying is, "Don't call my child illegitimate," while at the same time calling someone else a bastard and their relationship with the Lord illegitimate and decided by *us*. I point this out to help us all mature, because the Word says, "For whom the Lord loves He chastens, and scourges every son whom *He* receives.[7] If you endure chastening, *God* deals with you as with sons; for what son is he whom the *father* chastens not? [8] But if ye be without chastisement, whereof *all* are partakers, then you are bastards and not sons." [Heb. 12:6-8]Amen

The point is that we all are able to lift each other up in love and live in unity as a body of Christ and let *God* do the chastening only when we stay in prayer for one another. We are presented as no more pure before God by criticizing someone else, especially when it comes to their service to the Lord, according to the Word of God. Keep your flesh out of the church!

[Gal. 4:22-23, 4:29] "For it is written, that Abraham had two sons, the one by a handmaid, the other by a freewoman.[23] But he who was of the bondwoman was born after the flesh; but he of the freewoman was by promise.[29] But as then he that was born after the flesh, persecuted him that was born after the Spirit, even so it is now." Amen. God gives to, and God blesses whomever He pleases. Now, let's get some exercise equipment to the glory of the Lord! There's a storm a comin'!

When you use the right tools then you will be able to build up God's Kingdom *and* your temple of God. Unlike Jesus, this will take a lifetime, not three days. But what you will find is that every person, no matter how great or small and every duty performed, no matter how great or small are just as important to Jesus as the other. What Jesus needs and is looking for are people who seek *their* purpose and perform *their labor* of *love,* with the tools they have, within God's plan.

Sure, there's a bigger plan not controlled by you, but you control, by choice, whether or not to play your contributing role by your obedience. See, the temple of God lies in the hearts of men and is not made of brick and stones. It is your heart that you should ask God to search and to reveal to you your uncleanliness. You should fear God and not Satan. You should fear God and fear not *doing* all that He wants you do. There are no requirements as far as how rich or poor, tall or short, skinny or fat, educated or uneducated, skilled or unskilled or even how long or short a time you have been saved. God has a purpose for all of His children *right now*, even if what you are called on to do *right now* is not the fullness of your purpose.

[I Sam. 2:11, 2:17-18] "And Elkanah went to Ramah to his house. And the child did minister unto the Lord before Eli the priest. 17 Wherefore the sin of the young men was very great before the Lord; for men abhorred the offering of the Lord. [18] But Samuel ministered before the Lord, being a child, girded with a linen ephod.

[1Sam.3:7,19] [3:7] Now Samuel did not know the Lord, neither was the Word of the Lord yet revealed unto him. [3:19] And Samuel grew, and the Lord was with him, and did let none of his words fall to the ground." The Lord raised Samuel up in the temple, from a child to be His faithful priest, but first Samuel had to be faithful in the lighting of the lamps and other duties for Eli, the priest. Then he would be greater than Eli!

Here lies the storms. People are not thankful for the manna. People do not want the manna. People reject the manna. "Who fed thee in the wilderness with manna, which thy fathers knew not, that

He might humble thee, and He might prove thee, to do thee good at the latter end [Deut. 8:16-20]." Amen

When God starts to rebuild your wretched temple the first thing you have to do is to desire the manna. The first thing you have to do is get used to the manna. The first thing that you have to do is to depend on the manna. The first thing that you have to do is to be thankful for the manna. The first thing that you have to do is to be encouraged by the manna. The first thing that you have to do is to seek the manna. Then you will be strengthened by the manna! Only God knows what you need and all that you need comes from God!

I know you thought you did it all by yourself. I know that you've been looking over our shoulder at your college degrees hanging on the wall. I know that we thought that since we break down complex issues on our job we can bring that mindset to the church. I know that we thought that because we were a foreman, director, board chairman, or owner of a business that our natural talents have brought us to where we are today in the body of Christ. I also know that we have forgotten that is only God who gives you the power to get true wealth and true power!

I also know that without the *power* of the Holy Ghost, you have been building on the sand. I also know that without the *remembrance* of God and who He is that you are surely headed for destruction. I also know that it rains on the just and the unjust. I also know that there are a lot of folks that are so busy gloating over the blessings in their life that they count themselves as just, when in fact they are unjust, but can't see the spiritual storms around them. The truth is it is this goodness of God which calls men to repentance! The warning signs are all around us. But in our hearts we say, "My power and the might of mine hand has gotten me this wealth." People, in their hearts, feel that we are too good for the manna. Some people do not recognize God as the Author and Finisher of our faith. Carnal people don't want to build on the foundation of Jesus Christ, No, carnal people want to build wherever and however and with whatever they choose, using whichever people and tools they decide, in their carnality, are correct. When there is no unity, it is not of God. If we are not in one accord with each other and the Holy Spirit, it is not of God. If there is nothing but confusion and pride, it is not of God.

I went to visit at a church once where it was so loud and irreverent before the service began that I honestly had to bow my head and pray for the Lord to forgive us and for the Holy Spirit to enter into the minds, soul, and spirits of these people. Believe it or not, right in the middle of me praying I felt someone shake me really hard, so I looked up to find this woman usher glaring at me and saying to me, "Wake up! This is a church service!"

I had another person, whom I know didn't realize he needed the manna. We were involved in talking about Jesus one night. The next thing I hear is "You know, Gregory, I'll be honest with you. There was a time that I didn't like you. I mean, I couldn't even stand you. But you know, Gregory, you are all right with me. I like you!" I came a hair of telling him. "I don't' care if you like me or not!" That was exactly what I was thinking. I had never even been anywhere around that boy! Only angels and fools could go where I went. If you don't like someone how can you work in the harvest? Are you doing them a favor by liking them?

When you are thankful for the manna. You are saying, "God, I need you. God, I cannot build up this temple without You. And God, I trust You to provide me with what I need." You see, too many people want to start out on this spiritual journey without spiritual food. Too many people are running a spiritual race on empty. Too many people falsely believe that they can start out on this spiritual journey from the middle or near the end of the journey without ever having tasted the manna. Too many leaders fail to acknowledge that it is the manna [Deut. 8:2-3] which the Father uses ". . . to humble thee and to prove thee, to know what was in thine heart, whether thou wouldst keep His commandments, or no." You see, man does not live by bread alone, but by every Word that proceeds out of the mouth of the Lord does he live.

There are too many people leaving churches today because of a few simple-minded *leaders* who don't have the heart and the humility to get down in the ashes with their flock and be fed the manna. There are too many *leaders* in the church today who have no intention of giving up their status, job, self-righteousness, and graven images in order that they may seek the True and Mighty and Invisible God. Instead of seeking the Invisible God and the manna, which will strengthen them and do them good at the latter end, they surround themselves with graven images and find comfort in their own wisdom.

I don't trust myself or *my* wisdom to carry me right now, much less at the latter end! I may be good. I may be bad. I can try to be good and still my works are nothing. I have found out that without faith in the Lord God Almighty that I have no *power.* But when I place my trust and my faith in God and I walk in obedience to His commandments and thank Him for the manna, by surrendering my all to Jesus, then I have seen for myself, and I know with all that is within me, that I shall *rise up* and call myself blessed!! I have seen for myself that neither enemies nor hell can prevail against me as long as I keep returning to my first love, which is the Lord, and the manna which strengthens me.

You see, it is the foundation of my Lord and Savior, Jesus Christ and my *earnest desire* for *Him* to bring my hopes and dreams into reality that keep me from falling back into that old sinful life. I can stand here tonight and tell Satan that I will never go back to that lifestyle because I have the courage and the Holy Ghost boldness to stand on God's Word, all by myself, if no one else has the guts to face that Liar. I'm sick and tired of these Preachers and church leaders talking about, "Be careful or the Enemy will get you." Submit to God. Resist temptation and praise the Lord, commanding the Devil to leave in the Mighty Name of the Lion of Judah and he has got to go! Praise God! Thank Jesus! Bless the Holy Ghost! Pray without ceasing!

When you praise and worship the Lord and stand upon His foundation you have *power* over the Enemy! He knows that you have *power* over him, which is why he always works through other people to try to get you sidetracked or to stumble and fall. But you are *blessed,* for the Word tells you, "The steps of a good man are ordered by the Lord; and he delights in his way. [24] Though he fall, he shall not be utterly cast down; for the Lord upholds him with His hand. [25] I have been young, and now I am old; yet have I not seen the righteous forsaken, nor His seed begging bread." [Psalm 37:23-25]

Let me tell you this one last thing, and if you don't get it by then you really need to get down on your knees and pray to the Lord to release *you* from *your* bondage. See, it's *you holding on* to *your* self-pride, jealousies, bitterness, envy, fear, and hatred, and resentment, and *your* rebellion which is *manifesting* in your life and keeping you from true freedom in the Lord and not some outside demonic *force*. These evil *forces* can only have *power* when you feed them. You can feed your spirit with all the scripture you want to, but if are not starving the flesh, then you will find yourself fighting the same spiritual battle, just on a higher level, because your flesh will still be growing along with your spirit. It has an appetite all of its own and none of it is for spiritual things. Some people believe otherwise; that your spirit will itself push these fleshly things out. But according to the Word of God *you* must lay these fleshly desires down!! The spirits of the prophets are subject to the prophets. [1 Cor.14:32]

Paul says, "That *you* put off concerning the former conversation of the old man . . ." and that "*you* put on the new man . . ." [Eph.4:22,24]. The Word also tells us, ". . . let *us* lay aside every weight, and the sin which doth so easily beset us, and let us run with patience the race that is set before us." [Heb.12:1] You do it!! It's in God's power, but you do it! The Word also tells us in Rev.19:7 ". . . the marriage of the Lamb is come and His wife *has made herself ready.*" Quit waiting on God to take that mess from you and cast down evil imaginations and anything that exalts itself against the knowledge of God and bringing into captivity every thought to the obedience of Christ!![2Cor.10:5]

You see, once I began to starve my flesh and to feed my spirit through prayer, fasting, studying the Word in faith, obedience, and surrender to the will of God, I began to grow in the Lord to the point that He was able to pour out His Holy Spirit into my spirit, mind, and soul. Once filled with the Holy Spirit, I needed to *separate* myself from wickedness, so I began praying to the Lord to give me a Word and to show me and to place me where I could have the *freedom* to grow and to worship in spirit and in truth. I made a vow to serve Him for the rest of my life if He saw it in me. I prayed for Him to show me my purpose and to give me a Word for His children.

What I tell you now is that when God gives you an anointing to be a vessel for Him to pour out His Spirit upon His children, if that Spirit is rejected in one place, the anointing doesn't go away and the Spirit will move you to another place and still open up the floodgates of heaven and let it rain upon His other children. I have never in my life felt the love *of God* move in a place or in a child's life the way I did when the Spirit had me lay hands on my little cousins and see them baptized in the Holy Ghost and speaking in tongues. Amen

When I returned to my first love, what I had to do is the same thing that everyone must do, and that was to be thankful for the manna from heaven. You see, in order to return to your first love, there first must be a repentance to take place. True repentance means that you turn from your wickedness and follow the Lord, *no matter what*. Get used to the manna! True repentance means that you no longer are standing with one foot in Moab and one foot in Judah, but have now made the solemn declaration that Ruth made, "For whither thou goest, I will go; and where thou lodgest, I will lodge; thy people shall be my people, and thy God my God." When you return to your first love you leave the flesh behind and are reborn of the Spirit. It is this complete turnaround that took me from contentment in the flesh, to confusion in the flesh, to conviction of the flesh, to confession of the spirit, to conversion of the flesh, to a *new* contentment in the Spirit!!

What I have seen for myself is that in order for me to keep pressing forward, going from glory to glory, I must keep shedding this old flesh and bring that old carnal mind and tongue into subjection and leave behind anything or anybody which come between myself and a total surrender to the Holy Ghost. [James 3:14-18] I fully understand that before I can move on into the fullness of my purpose that I must first be thankful for the manna! And I thank You, God for the manna! I didn't realize it at the time I was a child growing up that You heard that little boy's cries. I didn't realize it growing up through my teenage years that You were feeding me that manna. I didn't realize that you were saying, "I don't have to bless sin, or sinful acts but I will feed you manna." I didn't realize that during an adult life full of every sin and wickedness that my mind would dream up that You, Jesus, had a plan for my life in the wilderness. That even after being so hardhearted and starved for love that only You could comfort me and only You could make me desire the manna which provided me with Your foundation!"

You see, God does not destroy families. He strengthens them! Jesus has not asked anyone to destroy another child of God. To the contrary, Jesus says we are to love one another just as He loves us. In unity and on one accord with the Holy Spirit is the way, the truth, and the life. There is only one way to the Father, which is through the Son. Only by faith in Jesus and believing in His Holy and righteous Word are we able to receive the promises of healing and deliverance from those things that keep us in bondage.

I personally have seen too many husbands who are not leading their wives and loving them as they should, just throw a marriage away. They never pray with their wife and kids. They never initiate a home Bible study. They never recognize that right now, she may be weaker than him. I've seen wives give up on their husbands because he just doesn't seem to want to change. They never pray with him and the kids. They give up asking when he doesn't want to go to church. Instead of going to God's Word, they take their problems to their crazy girlfriends. Then they both run to church and fight in public. I've seen grandmothers try to brainwash grandchildren into denying their heritage from the other side of their family. If they can't get them to deny it, then they want them to feel as if their other relatives are to be ignored, disrespected, or ashamed of in public.

But God is no respecter of persons. James 5:16 says, "Confess your faults to one another, and pray for one another that ye may be healed. The effectual fervent prayer of the righteous availeth much." Here lie the storms in so many churches today. [Haggai 1:9-10] "Ye looked for much, and lo it came to little; and when you brought it home, I did blow upon it. Why? Saith the Lord of hosts. Because of mine house that is waste, and ye run every man to his own house. Therefore the heaven over you is stayed from dew, and the earth is stayed from her fruit." Amen

The problem is that there are churches that count themselves as righteous when they are not living in righteousness! We are made the righteousness of God through our salvation and no one can take it from us but we still must walk in that righteousness! We don't give each other our best and we surely can't claim to give God our best when we don't walk in the righteousness of God.

You can have prayer, and you should. You can have fervent prayer, and you should. But you will not have *effectual* prayer until you become righteous in spirit and in truth through your walk of *faith* in the *righteousness* of God's Word! When you have *faith* in the righteousness of God's Word then you will *act* on that faith in accordance to God's will, which *releases* the *power* of the Holy Spirit! But first you have got to humble yourselves before God and confess your faith *to* God.

See, I've seen too many folks gather around the altar, pray, and get up from the altar, pat each other on the back, tell each other how righteous their church body is, and leave a church when all the praying is over with, that has broken windows, paint peeling everywhere, roaches in the kitchen, toilets nasty or broken, carpet torn, gutters falling off, and the lawn just as raggedy. I have seen trim missing for years, plywood patched in where window panes *were*, and people get in their Mercedes, Lexus, and SUV's and go home to their "cieled houses, and this house lie in waste!"[Hag.1:4-6] What were you expecting God to do for you when you don't do anything for Him? In order for your prayers to be *effectual*, you have to put and keep God first!!

This "dew" from heaven can represent the *power* of the Holy Ghost raining down from the floodgates of heaven, from God Almighty, Himself. This "dew" from heaven can be that healing of the cancer which has hold of you right now. This "dew" from heaven is the healing of your wife's Alzheimer's disease. This "dew" from heaven is that financial blessing that you need for a new church roof. This "dew" from heaven is what brings you back from the brink of suicide. This "dew" from heaven will deliver your children from drugs, alcohol, and sex. This "dew" from heaven will be your Comforter when everybody in the church wants to try to talk about you. This "dew" will deliver people who practice sexual perversions. This "dew" from heaven will comfort the widows, homeless, motherless and fatherless. This "dew" from heaven will forgive and forget all that sin, which you have confessed and laid at the feet of the Lamb, and do a new thing in your life! [Isaiah 44:21-28]

What God is telling you is that not only is His house in a physical state of waste, but a spiritual state of waste as well. The earth is stayed from its fruit because you first need the "fruit" from the Holy Ghost. This fruit from heaven will bring you joy when you give to the poor. This fruit from heaven will convict your mouth to keep the peace among God's children. This fruit from heaven will grant you longsuffering when your family and friends persecute you for standing on the Word of God. This fruit from heaven will grant you the gentleness to teach and to correct the feeble minded. This fruit from heaven will give you the goodness of heart to take warm meals to the sick and shut-in. This fruit from heaven will give you the faith to tithe before all your bills are paid. This fruit from heaven will grant you the meekness to consider others feelings before your own ambitions. This fruit from heaven has the temperance to be slow to anger and quick to listen. Above all this fruit of the Spirit brings into your heart a love for your brothers and sisters whether or not they know Jesus right now.

What God is telling each of us is that it is His will to build His kingdom up from the earth through people's relationships, which begin in the hearts of men and not in a structure made of brick and mortar. Without love in your hearts for each other, there will be no harvest of the earth. Without love in your hearts for each other you may grow upwardly a little bit but you will never see the template of love cross over your differences with others and connect all these separate columns of Christians together as one. Love is your cornerstone. Love is your template. And love is the keystone that locks everything together with the mortar of faith. It is only your love for God that will keep you from going astray. It is only your love for God that will keep you pressing on. It is only your love for God that will keep you safe. Amen

It is your love of Jesus that will keep you and your church family in one accord. Through fasting, righteous living, faith, love, and prayer for one another you will witness the Holy Ghost filled, Pentecostal power, pillars of the temple trembling, down to the foundation shaking, Holy Ghost dancing, prayer tongue speaking, smoke-filled sanctuary, Shekinah glory of the Lord!!!

It is my sincere hope that you have been or will be strengthened by the reading of this book. It is my hope that someone will be saved by its reading. I pray that those Pastors and leaders lost in the storm will reflect on their "first love" and pray for the Lord to renew, revive, and restore them in God's Holy precepts. It is my main hope that "sinners" of the world see that *they are not alone* on their journey to seek the Lord. I pray that you trust in the Lord and that He surrounds you with a church family, which knows the true meaning of fellowship and love for one another.

Thank you Pastor Willa Estell. You mean the world to me and I will love you until the day I die. Your prayers birthed a new creature. Remember Nehemiah.

Gregory
January 25, 2012